I0011659

Data Structures in Java

Noel Kalicharan

Senior Lecturer, Computer Science
The University of the West Indies
St. Augustine, Trinidad

Published March 2008

© Noel Kalicharan, 2008

noel.kalicharan@sta.uwi.edu

noelk@hotmail.com

All rights reserved

The text of this publication, or any part thereof, may not be reproduced or transmitted in any form or by any means, electronic or mechanical, including photocopying, recording, storage in an information retrieval system, the Internet, or otherwise, without prior written permission of the author.

Preface

Data Structures in Java is the third book in a sequence following *Java Programming – A Beginner's Course* and *Advanced Programming in Java*.

Data structures is concerned with the storage, representation and manipulation of data in a computer. In this book, we discuss some of the more versatile and popular data structures used to solve a variety of useful problems. Many books on data structures tend to go for over-kill and the student gets lost in complexity; such books are better used as references.

This books presents a wealth of basic knowledge in a simplified form. It is based on the premise that it is better to learn a few concepts well than many concepts poorly. As a result, it restricts itself to what can be reasonably covered in a one-semester course in data structures. The emphasis is on treating material in such a way that the student is comfortable without being overwhelmed by complexity and analysis.

The approach is practical rather than theoretical. With this in mind, we show *how* to implement the data structures and operations on them using Java. We also show how to write programs to solve problems using these structures. A basic knowledge of Java is assumed. This includes writing methods that use *if...then...else*, *while* and *for* loops. You should also be comfortable working with strings and arrays.

Chapter 1 deals with linked lists. It covers basic operations such as building, searching, insertion into and deletion from a linked list. The chapter ends with the merging of two sorted linked lists.

Chapter 2 covers stacks and queues. It shows how to implement these useful structures using linked lists and arrays. An important step in evaluating an arithmetic expression is converting it to postfix form. This chapter shows how.

Chapter 3 deals with that most versatile of data structures—the binary tree. It shows how to build and traverse a binary tree. The *binary search tree* is a special kind of tree that facilitates quick searching. We show how to build and manipulate such trees, and use one to produce a cross-reference listing of words in the input. We also show how to represent a binary tree compactly using an array.

Chapter 4 discusses several sorting methods, starting with a revision of the 'simple' ones—selection and insertion sort. This is followed by the faster methods—heapsort, quicksort and mergesort. The chapter ends with a discussion of Shell (diminishing increment) sort.

Chapter 5 deals with graphs. A very large number of problems/situations can be modelled using graphs. So learning about graphs is fundamental to solving many kinds of problems. Topics include how to represent, build and traverse a graph, topological sorting, finding shortest paths and mimimum spanning trees.

Chapter 6 is devoted to *hashing*, one of the fastest ways to search. It covers hashing fundamentals and discusses several ways to resolve collisions.

Chapter 7 deals with matrices, in particular the storage requirements of matrices and how this storage can be reduced. It covers triangular matrices, symmetric and skew-symmetric matrices, band matrices and sparse matrices.

Our goal is to provide a good, basic understanding of important data structures and how they can be implemented in Java. We hope that this will whet your appetite for deeper study of this exciting area of computer science.

Noel Kalicharan

Contents

1 Linked lists

In this chapter, we will explain:

- the notion of a linked list
- how to write declarations for working with a linked list
- how to count the nodes in a linked list
- how to search for an item in a linked list
- how to find the last node in a linked list
- the difference between static storage and dynamic storage allocation
- how to build a linked list by adding a new item at the end of the list
- how to build a linked list by adding a new item at the head of the list
- how to build a linked list by adding a new item in such a way that the list is always sorted
- how to delete items from a linked list
- how to use linked lists to determine if a phrase is a palindrome
- how to merge two sorted linked lists

When values are stored in a one-dimensional array ($x[1]$ to $x[n]$), say), they can be thought of as being organized as a 'linear list'. Consider each item in the array as a *node*. A linear list means that the nodes are arranged in a linear order such that

> $x[1]$ is the first node
> $x[n]$ is the last node
> if $1 < k <= n$, then $x[k]$ is preceded by $x[k - 1]$
> if $1 <= k < n$ then $x[k]$ is followed by $x[k + 1]$

Thus, given a node, the 'next' node is assumed to be in the next location, if any, in the array. The order of the nodes is the order in which they appear in the array, starting from the first. Consider the problem of inserting a new node between two existing nodes $x[k]$ and $x[k + 1]$.

This can be done only if $x[k + 1]$ and the nodes after it are moved to make room for the new node. Similarly, the deletion of $x[k]$ involves the movement of the nodes $x[k +1]$, $x[k + 2]$, etc. Accessing any given node is easy; all we have to do is provide the appropriate subscript.

In many situations, we use an array for representing a linear list. But we can also represent such a list by using an organization in which each node in the list points *explicitly* to the next node. This new organization is referred to as a *linked list*.

1

In a (singly) linked list, each node contains a pointer which points to the next node in the list. We can think of each node as a cell with two components:

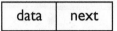

where **data** can actually be one or more fields (depending on what needs to be stored in a node), and **next** 'points to' the next node of the list. (You can use any names you want, instead of **data** and **next**.)

Since the **next** field of the *last* node does not point to anything, we must set it to a special value called the "null pointer". In Java, the "null pointer" value is denoted by **null**.

In addition to the cells of the list, we need an object variable (**top**, say) which 'points to' the first item in the list. If the list is empty, the value of **top** is **null**.

Pictorially, we represent a linked list as follows:

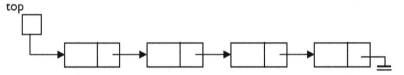

The electrical earth symbol ⏚ is used to represent the null pointer.

Traversing a linked list is like going on a treasure hunt. You are told where the first item is. This is what **top** does. When you get to the first item, *it* directs you to where the second item is (this is the purpose of **next**). When you get to the second item, *it* tells you where the third item is (via **next**), and so on. When you get to the last item, its "null pointer" tells you that that is the end of the hunt (the end of the list).

How can we represent a linked list in a Java program? Since each node consists of at least two fields, we will need to use a **class** to define the format of a node. The **data** component can consist of one or more fields (each of which can itself be an object with many fields). The *type* of these fields will depend on what kind of data needs to be stored.

But what is the type of the **next** field? We know it's a pointer, but a pointer to what? It's a pointer to an object which is just like the one being defined![1] As an example, suppose the data at each node is a positive integer. We can define the class from which nodes will be created as follows (using **num** instead of **data**):

```
class Node {
   int num;
   Node next;
}
```

---

[1] This is usually called a self-referencing object.

The variable **top** can now be defined as a **Node** variable, thus:

```
Node top;
```

As explained before, the declaration of **top** allocates storage for **top** but does not allocate storage for any nodes. The *value* of **top** can be the address of a **Node** object but, so far, there are no nodes in the list. As we know, we can create a **Node** object and assign its address to top with:

```
top = new Node();
```

This will create the following:

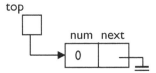

Recall that when an object is created, unless specified otherwise, Java will set a numeric field to 0 and an object field to **null**.

We will see how to create linked lists a little later but, first, we look at some basic operations which may be performed on a linked list.

1.1 Basic operations on a linked list

For illustrative purposes, we assume that we have a linked list of integers. We ignore, for the moment, *how* the list might be built.

1.1.1 Counting the nodes in a linked list

Perhaps the simplest operation is to count the number of nodes in a list. To illustrate, we write a function which, given a pointer to a linked list, returns the number of nodes in the list.

Before we write the function, let us see how we can traverse the items in the list, starting from the first one. Suppose **top** points to the head of the list. Consider the code

```
curr = top;
while (curr != null) curr = curr.next;
```

Initially, **curr** points to the first item, if any, in the list. If it is not **null**, the statement

```
curr = curr.next;
```

is executed. This sets **curr** to point to 'whatever the current node is pointing to'; in effect, the next node. For example, given the list:

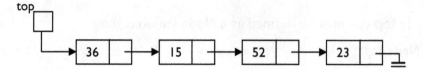

initially, **curr** points to (the node containing) 36. Since **curr** is not **null**, it is set to point to whatever 36 is pointing to, that is, (the node containing) 15.

The **while** condition is tested again. Since **curr** is not **null**, **curr** = **curr.next** is executed, setting **curr** to point to whatever 15 is pointing to, that is, 52.

The **while** condition is tested again. Since **curr** is not **null**, **curr** = **curr.next** is executed, setting **curr** to point to whatever 52 is pointing to, that is, 23.

The **while** condition is tested again. Since **curr** is not **null**, **curr** = **curr.next** is executed, setting **curr** to point to whatever 23 is pointing to, that is, **null**.

The **while** condition is tested again. Since **curr** *is* **null**, the while loop is no longer executed.

Note that each time **curr** is not **null**, we enter the **while** loop. But the number of times that **curr** is *not* **null** is exactly the same as the number of items in the list. So in order to count the number of items in the list, we just have count how many times the **while** body is executed.

To do this, we use a counter initialized to 0 and increment it by 1 inside the **while** loop. We can now write the function as follows (we call it **length**):

```java
public static int length(Node top) {
    int n = 0;
    Node curr = top;
    while (curr != null) {
        n++;
        curr = curr.next;
    }
    return n;
}
```

Note that if the list is empty, **curr** will be **null** the first time and the **while** loop will not be executed. The function will return 0, the correct result.

Strictly speaking, the variable **curr** is not necessary. The function will work fine if we omit **curr** and replace **curr** by **top** in the function. At the end of the execution of the function, **top** will be **null**.

You may be worried that you have lost access to the list. But do not be. Remember that **top** in **length** is a *copy* of whatever variable (**head**, say) is pointing to the list in the calling function. Changing **top** has no effect whatsoever on **head**. When **length** returns, **head** is still pointing to the first item in the list.

1.1.2 Searching a linked list

Another common operation is to search a linked list for a given item. For example, given the list

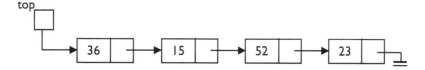

we may wish to search for the number 52. Our search should be able to tell us that 52 is in the list. On the other hand, if we search for 25, our search should report that 25 is not in the list.

Suppose the number we are searching for is stored in the variable, **key**. The search proceeds by comparing **key** with each number in the list, starting from the first one. If **key** matches with any item, we have found it. If we get to the end of the list and **key** did not match any item, we can conclude that **key** is not in the list.

We must write the logic so that the search ends if we find a match *or* we reach the end of the list. Put another way, the search continues if we have not reached the end of the list *and* we do not have a match. If **curr** points to some item in the list, we can express this logic as:

```
while (curr != null && key != curr.num) curr = curr.next;
```

The condition **curr != null** must be written first. If **curr** *is* **null**, the **&&** is false and the second condition **key != curr.num** is not evaluated.

If we wrote

```
while (key != curr.num && curr != null) curr = curr.next; //wrong
```

and **curr** happens to be **null**, our program will crash when it tries to retrieve **curr.num**; in effect, this asks for the number pointed to by **curr** but if **curr** is **null**, it does not point to anything. We say we are trying to "de-reference a **null** pointer", and that is an error.

Let us write the search as a function which, given a pointer to the list and **key**, returns the node containing **key** if it is found. If not found, the function returns **null**.

We assume the **Node** declaration from the previous section. Our function will return a value of type **Node**. Here it is:

```
public static Node search(Node top, int key) {
    while (top != null && key != top.num)
        top = top.next;
    return top;
}
```

If **key** is not in the list, **top** will become **null** and **null** will be returned. If **key** is in the list, the **while** loop is exited when **key** = **top.num**; at this stage, **top** is pointing to the node containing **key** and *this* value of **top** is returned.

1.1.3 Finding the last node in a linked list

Sometimes, we need to find the pointer to the last node in a list. Recall that the last node in the list is distinguished by *its* **next** pointer being **null**. Here is a function which returns a pointer to the last node in a given list. If the list is empty, the function returns **null**.

```
public static Node getLast(Node top) {
    if (top == null) return null;
    while (top.next != null)
        top = top.next;
    return top;
}
```

We get to the **while** statement if **top** is not **null**. It therefore makes sense to ask about **top.next**. If *this* is not **null**, the loop is entered and **top** is set to this non-**null** value. This ensures that the **while** condition is defined the next time it is executed. When **top.next** *is* **null**, **top** is pointing at the last node and *this* value of **top** is returned.

1.2 Building a linked list – adding new item at the tail

Consider the problem of reading positive integers (terminated by 0) and building a linked list which contains the numbers in the order in which they were read. For example, given the data

        36 15 52 23 0

we want to build the following linked list:

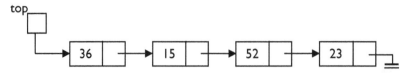

One question which arises is how many nodes will there be in the list? This, of course, depends on how many numbers are supplied. One disadvantage of using an array for storing a linear list is that the size of the array must be specified beforehand. If, when the program is run, it finds that it needs to store more items than this size allows, it may have to be aborted.

With the linked list approach, whenever a new node must be added to the list, storage is allocated for the node and the appropriate pointers are set. Thus we allocate just the right amount of storage for the list—no more, no less.

We do use extra storage for the pointers, but this is more than compensated for by more efficient use of storage as well as easy insertions and deletions. Allocating storage 'as needed' is usually referred to as *dynamic storage allocation*. (On the other hand, array storage is referred to as *static* storage.)

In our solution to building the list as described above, we start with an empty list. Our program will reflect this with the statement

        top = null;

When we read a new number, we must

- allocate storage for a node;
- put the number in the new node;
- make the new node the last one in the list.

Using our **Node** class on page 2, let us write a constructor which, given an integer argument, sets **num** to the integer and sets **next** to **null**.

```
public Node(int n) {
  num = n;
  next = null;
}
```

The statement

        Node p = new Node(36);

is executed as follows. First, storage for a new node is allocated. Assuming an **int** occupies 4 bytes and a pointer occupies 4 bytes, the size of **Node** is 8 bytes. So 8 bytes are allocated starting at address 4000, say. 36 is stored in the **num** field and **null** in the **next** field, thus:

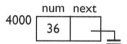

The value 4000 is then assigned to **p**; in effect **p** is pointing at the object just created. Since the actual address 4000 is not normally important, we usually depict this as:

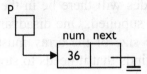

In other words, **p** is pointing to the object wherever it happens to be.

When we read the first number, we must create a node for it and set **top** to point to the new node. In our example, when we read 36, we must create the following:

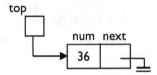

If **n** contains the new number, this can be accomplished with

```
if (top == null) top = new Node(n);
```

There are no arrows inside the computer but the effect is achieved with the following (assuming the new node is stored at location 4000):

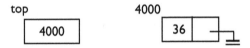

For each subsequent number, we must set the **next** field of the current last node to point to the new node. The new node becomes the last node. Suppose the new number is 15. We must create:

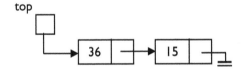

But how do we find the last node of the existing list? One method is to start at the top of the list and follow the **next** pointers until we encounter **null**. This is time-consuming if we have to do it for each new number. A better approach is to keep a pointer (**last**, say) to the last node of the list. This pointer is updated as new nodes are added. The code for this could be written like this:

```
np = new Node(n);          //create a new node
if (top == null) top = np;  //set top if first node
else last.next = np;        //set last.next for other nodes
last = np;                  //update last to new node
```

Suppose there is just one node in the list; this is also the last node. In our example, the value of **last** will be 4000. Suppose the node containing 15 is stored at location 2000. We have the following situation:

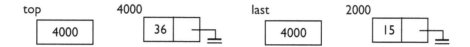

The above code will set the **next** field at location 4000 to 2000 and set **last** to 2000. The following is the result:

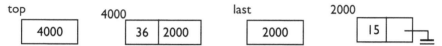

Now **top** (4000) points to the node containing 36; this node's **next** field is 2000 and, hence, points to the node containing 15. This node's **next** field is **null**, indicating the end of the list. The value of **last** is 2000, the address of the last node in the list. Program P1.1 reads the numbers and creates the linked list as discussed.

```
                            Program P1.1
import java.util.*;
public class BuildList1 {

  public static void main(String[] args) {
    Scanner in = new Scanner(System.in);
    Node top, np, last = null;

    top = null;
    System.out.printf("Enter some integers ending with 0\n");
    int n = in.nextInt();
    while (n != 0) {
      np = new Node(n);        //create a new node containing n
      if (top == null) top = np;        //set top if first node
      else last.next = np;     //set last.next for other nodes
      last = np;        //update last to new node
      n = in.nextInt();
    }
    printList(top);
  } //end main

  public static void printList(Node top) {
    while (top != null) {  //as long as there's a node
      System.out.printf("%d ", top.num);
      top = top.next;  //go on to the next node
    }
    System.out.printf("\n");
  } //end printList
} //end class BuildList1

//add Node class with constructor here
```

In order to verify that the list has been built correctly, we should print its contents. The method **printList** traverses the list from the first node to the last, printing the number at each node.

1.3 Insertion into a linked list

A list with one pointer in each node is called a *one-way linked list*. One important characteristic of such a list is that access to the nodes is via the 'top of list' pointer and the pointer field in each node[2]. This means that access is restricted to being sequential.

The only way to get to node 4, say, is via nodes 1, 2 and 3. Since we can't access the kth node directly, we will not be able, for instance, to perform a binary search on a linked list. The great advantage of a linked list is that it allows for easy insertions and deletions anywhere in the list.

Suppose we want to insert a new node between the second and third nodes. We can view this simply as insertion after the second node. For example, suppose **prev** points to the second node and **np** points to the new node:

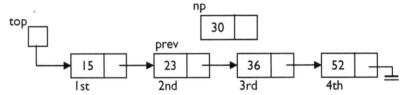

We can insert the new node by setting its **next** field to point to the third node and the **next** field of the second node to point to the new node. Note that all we need to do the insertion is the second node; *its* **next** field will give us the third node. The insertion can be done with:

```
np.next = prev.next;
prev.next = np;
```

The first statement says 'let the new node point to whatever the second node is pointing at, i.e., the third node'. The second statement says 'let the second node point to the new node'. The net effect is that the new node is inserted between the second and the third. The new node becomes the third node and the original third node becomes the fourth node. This changes the above list into:

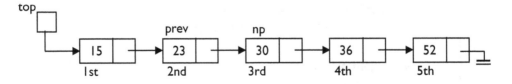

---

[2] However, other explicit pointers may point to specific nodes in the list, for example, the pointer **last**, above, which points to the last node in the list.

Does this code work if **prev** were pointing at the last node so that we are, in fact, inserting after the last node? Yes. If **prev** is the last node then **prev.next** is **null**. Therefore, the statement

> np.next = prev.next;

sets **np.next** to **null** so that the new node becomes the last node. As before, **prev.next** is set to point to the new node. This is illustrated by changing

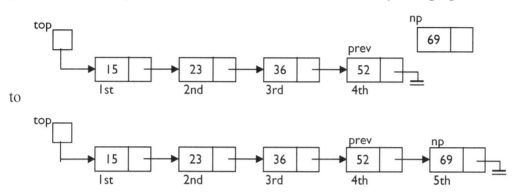

to

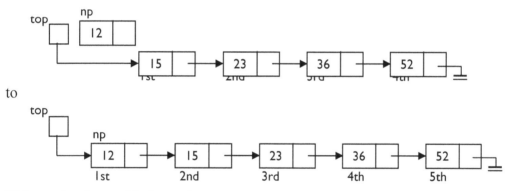

In many situations, it is required to insert a new node at the head of the list. That is, we want to make the new node the first node. Assuming that **np** points to the new node, we want to convert

to

This can be done with the code:

> np.next = top;
> top = np;

The first statement sets the new node to point to whatever **top** is pointing at (that is, the first node), and the second statement updates **top** to point to the new node.

You should observe that the code works even if the list is initially empty (that is, if **top** is **null**). In this case, it converts

into

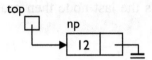

1.4 Building a linked list – adding new item at the head

Consider again the problem of building a linked list of positive integers but, this time, we insert each new number at the head of the list rather than at the end. The resulting list will have the number in reverse order to how they are given. If the incoming numbers are (0 terminates the data)

      36 15 52 23 0

we want to build the following linked list:

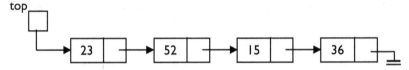

The program to build the list in reverse order is actually simpler than the previous one. It is almost identical to Program P1.1. Only the **while** loop needs to be changed to:

```
while (n != 0) {
    np = new Node(n);   //create a new node containing n
    np.next = top;      //set it to point to first node
    top = np;           //update top to point to new node
    n = in.nextInt();
}
```

As each new number is read, we set its link to point to the first node, and we set **top** to point to the new node, making it the (new) first node.

Program P1.1 inserts incoming numbers at the tail of the list. This is an example of adding an item to a *queue*. A queue is a linear list in which insertions occur at one end and deletions (see next) occur at the other end.

When we change the **while** loop as above, we insert incoming numbers at the head of the list. This is an example of adding an item to a *stack*. A stack is a linear list in which insertions and deletions occur *at the same end*. In stack terminology, when we add an item, we say the item is *pushed* onto the stack. Deleting an item from a stack is referred to as *popping* the stack.

We will discuss stacks and queues in detail in the next chapter.

1.5 Deletion from a linked list

Deleting a node from the top of a linked list is accomplished by

```
top = top.next;
```

This says let **top** point to whatever the first node was pointing at (that is, the second node, if any). Since **top** is now pointing at the second node, effectively, the first node has been deleted from the list. This statement changes

to

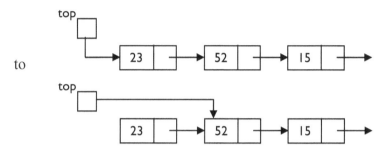

Of course, before we delete, we should check that there *is* something to delete, that **top** is not **null**.

If there is only one node in the list, deleting it will result in the empty list; **top** will become **null**.

To delete an arbitrary node from a linked list requires more information. Suppose **curr** (for 'current') points to the node to be deleted. Deleting this node requires that we change the **next** field of the *previous* node. This means we must know the pointer to the previous node; suppose it is **prev** (for 'previous'). Then deletion of node **curr** can be accomplished by

```
prev.next = curr.next;
```

This changes

to

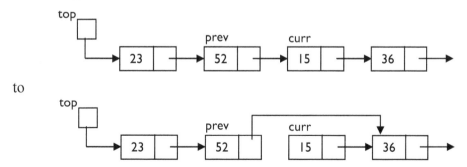

Effectively, the node pointed to by **curr** is no longer in the list—it has been deleted.

One may wonder what happens to nodes which have been deleted. In our discussion above, 'deletion' meant 'logical deletion', that is, as far as processing the list is concerned, the deleted nodes are not present. But the nodes are still in memory, occupying storage, even though we may have lost the pointers to them.

If we have a large list in which many deletions have occurred, then there will be a lot of 'deleted' nodes scattered all over memory. These nodes occupy storage even though they will never, and cannot, be processed.

Java's solution to this problem is "automatic garbage collection". From time to time, Java checks for these 'unreachable' nodes and removes them, reclaiming the storage they occupy. The programmer never has to worry about these 'deleted' nodes.

1.6 Building a sorted linked list

As a third possibility, suppose we want to build the list so that the numbers are always sorted in ascending order. If the incoming numbers are (0 terminates the data)

        36 15 52 23 0

we want to build the following list:

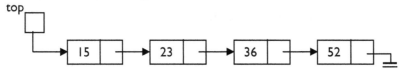

When a new number is read, it is inserted in the existing list (which is initially empty) in its proper place. The first number is simply added to the empty list.

Each subsequent number is compared with the numbers in the existing list. As long as the new number is greater than a number in the list, we move down the list until the new number is smaller than, or equal to, an existing number or we come to the end of the list.

To facilitate the insertion of the new number, before we leave a node and move on to the next one, we must save the pointer to it in case the new number must be inserted after this node. However, we can only know this when we compare the new number with the number in the next node.

To illustrate these ideas, consider the sorted list

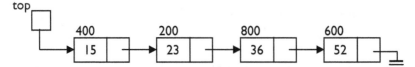

and suppose we want to add a new number (30, say) to the list so that it remains sorted. Assume the number above a node is the address of the node. Thus the value of **top** is 400.

First, we compare 30 with 15. It is bigger, so we move on to the next number, 23, saving the address (400) of 15.

Next, we compare 30 with 23. It is bigger, so we move on to the next number, 36, saving the address (200) of 23. We no longer need the address (400) of 15.

Next, we compare 30 with 36. It is smaller, so we have found the number *before* which we must insert 30. This is the same as inserting 30 *after* 23. Since we had saved the address of 23, we can now perform the insertion.

We will use the following code to process the new number, **n**:

```
prev = null;
curr = top;
while (curr != null && n > curr.num) {
  prev = curr;
  curr = curr.next;
}
```

Initially, **prev** is **null** and **curr** is 400. The insertion of 30 proceeds as follows:

- 30 is compared with **curr.num**, 15. It is bigger so we set **prev** to **curr** (400) and set **curr** to **curr.next**, 200; **curr** is not **null**.
- 30 is compared with **curr.num**, 23. It is bigger so we set **prev** to **curr** (200) and set **curr** to **curr.next**, 800; **curr** is not **null**.
- 30 is compared with **curr.num**, 36. It is smaller so we exit the **while** loop with **prev** being 200 and **curr** being 800.

We have the following situation:

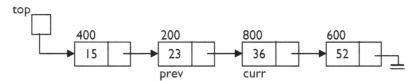

If the new number is stored in a node pointed to by **np**, we can now add it to the list with the following code:

```
np.next = curr;  //we could also use prev.next for curr
prev.next = np;
```

This will change

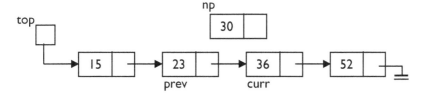

to

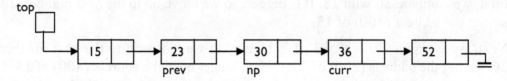

As an exercise, verify that this code will work if the number to be added is bigger than all the numbers in the list. Hint: when will the **while** loop exit?

If the number to be added is *smaller* than all the numbers in the list, it must be added at the head of the list and becomes the new first node in the list. This means that the value of **top** has to be changed to the new node.

The **while** loop above will work in this case as well. The **while** condition will be false on the very first test (since **n** will be smaller than **curr.num**). On exit, we simply test if **prev** is *still* **null**; if it is, the new node must be inserted at the top of the list.

If the list were initially empty, the **while** loop will exit immediately (since **curr** will be **null**). In this case also, the new node must be inserted at the top of the list, becoming the only node in the list.

Program P1.2 contains all the details. The insertion of a new node in its proper position in the list is delegated to the function **addInPlace**. This function returns a pointer to the top of the modified list.

Program P1.2

```java
import java.util.*;
public class BuildList3 {

   public static void main(String[] args) {
      Scanner in = new Scanner(System.in);
      Node top, np, last = null;

      top = null;
      System.out.printf("Enter some integers ending with 0\n");
      int n = in.nextInt();
      while (n != 0) {
         top = addInPlace(top, n);
         n = in.nextInt();
      }
      printList(top);
   } //end main
```

```
public static Node addInPlace(Node top, int n) {
// This functions inserts n in its ordered position in a (possibly empty)
// list pointed to by top, and returns a pointer to the new list
   Node np, curr, prev;

   np = new Node(n);
   prev = null;
   curr = top;
   while (curr != null && n > curr.num) {
     prev = curr;
     curr = curr.next;
   }
   np.next = curr;
   if (prev == null) return np; //top of list is now the new node
   prev.next = np;
   return top; //the top of the list has not changed
 } //end addInPlace

   // printList goes here; same as for P1.1
} //end class BuildList3

// class Node goes here
```

The following is a sample run of P1.2:

```
Enter some integers ending with 0
8 3 5 9 1 7 2 4 6 0
1 2 3 4 5 6 7 8 9
```

1.7 A linked list class

We have discussed many of the basic ideas involved in the processing of linked lists and we have seen how to implement common operations on linked lists. We used **static** methods (**printList**, **addInPlace**) and passed the "head node" of the list as an argument.

Let us now change our viewpoint slightly. Our goal is to write a "linked list class" from which we can create "linked list objects" which we can use for working with linked lists.

The first question to answer is "What defines a linked list?" That's easy. It's the (object) variable, essentially a pointer, which points to the first node in the list. So our class will begin as follows:

```
public class LinkedList {
   Node head = null;
      .
```

```
} //end class LinkedList
```

We will use **head** as our "top of list" variable. Even though Java will initialize it to **null** when we use a statement like

```
LinkedList LL = new LinkedList();
```

we do so explicitly to draw attention to its initial value.

How do we define **Node**? Well, it depends on the kind of items (the "data") that we wish to store in the list. If we want a list of integers, we can use

```
class Node {
  int num;
  Node next;
}
```

If we want a list of characters, we can use

```
class Node {
  char ch;
  Node next;
}
```

And if we want a list of parts, we can use

```
class Node {
  Part part;
  Node next;
}
```

As you can see, we would need to change the definition of **Node** each time we want a different kind of linked list. But we would also need to change a method if its code depends on the kind of item in the list. Consider, for example, a method which adds a new node at the head of a list of integers:

```
public void addHead(int n) {
  Node p = new Node(n); //assume Node has the appropriate constructor
  p.next = head;
  head = p;
}
```

This can be used, for instance, as follows (**LL** is a **LinkedList**):

```
LL.addHead(25);
```

This will add a node containing 25 at the head of the list, **LL**.

But if we need a list of characters, we would need to change the heading to

```
public void addHead(char c)
```

and, for a list of **Part** objects, to

```
public void addHead(Part p)
```

If there are many methods in the class, these changes could become quite tedious every time we need to change the kind of data stored in our list.

We will use an approach that will minimize the changes required in **LinkedList**.

Let us define the class **Node** as follows:

```
class Node {
  NodeData data;
  Node next;

  public Node(NodeData nd) {
    data = nd;
    next = null;
  }
} //end class Node
```

We write the class in terms of an unspecified, as yet, data type, **NodeData**. There are two fields, **data** and **next**. Without knowing anything more about **NodeData**, we can write **addHead** as follows:

```
public void addHead(NodeData nd) {
  Node p = new Node(nd);
  p.next = head;
  head = p;
}
```

A class (**TestList**, say) that wants to use **LinkedList** must provide a definition of **NodeData** that is available to **LinkedList**. Suppose we want a linked list of integers. We can define **NodeData** as follows (we will explain the need for **toString** shortly):

```
public class NodeData {
  int num;

  public NodeData(int n) {
    num = n;
  }

  public String toString() {
    return num + " ";
    //" " needed to convert num to a string; may also use "" (empty string)
  }
} //end class NodeData
```

and build a linked list in reverse order with code such as:

```
LinkedList LL = new LinkedList();
System.out.printf("Enter some integers ending with 0\n");
int n = in.nextInt();
while (n != 0) {
    LL.addHead(new NodeData(n)); //NodeData argument required
    n = in.nextInt();
}
```

Note that since **addHead** requires a **NodeData** argument, we must create a **NodeData** object with the integer **n** to be passed to **addHead**.

How can we print the items in a list? Presumably, we would like a method (**printList**, say) in the **LinkedList** class which does the job. But since **LinkedList** does not know what **NodeData** might contain (and it could vary from one run to the next) how can it print the data in a node?

The trick is to let **NodeData** print itself using the **toString** method. Here is one way to write **printList**:

```
public void printList() {
    Node curr = head;
    while (curr != null) {
        System.out.printf("%s", curr.data); //invokes curr.data.toString()
        curr = curr.next;
    }
    System.out.printf("\n");
} //end printList
```

Recall that **curr.data** is a **NodeData** object. Since we use it in a context where a string is required, Java will look in the **NodeData** class for a **toString** method. Since it finds one, it will use it to print **curr.data**. The **printf** statement could also have been written as follows where we call **toString** explicitly:

```
System.out.printf("%s ", curr.data.toString());
```

If **LL** is a **LinkedList**, the list can be printed with:

```
LL.printList();
```

So far, our **LinkedList** class consists of the following:

```
public class LinkedList {
    Node head = null;

    public void addHead(NodeData nd) {
        Node p = new Node(nd);
        p.next = head;
        head = p;
    }
```

```
      public void printList() {
        Node curr = head;
        while (curr != null) {
          System.out.printf("%s", curr.data); //invokes curr.data.toString()
          curr = curr.next;
        }
        System.out.printf("\n");
      } //end printList

  } //end class LinkedList
```

We could add a method to check if a linked list is empty:

```
      public boolean empty() {
        return head == null;
      }
```

If **LL** is a **LinkedList**, we can use **empty** as in:

```
      while (!LL.empty()) { ...
```

Now suppose we want to add a method which will build a linked list in 'sorted order'. Again, since **LinkedList** does not know what **NodeData** might contain, how do we define 'sorted order' in **LinkedList**? Again, the solution is to let **NodeData** tell us when one **NodeData** item is less than, equal to or greater than another **NodeData** item.

We can do this by writing an instance method (we'll call it **compareTo**) in **NodeData**:

```
      public int compareTo(NodeData nd) {
        if (this.num == nd.num) return 0;
        if (this.num < nd.num) return -1;
        return 1;
      }
```

Here, we use the Java keyword **this** for the first time. If **a** and **b** are two **NodeData** objects, remember that we can call the method with **a.compareTo(b)**. In the method, **this** refers to the object used to call it. Thus, **this.num** refers to **a.num**. We note that the method will work just the same without **this**, for **num**, by itself, does refer to **a.num**.

Since the **NodeData** class we are using has one integer field, **num**, **compareTo** reduces to comparing two integers. The expression **a.compareTo(b)** returns 0 if **a.num** is equal to **b.num**, −1 if **a.num** is less than **b.num** and 1 if **a.num** is greater than **b.num**.

Using **compareTo**, we can write **addInPlace** as follows:

```
public void addInPlace(NodeData nd) {
  Node np, curr, prev;
  np = new Node(nd);
  prev = null;
  curr = head;
  while (curr != null && nd.compareTo(curr.data) > 0) { //new value is bigger
    prev = curr;
    curr = curr.next;
  }
  np.next = curr;
  if (prev == null) head = np;
  else prev.next = np;
} //end addInPlace
```

It is similar to the method on page 17. If **LL** is a **LinkedList**, we can use it as in:

```
LL.addInPlace(new NodeData(25));
```

This will create a **Node** with a **NodeData** object containing 25 and insert this node in the list so that the list is in ascending order.

The following class reads integers, builds a linked list in ascending order and prints the sorted list:

```
import java.util.*;
public class LinkedListTest {
  public static void main(String[] args) {
    Scanner in = new Scanner(System.in);
    LinkedList LL = new LinkedList();
    System.out.printf("Enter some integers ending with 0\n");
    int n = in.nextInt();
    while (n != 0) {
      LL.addInPlace(new NodeData(n));
      n = in.nextInt();
    }
    LL.printList();
  } //end main
} //end LinkedListTest
```

How to organize Java files

So far, we have been dealing with 4 classes—**LinkedList, Node, NodeData** and **LinkedListTest**. You may be wondering where do we store these classes.

For starters, we can store the **LinkedListTest** class, above, in a file which must be called **LinkedListTest.java**. Remember that a **public** class **x** must be stored in a file called **x.java**. We can store the other classes in the *same* file provided we write the class header as **class xxx** rather than **public class xxx**.

However, in order for our classes to be usable by other classes, we will organize them differently. We will store the **NodeData** class in a file by itself. The file must be called **NodeData.java** and, so far, will contain the following:

```java
public class NodeData {
  int num;
  public NodeData(int n) {
    num = n;
  }
  public int compareTo(NodeData nd) {
    if (this.num == nd.num) return 0;
    if (this.num < nd.num) return -1;
    return 1;
  }
  public String toString() {
    return num + " ";
    //" " needed to convert num to a string; may also use "" (empty string)
  }
} //end class NodeData
```

We will store the **LinkedList** class in a file **LinkedList.java**. Since the **Node** class is used only by the **LinkedList** class, we will store it in the same file which, so far, will contain the following:

```java
public class LinkedList {
  Node head = null;
  public void addHead(NodeData nd) {
    Node p = new Node(nd);
    p.next = head;
    head = p;
  }
  public void printList() {
    Node curr = head;
    while (curr != null) {
      System.out.printf("%s", curr.data); //invokes curr.data.toString()
      curr = curr.next;
    }
    System.out.printf("\n");
  } //end printList
```

```
    public void addInPlace(NodeData nd) {
      Node np, curr, prev;

      np = new Node(nd);
      prev = null;
      curr = head;
      while (curr != null && nd.compareTo(curr.data) > 0) { //nd is bigger
        prev = curr;
        curr = curr.next;
      }
      np.next = curr;
      if (prev == null) head = np;
      else prev.next = np;
    } //end addInPlace

} //end class LinkedList

class Node {              -
  NodeData data;
  Node next;

  public Node(NodeData d) {
    data = d;
    next = null;
  }
} //end class Node
```

We note that if the **Node** class were needed by another class, it would be best to declare it **public** and put it in a file called **Node.java**.

Expanding the *LinkedList* class

In order to prepare for the next example, we will expand the **LinkedList** class with the following methods. The function **getHeadData** returns the **data** field of the first node, if any, in the list.

```
    public NodeData getHeadData() {
      if (head == null) return null;
      return head.data;
    }
```

The method **deleteHead** removes the first node, if any, in the list.

```
    public void deleteHead() {
      if (head != null) head = head.next;
    }
```

24

The method **addTail** adds a new node at the end of the list. It finds the last node (for which **next** is **null**) and sets it to point to the new node.

```
public void addTail(NodeData nd) {
  Node p = new Node(nd);
  if (head == null) head = p;
  else {
    Node curr = head;
    while (curr.next != null) curr = curr.next;
    curr.next = p;
  }
} //end addTail
```

The function **copyList** makes a copy of the list used to call it and returns the copy.

```
public LinkedList copyList() {
  LinkedList temp = new LinkedList();
  Node curr = this.head;
  while (curr != null) {
    temp.addTail(curr.data);
    curr = curr.next;
  }
  return temp;
} //end copyList
```

The method **reverseList** reverses the order of the nodes in the given list. It works on the original list, not a copy.

```
public void reverseList() {
  Node p1, p2, p3;
  if (head == null || head.next == null) return;
  p1 = head;
  p2 = p1.next;
  p1.next = null;
  while (p2 != null) {
    p3 = p2.next;
    p2.next = p1;
    p1 = p2;
    p2 = p3;
  }
  head = p1;
} //end reverseList
```

The function **equals** compares two linked lists. If **L1** and **L2** are two linked lists, the expression **L1.equals(L2)** is **true** if they contain identical elements in the same order and **false**, otherwise.

```
public boolean equals(LinkedList LL) {
   Node t1 = this.head;
   Node t2 = LL.head;
   while (t1 != null && t2 != null) {
      if (t1.data.compareTo(t2.data) != 0) return false;
      t1 = t1.next;
      t2 = t2.next;
   }
   if (t1 != null || t2 != null) return false; //if one ended but not the other
   return true;
} //end equals
```

1.8 Example - palindrome

Consider the problem of determining if a given string is a *palindrome* (the same when spelt forwards or backwards). Examples of palindromes (ignoring case, punctuation and spaces) are:

> **civic**
> **Racecar**
> **Madam, I'm Adam.**
> A man, a plan, a canal, Panama.

If all the letters were of the same case (upper or lower) and the string (**word**, say) contained no spaces or punctuation marks, we *could* solve the problem as follows:

> compare the first and last letters
> if they are different, the string is not a palindrome
> if they are the same, compare the second and second to last letters
> if they are different, the string is not a palindrome
> if they are the same, compare the third and third to last letters

and so on; we continue until we find a non-matching pair (and it's not a palindrome) or there are no more pairs to compare (and it is a palindrome).

This method is efficient but it requires us to be able to access any letter in the word directly. This is possible if the word is stored in an array and we use a subscript to access any letter. However, if the letters of the word are stored in a linked list, we cannot use this method since we can only access the letters sequentially.

In order to illustrate how linked lists may be manipulated, we will use linked lists to solve the problem using the following idea:

> (1) store the original phrase in a linked list, one character per node
> (2) create another list containing the letters only of the phrase, all converted to lowercase; call this list1
> (3) reverse list1 to get list2

(4) compare list1 with list2, node by node, until we get a mismatch (phrase is not a palindrome) or we come to the end of the lists (phrase is a palindrome)

Consider the phrase **Damn Mad!**; this will be stored as:

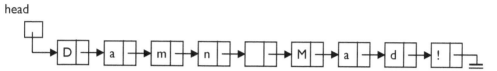

Step (2), above, will convert this to

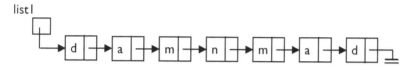

Step (3), above, will then convert this to

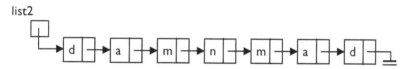

Comparing **list1** and **list2** will reveal that **Damn Mad!** is a palindrome.

We will write a program which prompts the user to type a phrase and tells her if it is a palindrome or not. It then prompts for another phrase. To stop, the user must press "Enter" only. The following is a sample run:

```
Type a phrase. (To stop, press "Enter" only): Damn Mad!
is a palindrome
Type a phrase. (To stop, press "Enter" only): So Many Dynamos!
is a palindrome
Type a phrase. (To stop, press "Enter" only): Rise to vote, sir.
is a palindrome
Type a phrase. (To stop, press "Enter" only): Thermostat
is not a palindrome
Type a phrase. (To stop, press "Enter" only): A Toyota's a Toyota.
is a palindrome
Type a phrase. (To stop, press "Enter" only):
```

Previously, we worked with a linked list of integers. But, now, we need a linked list of characters. If we did things right, we should only need to make changes in the **NodeData** class. We should not have to change *anything* in the **LinkedList** class, and we won't. Here is what **NodeData** should look like:

```
public class NodeData {
    char ch;

    public NodeData(char c) {
        ch = c;
    }

    public char getData() {return ch;}

    public int compareTo(NodeData nd) {
        if (this.ch == nd.ch) return 0;
        if (this.ch < nd.ch) return -1;
        return 1;
    }

    public String toString() {
        return ch + "";
    }
} //end class NodeData
```

We have added an accessor, **getData**, to return the value in the only data field, **ch**. The other changes essentially involve changing **int** to **char**.

We will write a function, **getPhrase**, which will read the data and store the characters of the phrase in a linked list, one character per node. The function returns the newly-created list. This function must build the linked list in the order in which the characters in the phrase are typed.

The function achieves this by first reading the entire phrase using **nextLine**. Then, starting at the last character and going backwards, it inserts each new character at the *head* of the list. (We could also start at the first character and add each new character at the *tail* of the list but this requires more work.) Here is the function:

```
public static LinkedList getPhrase(Scanner in) {
    LinkedList phrase = new LinkedList();
    String str = in.nextLine();
    for (int j = str.length() - 1; j >= 0; j--)
        phrase.addHead(new NodeData(str.charAt(j)));
    return phrase;
}
```

Next, we write a function, **lettersLower**, which, given a linked list of characters, creates another list containing the letters only, all converted to lowercase. As each letter is encountered, it is converted to lowercase and added to the *tail* of the new list using **addTail**. The function is shown on the next page.

The expression **phrase.getHeadData()** returns the **data** field (of type **NodeData**) of the first node in the list. The accessor, **getData**, in the **NodeData** class, returns the character stored in the node.

```
public static LinkedList lettersLower(LinkedList phrase) {
  LinkedList word = new LinkedList();

  while (!phrase.empty()) {
    char ch = phrase.getHeadData().getData();
    if (Character.isLetter(ch))
        word.addTail(new NodeData(Character.toLowerCase(ch)));
    phrase.deleteHead();
  }
  return word;
}
```

We now have everything we need to write Program P1.3 which solves the palindrome problem as described on page 26.

Program P1.3

```
import java.util.*;
public class Palindrome {
  public static void main(String[] args) {
    Scanner in = new Scanner(System.in);
    System.out.printf("Type a phrase. (To stop, press 'Enter' only): ");
    LinkedList aPhrase = getPhrase(in);
    while (!aPhrase.empty()) {
      LinkedList w1 = lettersLower(aPhrase);
      System.out.printf("Converted to: ");
      w1.printList();
      LinkedList w2 = w1.copyList();
      w2.reverseList();
      if (w1.equals(w2)) System.out.printf("is a palindrome\n");
      else System.out.printf("is not a palindrome\n");
      System.out.printf("Type a phrase. (To stop, press 'Enter' only): ");
      aPhrase = getPhrase(in);
    }
  } //end main

  // getPhrase and lettersLower go here

} //end class Palindrome
```

1.9 Merging two sorted linked lists

We consider the problem of merging two ordered linked lists to produce one ordered list. Suppose the given lists are:

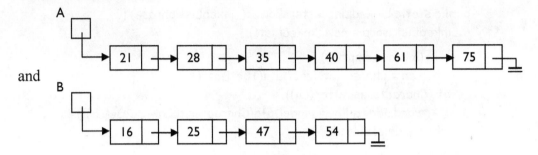

and

We wish to create one linked list with all the numbers in ascending order, thus:

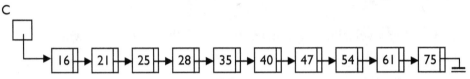

We will create the merged list by creating a new node for each number that we add to the list **C**; we leave the lists **A** and **B** untouched. We will use the following algorithm:

```
while (at least one number remains in both A and B) {
  if (smallest in A < smallest in B)
    add smallest in A to C
    move on to next number in A
  else
    add smallest in B to C
    move on to next number in B
  endif
}
//at this stage, at least one of the lists has ended
while (A has numbers) {
  add smallest in A to C
  move on to next number in A
}
while (B has numbers) {
  add smallest in B to C
  move on to next number in B
}
```

If **A** and **B** are of type **LinkedList**, we will write an instance method, **merge**, in the **LinkedList** class such that **A.merge(B)** will return a **LinkedList** containing the merged elements of **A** and **B**. The method is shown on the next page.

As implemented, **addTail** has to traverse the entire list to find the end before adding each new node. This is inefficient. We *could* keep a pointer (**tail**, say) to the end of the list to facilitate adding a node at the end. But this would complicate the class unnecessarily at this stage.

```
public LinkedList merge(LinkedList LL) {
   Node A = this.head;
   Node B = LL.head;
   LinkedList C = new LinkedList();
   while (A != null && B != null) {
      if (A.data.compareTo(B.data) < 0) {
         C.addTail(A.data);
         A = A.next;
      }
      else {
         C.addTail(B.data);
         B = B.next;
      }
   }
   while (A != null) {
      C.addTail(A.data);
      A = A.next;
   }
   while (B != null) {
      C.addTail(B.data);
      B = B.next;
   }
   return C;
} //end merge
```

Since adding a node at the head is a simple operation, it would be more efficient here to add a new node at the head and, when the merge is completed, reverse the list. We simply replace **addTail** by **addHead** and, just before **return C**, we insert the statement **C.reverseList();**.

To test **merge**, we write Program P1.4 (next page). It requests the user to enter data for two lists. The data can be entered in any order. The lists will be built in sorted order by adding each new number 'in place'. A sample run is shown below:

```
Enter some integers ending with 0
8 4 12 6 10 2 0
Enter some integers ending with 0
5 7 15 1 3  0

When we merge
2 4 6 8 10 12
with
1 3 5 7 15
we get
1 2 3 4 5 6 7 8 10 12 15
```

```
                          Program P1.4
        import java.util.*;
        public class MergeLists {
          public static void main(String[] args) {
            Scanner in = new Scanner(System.in);
            LinkedList A = createSortedList(in);
            LinkedList B = createSortedList(in);
            System.out.printf("\nWhen we merge\n");
            A.printList();
            System.out.printf("with\n");
            B.printList();
            System.out.printf("we get\n");
            A.merge(B).printList();
          } //end main

          public static LinkedList createSortedList(Scanner in) {
            LinkedList LL = new LinkedList();
            System.out.printf("Enter some integers ending with 0\n");
            int n = in.nextInt();
            while (n != 0) {
              LL.addInPlace(new NodeData(n));
              n = in.nextInt();
            }
            return LL;
          }
        } //end MergeLists
```

Exercises 1

1. Write an instance method in the **LinkedList** class which returns **true** if the list is sorted in ascending order and **false**, otherwise.

2. Write an instance method to reverse the nodes of a linked list by creating a new list. The method returns the newly-created list.

3. Write a method to sort a linked list of integers as follows:

    (a) Find the largest value in the list.
    (b) Delete it from its position and insert it at the head of the list.
    (c) Starting from what is now the second element, repeat (a) and (b).
    (d) Starting from what is now the third element, repeat (a) and (b).

    Continue until the list is sorted.

4. Write a function which takes 3 arguments—a pointer to a linked list of integers, and two integers **n** and **j**—and inserts **n** after the **j**th element of the list. If **j** is 0, **n** is inserted at the head of the list. If **j** is greater than the number of elements in the list, **n** is inserted after the last one.

5. The characters of a string are held on a linked list, one character per node.

(a) Write a method which, given a pointer to a string and two characters, **c1** and **c2**, replaces all occurrences of **c1** with **c2**.

(b) Write a function which, given a pointer to a string and a character, **c**, deletes all occurrences of **c** from the string. Return a pointer to the modified string.

(c) Write a function which creates a new list consisting of the letters only in the given list, all converted to lowercase and stored in alphabetical order. Return a pointer to the new list.

(d) Write a function which, given pointers to two strings, returns **true** if the first is a substring of the other and **false**, otherwise.

6. Write a function which, given an integer **n**, converts **n** to binary, and stores each bit in one node of a linked list with the *least* significant bit at the head of the list and the *most* significant bit at the tail. For example, given 13, the bits are stored in the order 1 0 1 1, from head to tail. Return a pointer to the head of the list.

7. Write a function which, given a pointer to a linked list of bits stored as in 6, *traverses the list once* and returns the decimal equivalent of the binary number.

8. You are given two pointers **b1** and **b2** each pointing to a binary number stored as in 6. You must return a pointer to a newly-created linked list representing the binary sum of the given numbers with the *least* significant bit at the head of the list and the *most* significant bit at the tail of the list. Write functions to do this in two ways:

(i) using the functions from 6 and 7

(ii) performing a 'bit by bit' addition

9. Repeat exercises 6, 7 and 8 but, this time, store the bits with the *most* significant bit at the head of the list and the *least* significant bit at the tail.

10. Two words are anagrams if one word can be formed by rearranging all the letters of the other word, for example: treason, senator. A word is represented as a linked list with one letter per node of the list.

Write a function which, given **w1** and **w2** each pointing to a word of lowercase letters, returns 1 if the words are anagrams and 0 if they are not. Base your algorithm on the following: for each letter in **w1**, search **w2** for it; if found, delete it and continue; otherwise, return 0.

11. The children's game of 'count-out' is played as follows: *n* children (numbered 1 to *n*) are arranged in a circle. A sentence consisting of *m* words is used to eliminate one child at a time until one child is left.

Starting at child 1, the children are counted from 1 to *m* and the *m*th child is eliminated. Starting with the child after the one just eliminated, the children are again counted from 1 to *m* and the *m*th child eliminated. This is repeated until one child is left. Counting is done circularly and eliminated children are not counted.

Write a program to read values for *n* and *m* and print the number of the last remaining child. Use a linked list to hold the children.

Hint: let the last node point to the first, creating a *circular* list.

12. The digits of an integer are held on a linked list in reverse order, one digit per node. Write a function which, given pointers to two integers, performs a digit by digit addition and returns a pointer to the digits of the sum stored in reverse order. Note: this idea can be used to add arbitrarily large integers.

2 Stacks and Queues

In this chapter, we will explain:

- the notion of an abstract data type
- what is a stack
- how to implement a stack using an array
- how to implement a stack using a linked list
- how to implement a stack for a general data type
- how to convert an expression from infix to postfix
- how to evaluate an arithmetic expression
- what is a queue
- how to implement a queue using an array
- how to implement a queue using a linked list

2.1 Abstract data types

We are familiar with the notion of declaring variables of a given type (**double**, say) and then performing operations on those variables (e.g. add, multiply, assign) *without needing to know **how** those variables are stored inside the computer*. In this scenario, the compiler designer can change the way a **double** variable is stored and a programmer would *not* have to change his programs which use **double** variables. This is an example of an *abstract data type*.

An *abstract data type* is one which allows a user to manipulate the data type without any knowledge of *how* the data type is represented inside the computer. In other words, as far as the *user* is concerned, all he needs to know are the *operations* which can be performed on the data type. The person who is *implementing* the data type is free to change its implementation without affecting the users.

In this chapter, we will show how to implement stacks and queues as abstract data types.

2.2 Stacks

A *stack* as a linear list in which items are added at one end and deleted from the same end. The idea is illustrated by a "stack of plates" placed on a table, one on top the other. When a plate is needed, it is taken from the top of the stack. When a plate is washed, it is added at the top of the stack. Note that if a plate is now

---

34

needed, this 'newest' plate is the one that is taken. A stack exhibits the "last in, first out" property.

To illustrate the stack ideas, we will use a stack of integers. Our goal is to define a *data type* (implemented as a **class**) called a *stack* so that a user can declare variables of this type and manipulate it in various ways. What are some of these ways?

As indicated above, we will need to add an item to the stack—the term commonly used is *push*. We will also need to take an item off the stack—the term commonly used is *pop*.

Before we attempt to take something off the stack, it is a good idea to ensure that the stack *has* something on it, that it is not empty. We will need an operation which tests if a stack is empty.

Given these three operations—*push*, *pop* and *empty*—let us illustrate how they can be used to read some numbers and print them in *reverse* order. For example, given the numbers

        36 15 52 23

we wish to print

        23 52 15 36

We can solve this problem by adding each new number to the top of a stack, **S**. After all the numbers have been placed on the stack, we can picture the stack as as follows:

        23 (top of stack)
        52
        15
        36 (bottom of stack)

Next, we remove the numbers, one at a time, printing each as it is removed.

We will need a way of telling when all the numbers have been read. We will use 0 to end the data. The logic for solving this problem can be expressed as:

```
create an empty stack, S
read(num)
while (num != 0) {
  push num onto S
  read(num)
}
while (S is not empty) {
  pop S into num //store the number at the top of S in num
  print num
}
```

We now show how we can implement a stack of integers and its operations.

2.2.1 Implementing a stack using an array

In order to simplify the presentation of the basic principles, we will work with a stack of integers. Later, we will see how to implement a stack for a general data type.

In the array implementation of a stack (of integers), we use an integer array (**ST**, say) for storing the numbers and an integer variable (**top**, say) which contains the subscript of the item at the top of the stack.

Since we are using an array, we will need to know its size in order to declare it. We will need to have some information about the problem to determine a reasonable size for the array. We will use the symbolic constant, **MaxStack**. If we attempt to push more than **MaxStack** elements onto the stack, a *stack overflow* error will be reported.

We begin our definition of the class **Stack** as follows:

```
public class Stack {
   final static int MaxStack = 100;
   int top = -1;
   int[] ST = new int[MaxStack];
        .
} //end class Stack
```

Valid values for **top** will range from 0 to **MaxStack - 1**. When we create a new stack, as in

```
Stack S = new Stack();
```

top will be set to the "invalid subscript", -1.

When this statement is executed, we can picture memory as follows:

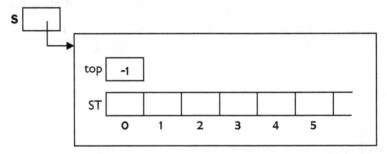

This represents an empty stack. We will need a function which tells us whether a stack is empty or not. We can add the following instance method to the class:

```
public boolean empty() {
   return top == -1;
}
```

This simply checks whether **top** has the value -1.

The major operations on a stack are *push* and *pop*. To push an item, **n**, onto a stack, we must store it in **ST** and update **top** to point to it. The basic idea is:

```
add 1 to top
set ST[top] to n
```

However, we must guard against trying to add something to the stack when it is already full. The stack is full when **top** has the value **MaxStack - 1**, the subscript of the last element. In this case, we will report that the stack is full and halt the program. Here is the instance method, **push**, in the **Stack** class:

```
public void push(int n) {
  if (top == MaxStack - 1) {
    System.out.printf("\nStack Overflow\n");
    System.exit(1);
  }
  ++top;
  ST[top] = n;
} //end push
```

To illustrate, after the numbers 36, 15, 52 and 23 have been pushed onto **S**, our picture in memory looks like this:

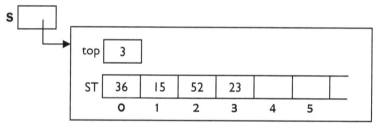

To pop an item, we return the value in location **top** and decrease **top** by 1:

```
set hold to ST[top]
subtract 1 from top
return hold
```

Again, we must guard against trying to take something off an empty stack. What should we do if the stack is empty and **pop** is called? We will simply report an error and halt the program. Here is the instance method, **pop**, in the **Stack** class:

```
public int pop() {
  if (this.empty()) {
    System.out.printf("\nAttempt to pop an empty stack\n");
    System.exit(2);
  }
  int hold = ST[top];
  --top;
  return hold;
}
```

Note that even though we have written **pop** to do something reasonable if it is called and the stack is empty, it is better if the programmer establishes that the stack is *not* empty (using the **empty** function) before calling **pop**.

Given the class **Stack**, we can now write Program P2.1 which reads some numbers, terminated by 0, and prints them in reverse order.

Program P2.1

```java
import java.util.*;
public class StackTest {
  public static void main(String[] args) {
    Scanner in = new Scanner(System.in);
    Stack S = new Stack();
    System.out.printf("Enter some integers ending with 0\n");
    int n = in.nextInt();
    while (n != 0) {
      S.push(n);
      n = in.nextInt();
    }
    System.out.printf("\nNumbers in reverse order\n");
    while (!S.empty())
      System.out.printf("%d ", S.pop());
    System.out.printf("\n");
  } //end main
} //end StackTest
```

The following shows a sample run of the program:

```
Enter some integers ending with 0
1 2 3 4 5 6 7 8 9 0

Numbers in reverse order
9 8 7 6 5 4 3 2 1
```

It is important to observe that the code in P2.1, which uses the stack, does so via the methods **push**, **pop** and **empty** and makes *no* assumption about *how* the stack elements are stored. This is the hallmark of an abstract data type—it can be used without the user needing to know how it is implemented.

Next, we will implement the stack using a linked list and P2.1 will remain exactly the same for solving the problem of printing the numbers in reverse order.

2.2.2 *Implementing a stack using a linked list*

The array implementation of a stack has the advantages of simplicity and efficiency. However, one major disadvantage is the need to know what size to declare the array. Some reasonable guess has to be made but this may turn out to be too small (and the program has to halt) or too big (and storage is wasted).

To overcome this disadvantage, a linked list can be used. Now, we will allocate storage for an element only when it is needed.

The stack is implemented as a linked list with new items added at the head of the list. When we need to pop the stack, the item at the head is removed.

Again, we illustrate the principles using a stack of integers. First, we will need to define a **Node** class which will be used to create nodes for the list. We will use the following:

```
class Node {
  int data;
  Node next;

  public Node(int d) {
    data = d;
    next = null;
  }
} //end class Node
```

Next, we will write the class, **Stack**, which begins as follows:

```
public class Stack {
  Node top = null;

  public boolean empty() {
    return top == null;
  }
  ...
```

There is one instance variable—**top** of type **Node**. It is initialized to **null** to denote the empty stack. The function **empty** simply checks if **top** is **null**. The empty stack, **S**, is depicted as follows:

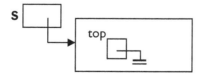

The method, **push**, is the same as **addHead** of the last chapter (page 18):

```
public void push(int n) {
   Node p = new Node(n);
   p.next = top;
   top = p;
} //end push
```

After 36, 15, 52 and 23 (in that order) have been pushed onto a stack, **S**, we can picture it thus:

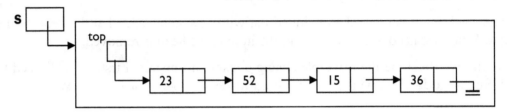

Next, we write **pop**. Again, the question arises as to what action to take if the user attempts to pop an empty stack. We will treat this as an error, print a message and halt the program. Here is **pop**:

```
public int pop() {
   if (this.empty()) {
      System.out.printf("\nAttempt to pop an empty stack\n");
      System.exit(2);
   }
   int hold = top.data;
   top = top.next;
   return hold;
} //end pop
```

Even with this changed definition of the **Stack** class, Program P2.1 will run exactly the same as before. It can do so since it makes no assumptions as to how the stack is implemented.

2.3 A general stack type

In order to simplify our presentation, we have worked with a stack of integers. We remind you of those places which are tied to the decision to use integers:

- in the declaration of **Node**, we declare an **int** called **num**;
- in **push**, we pass an **int** argument;
- in **pop**, we return an **int** result.

This means that if we need a stack of characters, say, we will have to change **int** to **char** in all of the above places. Similar changes will have to be made for stacks of other types.

It would be nice if we could minimize the changes needed when a different type of stack is required. We now show how this could be done.

Following the ideas developed in the last chapter, we define **Node** as follows:

```
class Node {
  NodeData data;
  Node next;

  public Node(NodeData d) {
    data = d;
    next = null;
  }
} //end class Node
```

The data at a node consists of the general type, **NodeData**. When the user defines the **NodeData** class, she will decide what kind of items will be stored on the stack.

The **Stack** class starts off the same as before:

```
public class Stack {
  Node top = null;

  public boolean empty() {
    return top == null;
  }
  ...
```

But now, **push** will require a **NodeData** argument and can be written as:

```
public void push(NodeData nd) {
  Node p = new Node(nd);
  p.next = top;
  top = p;
} //end push
```

Similarly, we write **pop** as:

```
public NodeData pop() {
  if (this.empty()) {
    System.out.printf("\nAttempt to pop an empty stack\n");
    System.exit(2);
  }
  NodeData hold = top.data;
  top = top.next;
  return hold;
} //end pop
```

The observant reader will notice that all we have done so far is change **int** to **NodeData** in **Node**, **push** and **pop**.

If we want to implement a stack of integers, we can use the **NodeData** class from page 23, with the addition of the following accessor:

```
public int getData() {return num;}
```

Even with these changes to **Node**, **Stack** and **NodeData**, Program P2.1 will work as before if we change **S.push(n)** to **S.push(new NodeData(n))** and **S.pop()** to **S.pop().getData()**.

If we need a stack of characters, we can use the **NodeData** class from page 28.

2.3.1 Example – convert from decimal to binary

Consider the problem of converting a positive integer from decimal to binary. We can use an integer stack, **S**, to do this using repeated division by 2 and saving the remainders. Here is the algorithm:

```
initialize S to empty
read the number, n
while (n > 0) {
  push n % 2 onto S
  n = n / 2
}
while (S is not empty) print pop(S)
```

This algorithm is implemented as Program P2.2.

```
                      Program P2.2
import java.util.*;
public class DecimalToBinary {
  public static void main(String[] args) {
    Scanner in = new Scanner(System.in);
    Stack S = new Stack();
    System.out.printf("Enter a positive integer: ");
    int n = in.nextInt();
    while (n > 0) {
      S.push(new NodeData(n % 2));
      n = n / 2;
    }
    System.out.printf("\nIts binary equivalent is ");
    while (!S.empty())
      System.out.printf("%d", S.pop().getData());
    System.out.printf("\n");
  } //end main
} //end DecimalToBinary
```

A sample run is shown on the next page:

```
Enter a positive integer: 99

Its binary equivalent is 1100011
```

2.4 How to convert from infix to postfix

Consider the expression: 7 + 3 * 4. What is its value? Without any knowledge about which operation should be performed first, we would probably work out the value from left to right as (7 + 3 = 10) * 4 = 40. However, normal rules of arithmetic state that multiplication *has higher precedence* than addition. This means that, in an expression like the one above, multiplication (*) is performed before addition (+). Knowing this, the value is 7 + 12 = 19.

We can, of course, force the addition to be performed first by using brackets, as in (7 + 3) * 4. Here, the brackets mean that + is done first.

These are examples of *infix* expressions; the operator (+, *) is placed *between* its operands. One disadvantage of infix expressions is the need to use brackets to override the normal *precedence rules*.

Another way of representing expressions is to use *postfix* notation. Here, the operator comes *after* its operands and there is no need to use brackets to specify which operations to perform first. For example, the postfix form of

  7 + 3 * 4 is 7 3 4 * +

and the postfix form of

  (7 + 3) * 4 is 7 3 + 4 *

One useful observation is that the operands appear in the same order in both the infix and postfix forms but they differ in the order and placement of the operators.

Why is postfix notation useful? As mentioned above, we do not need brackets to specify precedence of operators. More importantly, though, it is a convenient form for evaluating the expression.

Given the postfix form of an expression, it can be evaluated as follows:

```
initialize a stack, S, to empty
while we have not reached the end of the expression
    get the next item, x, from the expression
    if x is an operand, push it onto S
    if x is an operator, pop its operands from S, apply the operator and
        push the result onto S
endwhile
pop S; // this is the value of the expression
```

Consider the expression $(7 + 3) * 4$ whose postfix form is $7\ 3 + 4\ *$. It is evaluated by traversing from left to right:

- the next item is 7; push 7 onto **S**; **S** contains 7
- the next item is 3; push 3 onto **S**; **S** contains 7 3 (the top is on the right)
- the next item is +; pop 3 and 7 from **S**; apply + to 7 and 3, giving 10; push 10 onto **S**; **S** contains 10
- the next item is 4; push 4 onto **S**; **S** contains 10 4
- the next item is *; pop 4 and 10 from **S**; apply * to 10 and 4, giving 40; push 40 onto **S**; **S** contains 40
- we have reached the end of the expression; we pop **S**, getting 40—the result of the expression.

Note that when operands are popped from the stack, the first one popped is the second operand and the second one popped is the first operand. This does not matter for addition and multiplication, but would be important for subtraction and division. As an exercise, convert the following to postfix form and step through its evaluation using the above algorithm: $(7 - 3) * (9 - 8 / 4)$

The big question, of course, is how do we convert an infix expression to postfix? Before presenting the algorithm, we observe that it will use an "operator" stack. We will also need a "precedence table" which gives the relative precedence of the operators. Given any two operators, the table will tell us if they have the same precedence (like + and -) and, if not, which has greater precedence.

As the algorithm proceeds, it will "output" the postfix form of the given expression.

Here is the algorithm:

1. Initialize a stack of operators, **S**, to empty
2. Get the next item, **x**, from the infix expression; if none, go to step 8; (**x** is either an operand, a left bracket, a right bracket or an operator)
3. If **x** is an operand, output **x**
4. If **x** is a left bracket, push it onto **S**
5. If **x** is a right bracket, pop items off **S** and output popped items until a left bracket appears on top of **S**; pop the left bracket and discard
6. If **x** is an operator then
   > while (**S** is not empty) and (a left bracket is not on top of **S**) and
   > > (an operator of equal or higher precedence than **x** is on top of **S**)
   > > pop **S** and output popped item
   > push **x** onto **S**
7. Repeat from step 2.
8. Pop **S** and output popped item until **S** is empty

You are advised to step through the algorithm for the following expressions:

```
3 + 5
7 - 3 + 8
7 + 3 * 4
(7 + 3) * 4
(7 + 3) / (8 - 2 * 3)
(7 - 8 / 2 / 2) * ((7 - 2) * 3 - 6)
```

Let us write a program to read a simplified infix expression and output its postfix form. We assume that an operand is a single-digit integer. An operator can be one of +, −, * or /. Brackets are allowed. The usual precedence of operators apply: + and − have the same precedence which is lower than that of * and /, which have the same precedence. The left bracket is treated as an operator with very low precedence, less than that of + and −.

We will implement this as a function **precedence** which, given an operator, returns an integer representing its precedence. The actual value returned is not important as long as the relative precedence of the operators is maintained. We will use the following:

```
public static int precedence(char c) {
    if (c == '(') return 0;
    if (c == '+' || c == '-') return 3;
    if (c == '*' || c == '/') return 5;
    return -99; //error
}
```

The actual values 0, 3 and 5 are not important. Any values can be used as long as they represent the relative precedence of the operators.

We will need a function to read the input and return the next non-blank character. The end-of-line character will indicate the end of the expression. Here is the function (we call it **getToken**):

```
public static char getToken() throws IOException {
    int n;
    while ((n = System.in.read()) == ' ') ; //read over blanks
    if (n == '\r' || n == '\n') return '\0';
        //'\r' on Windows, MacOS and DOS; '\n' on Unix
    return (char) n;
} //end getToken
```

The operator stack is simply a stack of characters which we will implement using the **NodeData** class on page 28.

Step 6 of the algorithm requires us to compare the precedence of the operator on top of the stack with the current operator. This would be easy if we could "peek" at the element on top of the stack without taking it off. To do this, we write the instance method, **peek**, and add it to the **Stack** class on page 41:

```
        NodeData peek(Stack S) {
          if (!empty(S)) return S.top.data;
          return null;
        }
```

Putting all these together, we write Program P2.3 which implements the algorithm for converting an infix expression to postfix.

```
                            Program P2.3
      import java.io.*;
      public class InfixToPostfix {
        public static void main(String[] args) throws IOException {
          char[] post = new char[255];
          int n = readConvert(post);
          printPostfix(post, n);
        } //end main

        public static int readConvert(char[] post) throws IOException {
          Stack S = new Stack();
          int j = 0;
          char c;
          System.out.printf("Type an infix expression and press Enter\n");
          char token = getToken();
          while (token != '\0') {
            if (Character.isDigit(token)) post[j++] = token;
            else if (token == '(') S.push(new NodeData('('));
            else if (token == ')')
              while ((c = S.pop().getData()) != '(') post[j++] = c;
            else {
              while (!S.empty() &&
                    precedence(S.peek().getData()) >= precedence(token))
                post[j++] = S.pop().getData();
              S.push(new NodeData(token));
            }
            token = getToken();
          }
          while (!S.empty()) post[j++] = S.pop().getData();
          return j;
        } //end readConvert
        public static void printPostfix(char[] post, int n) {
          int j;
          System.out.printf("\nThe postfix form is \n");
          for (j = 0; j < n; j++) System.out.printf("%c ", post[j]);
          System.out.printf("\n");
        } //end printPostfix
```

```
public static char getToken() throws IOException {
    int n;
    while ((n = System.in.read()) == ' ') ; //read over blanks
    if (n == '\r') return '\0';
    return (char) n;
} //end getToken

public static int precedence(char c) {
    if (c == '(') return 0;
    if (c == '+' || c == '-') return 3;
    if (c == '*' || c == '/') return 5;
    return -99; //error
} //end precedence

} //end class InfixToPostfix
```

The job of reading the expression and converting to postfix is delegated to **readConvert**. This "outputs" the postfix form to a character array, **post**. So as not to clutter the code with error checking, we assume that **post** is big enough to hold the converted expression. The function returns the number of elements in the postfix expression.

The method, **printPostfix**, simply prints the postfix expression.

The following is a sample run of P2.3:

```
Type an infix expression and press Enter
(7 - 8 / 2 / 2) * ((7 - 2) * 3 - 6)

The postfix form is
7 8 2 / 2 / - 7 2 - 3 * 6 - *
```

Program P2.3 assumes that the given expression is a valid one. However, it can be easily modified to recognize some kinds of invalid expressions. For instance, if a right bracket is missing, when we reach the end of the expression there would be a left bracket on the stack. (If the brackets match, there would be none.) Similarly, if a left bracket is missing, when a right one is encountered and we are scanning the stack for the (missing) left one, we would not find it.

You are urged to modify P2.3 to catch expressions with mismatched brackets. You should also modify it to handle any integer operands, not just single-digit ones. Yet another modification is to handle other operations such as %, sqrt (square root), sin (sine), cos (cosine), tan (tangent), log (logarithm), exp (exponential), etc.

2.4.1 How to evaluate a postfix expression

Program P2.3 stores the postfix form of the expression in a character array, **post**. We now write a function, **eval**, which, given **post**, evaluates the expression and returns its value. The function uses the algorithm on page 43.

We will need an *integer* stack to hold the operands and intermediate results. Recall that we needed a *character* stack to hold the operators. We can neatly work with both kinds of stacks if we define **NodeData** as:

```
public class NodeData {
    char ch;
    int num;
    public NodeData(char c) {
        ch = c;
    }
    public NodeData(int n) {
        num = n;
    }
    public char getCharData() {return ch;}
    public int getIntData() {return num;}
} //end class NodeData
```

We use the **char** field for the operator stack and the **int** field for the operand stack. Note the two constructors and the two accessors for setting and retrieving, respectively, **ch** and **num**.

Using *this* definition of **NodeData**, Program P2.3 will work fine if we simply replace all occurrences of **getData** with **getCharData**.

The function, **eval**, is shown on the next page. We can test **eval** by adding it to P2.3 and placing the following as the last statement in **main**:

```
System.out.printf("\nIts value is %d\n", eval(post, n));
```

The following is a sample run of the modified program:

```
Type an infix expression and press Enter
(7 - 8 / 2 / 2) * ((7 - 2) * 3 - 6)

The postfix form is
7 8 2 / 2 / - 7 2 - 3 * 6 - *

Its value is 45
```

```
public static int eval(char[] post, int n) {
  int j, a, b, c;
  Stack S = new Stack();
  for (j = 0; j < n; j++) {
    if (Character.isDigit(post[j]))
      S.push(new NodeData(post[j] - '0'));
    else {
      b = S.pop().getIntData();
      a = S.pop().getIntData();
      if (post[j] == '+') c = a + b;
      else if (post[j] == '-') c = a - b;
      else if (post[j] == '*') c = a * b;
      else c = a / b;
      S.push(new NodeData(c));
    }
  }
  return S.pop().getIntData();
} //end eval
```

2.5 Queues

A queue is a linear list in which items are added at one end and deleted from the other end. Familiar examples are queues at a bank, supermarket, a concert or a sporting event. People are supposed to join the queue at the rear and exit from the front. We would expect that a queue data structure would be useful for simulating these real-life queues.

Queues are also found inside the computer. There may be several jobs waiting to be executed and they are held in a queue. For example, several persons may each request something to be printed on a network printer. Since the printer can handle only one job at a time, the others have to be queued.

The basic operations we wish to perform on a queue are:

- add an item to the queue; we say *enqueue*
- take an item off the queue; we say *dequeue*
- check if the queue is empty
- inspect the item at the head of the queue

Like stacks, we can easily implement the queue data structure using arrays or linked lists. We will use a queue of integers for illustration purposes.

2.5.1 *Implementing a queue using an array*

In the array implementation of a queue (of integers), we use an integer array (**QA**, say) for storing the numbers and two integer variables (**head** and **tail**, say) which indicate the item at the head of the queue and the item at the tail of the queue, respectively.

Since we are using an array, we will need to know its size in order to declare it. We will need to have some information about the problem to determine a reasonable size for the array. We will use the symbolic constant, **MaxQ**. In our implementation, the queue will be declared full if there are **MaxQ - 1** elements in it and we attempt to add another.

We begin to define the class **Queue** as follows:

```
public class Queue {
    final static int MaxQ = 100;
    int head = 0, tail = 0;
    int[] QA = new int[MaxQ];

    ...
}
```

Valid values for **head** and **tail** will range from 0 to **MaxQ - 1**. To initialize a queue, we set **head** and **tail** to 0. Later, we will see why 0 is a good value to use.

As usual, we can create an empty queue, **Q**, with

```
Queue Q = new Queue();
```

When this statement is executed, the situation in memory can be represented by:

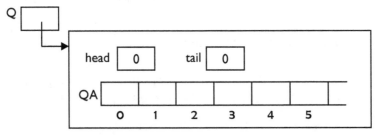

This represents the empty queue. In working with queues, we will need a function which tells us whether a queue is empty or not. We can use the following:

```
public boolean empty() {
    return head == tail;
}
```

Shortly, we will see that, given the way we will implement the *enqueue* and *dequeue* operations, the queue will be empty whenever **head** and **tail** have the same value. This value will not necessarily be 0. In fact, it may be any of the values from 0 to **MaxQ - 1**, the valid subscripts of **QA**.

Consider how we might add an item to the queue. In a real queue, a person joins at the tail. We will do the same here by incrementing **tail** and storing the item at the location indicated by **tail**.

For example, to add 36, say, to the queue, we increment **tail** to 1 and store 36 in **QA[1]**; **head** remains at 0.

If we then add 15 to the queue, it will be stored in **QA[2]** and **tail** will be 2.

If we now add 52 to the queue, it will be stored in **QA[3]** and **tail** will be 3.

Our picture in memory will look like this:

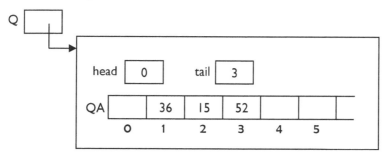

Note that **head** points "just in front of" the item which is actually at the head of the queue and **tail** points at the last item in the queue.

Now consider taking something off the queue. The item to be taken off is the one at the head. To remove it, we must *first* increment **head** and then return the value pointed to by **head**.

For example, if we remove 36, **head** will become 1 and it points "just in front of" 15, the item now at the head. Note that 36 still remains in the array but, to all intents and purposes, it is not in the queue.

Suppose we now add 23 to the queue. It will be placed in location 4 with **tail** being 4 and **head** being 1. The picture now looks like this:

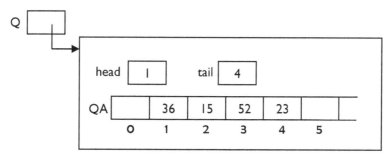

There are 3 items in the queue; 15 is at the head and 23 at the tail.

Consider what happens if we continuously add items to the queue without taking off any. The value of **tail** will keep increasing until it reaches **MaxQ - 1**, the last valid subscript of **QA**. What do we do if another item needs to be added?

We *could* say that the queue is full and stop the program. However, there are two free locations, 0 and 1. It would be better to try and use one of these. This leads us to the idea of a *circular queue*. Here, we think of the locations in the array as arranged in a circle: location **MaxQ - 1** is followed by location 0.

So if **tail** has the value **MaxQ - 1**, incrementing it will set it to 0.

Suppose we had not taken off any item from the queue. The value of **head** will still be 0. Now, what if, in attempting to add an item, **tail** is incremented from **MaxQ - 1** to 0? It now has the same value as **head**. In this situation, we declare that the queue is full.

We do this even though nothing is stored in location 0 which is, therefore, available to hold another item. The reason for taking this approach is that it simplifies our code for detecting when the queue is empty and when it is full.

To emphasize, when the queue is declared full, it contains **MaxQ - 1** items.

We can now write **enqueue**, an instance method to add an item to the queue.

```
public void enqueue(int n) {
   if (tail == MaxQ - 1) tail = 0;
   else ++tail;
   if (tail == head) {
      System.out.printf("\nQueue is full\n");
      System.exit(1);
   }
   QA[tail] = n;
} //end enqueue
```

We first increment **tail**. If, by doing so, it has the same value as **head**, we declare that the queue is full. If not, we store the new item in position **tail**.

Consider the diagram above. If we delete 15 and 52, it changes to

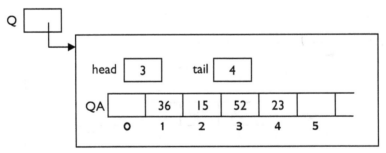

Now, **head** has the value 3, **tail** has the value 4, and there is 1 item in the queue, 23 in location 4. If we delete this last item, **head** and **tail** would both have the value 4 and the queue would be empty. This suggests that we have an empty queue when **head** has the same value as **tail**, as indicated earlier.

We can now write **dequeue**, a method which removes an item from the queue.

```
public int dequeue() {
  if (this.empty()) {
    System.out.printf("\nAttempt to remove from an empty queue\n");
    System.exit(2);
  }
  if (head == MaxQ - 1) head = 0;
  else ++head;
  return QA[head];
} //end dequeue
```

If the queue is empty, an error is reported and the program halted. If not, we increment **head** and return the value in location **head**. Note, again, that if **head** has the value **MaxQ - 1**, incrementing it sets it to 0.

To test our queue operations, we write Program P2.4 which reads an integer and prints its digits in reverse order. For example, if 12345 is read, the program prints 54321. The digits are extracted, from the right, and stored in a queue. The items in the queue are taken off, one at a time, and printed.

Program P2.4

```
import java.util.*;
public class QueueTest {
  public static void main(String[] args) {
    Scanner in = new Scanner(System.in);
    Queue Q = new Queue();
    System.out.printf("Enter a positive integer: ");
    int n = in.nextInt();
    while (n > 0) {
      Q.enqueue(n % 10);
      n = n / 10;
    }
    System.out.printf("\nDigits in reverse order: ");
    while (!Q.empty())
      System.out.printf("%d", Q.dequeue());
    System.out.printf("\n");
  } //end main
} //end QueueTest
```

2.5.2 Implementing a queue using a linked list

As with stacks, we can implement a queue using linked lists. This has the advantage of not having to decide beforehand how many items to cater for. We will use two pointers, **head** and **tail**, to point to the first and last items in the queue, respectively. The following diagram shows the data structure when four items (36, 15, 52, 23) are added to the queue:

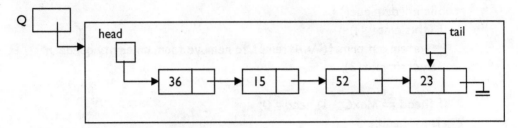

We will implement the queue so that it works with a general data type which we will call **NodeData**. Each node in the queue will be created from a **Node** class which we define as follows:

```
class Node {
    NodeData data;
    Node next;

    public Node(NodeData d) {
        data = d;
        next = null;
    }
} //end class Node
```

When the user defines the **NodeData** class, he will decide what kind of items will be stored in the queue.

The **Queue** class starts off as follows:

```
public class Queue {
    Node head = null, tail = null;

    public boolean empty() {
        return head == null;
    }
    ...
```

We can create an empty queue with:

```
Queue Q = new Queue();
```

This will create the following structure:

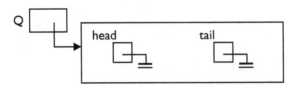

To enqueue an item, we must add it at the tail of the list. However, if the queue is empty, the new item becomes the only one in the queue; **head** and **tail** are set to point to it. If the queue is not empty, the item at the tail is set to point to the new one, and **tail** is updated to point to the new one. Here is **enqueue**:

```
public void enqueue(NodeData nd) {
    Node p = new Node(nd);
    if (this.empty()) {
        head = p;
        tail = p;
    }
    else {
        tail.next = p;
        tail = p;
    }
} //end enqueue
```

To take an item off the queue, we first check if the queue is empty. If it is, we print a message and end the program. If not, the item at the head of the queue is returned and the node containing the item is deleted.

If, by removing an item, **head** becomes **null**, it means that the queue is empty. In this case, **tail** is also set to **null**. Here is **dequeue**:

```
public NodeData dequeue() {
    if (this.empty()) {
        System.out.printf("\nAttempt to remove from an empty queue\n");
        System.exit(1);
    }
    NodeData hold = head.data;
    head = head.next;
    if (head == null) tail = null;
    return hold;
} //end dequeue
```

To use the **Queue** class, a user only needs to declare what he wants **NodeData** to be. To illustrate, suppose he wants a queue of integers. He can define **NodeData** as follows:

```
public class NodeData {
    int num;
    public NodeData(int n) {
        num = n;
    }
    public int getIntData() {return num;}
} //end class NodeData
```

Previously, we wrote Program P2.4 which reads an integer and prints its digits in reverse order. We now rewrite it as P2.5 using our new **Node**, **Queue** and **NodeData** classes.

```
                        Program P2.5
    import java.util.*;
    public class QueueTest {
      public static void main(String[] args) {
        Scanner in = new Scanner(System.in);
        Queue Q = new Queue();
        System.out.printf("Enter a positive integer: ");
        int n = in.nextInt();
        while (n > 0) {
          Q.enqueue(new NodeData(n % 10));
          n = n / 10;
        }
        System.out.printf("\nDigits in reverse order: ");
        while (!Q.empty())
          System.out.printf("%d", Q.dequeue().getIntData());
        System.out.printf("\n");
      } //end main
    } //end QueueTest
```

Stacks and queues are important to systems programmers and compiler writers. We have seen how to use stacks to evaluate arithmetic expressions. We can also use them to implement the "calling" and "return" mechanism for methods. Consider the situation where method **A** calls method **C** which calls method **B** which calls method **D**. When a method "returns", how does the computer figure out where to return to? We show how a stack can be used to do this.

Assume we have the following situation:

method A	method B	method C	method D
.	.	.	.
C;	D;	B;	.
100:	200:	300:	.
.	.	.	.

where a number, like 100, represents the "return address", the address of the next instruction to be executed when the function returns. When **A** calls **C**, the address 100 is pushed onto a stack, **S**. When **C** calls **B**, 300 is pushed onto **S**. When **B** calls **D**, 200 is pushed onto **S**. At this stage, the stack looks like this:

(bottom of stack) 100 300 200 (top of stack)

and control is in **D**. When **D** finishes and is ready to return, the address at the top of the stack (200) is popped and execution continues at this address. Note that this is the address immediately following the call to **D**.

Next, when **B** finishes and is ready to return, the address at the top of the stack (300) is popped and execution continues at this address. Note that this is the address immediately following the call to **B**.

Finally, when **C** finishes and is ready to return, the address at the top of the stack (100) is popped and execution continues at this address. Note that this is the address immediately following the call to **C**.

Naturally, queue data structures are used in simulating real-life queues. They are also used to implement queues "inside" the computer. In a multi-programming environment, several jobs may have to be queued waiting on a particular resource such as processor time or a printer.

Stacks and queues are also used extensively in working with more advanced data structures such as trees and graphs. While many of these algorithms are particularly interesting, they are beyond the scope of this book.

Exercises 2

1. What is an *abstract data type*?
2. What is a *stack*? What are the basic operations that can be performed on a stack?
3. What is a *queue*? What are the basic operations that can be performed on a queue?
4. Modify Program P2.3 (p. 90) to recognize infix expressions with mismatched brackets.
5. Program P2.3 works with single-digit operands. Modify it to handle any integer operands.
6. Modify Program P2.3 to handle expressions with operations such as %, square root, sine, cosine, tangent, logarithm and exponential.
7. Write declarations/functions to implement a stack of **double** values.
8. Write declarations/functions to implement a queue of **double** values.
9. An integer array **post** is used to hold the postfix form of an arithmetic expression such that:

    a positive number represents an operand;

    -1 represents +;

    -2 represents -;

    -3 represents *;

    -4 represents /;

    0 indicates the end of the expression.

    Show the contents of **post** for the expression (2 + 3) * (8 / 4) - 6.

    Write a function **eval** which, given **post**, returns the value of the expression.
10. An input line contains a word consisting of lowercase letters only. Explain how a stack can be used to determine if the word is a palindrome.
11. Show how to implement a queue using two stacks.

12. Show how to implement a stack using two queues.

13. A *priority queue* is one in which items are added to the queue based on a *priority number*. Jobs with higher priority numbers are closer to the head of the queue than those with lower priority numbers. A job is added to the queue in front of all jobs of lower priority but after all jobs of greater or equal priority.

    Write classes to implement a priority queue. Each item in the queue has a job number (integer) and a priority number. Implement, at least, the following: (i) add a job in its appropriate place in the queue (ii) delete the job at the head of the queue (iii) given a job number, remove that job from the queue.

    Ensure your methods work regardless of the state of the queue.

14. A stack, **S1**, contains some numbers in arbitrary order. Using another stack, **S2**, for temporary storage, show how to sort the numbers in **S1** such that the smallest is at the top of **S1** and the largest is at the bottom.

3 Binary trees

In this chapter, we will explain:

- the difference between a *tree* and a *binary tree*
- how to perform *pre-order*, *in-order* and *post-order* traversals of a binary tree
- how to represent a binary tree in a computer program
- how to build a binary tree from given data
- what is a *binary search tree* and how to build one
- how to write a program to do a word-frequency count of words in a passage
- how to write a program to cross-reference the words in a passage
- how to perform binary tree traversals using non-recursive algorithms
- how to perform a *level-order* traversal of a binary tree
- how to write some useful binary tree functions
- how to *delete* a node from a binary search tree
- how to build a 'best' binary search tree from sorted values
- how an *array* can represent a binary tree
- what is a *heap* and how to perform '*heapsort*'
- how a heap can be used to implement a *priority queue*

In this chapter, we discuss a very versatile data structure—the binary tree. The binary tree is a classic example of a non-linear data structure—compare a linear list where we identify a 'first' item, a 'next' item and a 'last' item. A binary tree is a special case of the more general *tree* data structure but it is the most useful and most widely used kind of tree.

3.1 Trees

A *tree* is a finite set of nodes such that

(a) there is one specially designated node called the *root* of the tree, and

(b) the remaining nodes are partitioned into $m \geq 0$ disjoint sets T_1, T_2, ..., T_m, and each of these sets is a tree.

The trees T_1, T_2, ..., T_m, are called the *subtrees* of the root. We use a recursive definition since recursion is an innate characteristic of tree structures. Figure 3.1 (next page) illustrates a tree. By convention, the root is drawn at the top and the tree grows downwards.

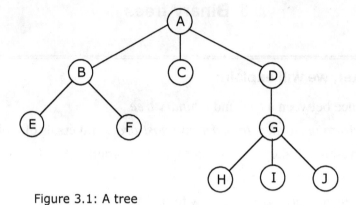

Figure 3.1: A tree

The root is **A**. There are 3 subtrees rooted at **B**, **C** and **D**, respectively. The tree rooted at **B** has 2 subtrees; the one rooted at **C** has no subtrees and the one rooted at **D** has 1 subtree. Each node of a tree is the root of a subtree.

The *degree* of a node is the number of subtrees of the node. Think of it as the number of lines leaving the node. For example, degree(**A**) = 3, degree(**C**) = 0, degree(**D**) = 1 and degree(**G**) = 3.

We use the terms *parent*, *child* and *sibling* to refer to the nodes of a tree. For example, the parent **A** has three children—**B**, **C** and **D**; the parent **B** has 2 children—**E** and **F**—and the parent **D** has one child, **G**, which has 3 children **H**, **I** and **J**. Note that a node may be the child of one node but the parent of another.

Sibling nodes are child nodes of the same parent. For example, **B**, **C** and **D** are siblings; **E** and **F** are siblings and **H**, **I** and **J** are siblings.

In a tree, a node may have several children but, except for the root, only 1 parent. The root has no parent. Put another way, a non-root node has exactly one line leading *into* it.

A *terminal* node (also called a *leaf*) is a node of degree 0. A *branch* node is a non-terminal node. In the diagram, **C**, **E**, **F**, **H**, **I** and **J** are leaves while **A**, **B**, **D** and **G** are branch nodes.

The *moment* of a tree is the number of nodes in the tree. The above tree has moment 10.

The *weight* of a tree is the number of leaves in the tree. The above tree has weight 6.

The *level* (or *depth*) of a node is the number of branches which must be traversed on the path to the node from the root. The root has level 0.

In the tree above, **B**, **C** and **D** are at level 1; **E**, **F** and **G** are at level 2; and **H**, **I** and **J** are at level 3. The level of a node is a measure of the depth of the node in the tree.

The *height* of a tree is the number of levels in the tree. The above tree has height 4. Note that the height of a tree is one more than its highest level.

If the relative order of the subtrees T_1, T_2, ..., T_m is important, the tree is an *ordered* tree. If order is unimportant, the tree is *oriented*.

A *forest* is a set of 0 or more disjoint trees. For example,

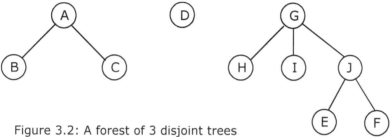

Figure 3.2: A forest of 3 disjoint trees

While general trees are of some interest, by far the most important kind of tree is a binary tree.

3.2 Binary trees

A *binary tree* can

(a)   be empty

(b)   consist of a root and two subtrees—a left and a right—each subtree being a binary tree.

A consequence of this definition is that a node always has two subtrees, any of which may be empty. Another consequence is that if a node has *one* non-empty subtree, it is important to distinguish whether it is on the left or right. For example,

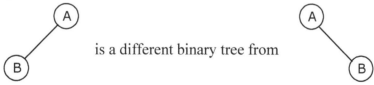

is a different binary tree from

The first has an empty right subtree while the second has an empty left subtree. However, as *trees*, they are the same.

The following are examples of binary trees:

(i) binary tree of 1 node, the root

(ii) binary trees with 3 nodes

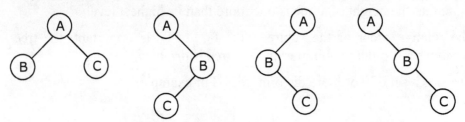

(iii) binary tree with all left subtrees empty;   all right subtrees empty

(iv) binary tree where each node, except the leaves, has exactly two subtrees; this
is called a *complete* binary tree.

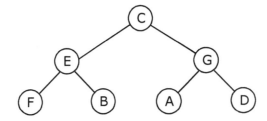

(v) a general binary tree

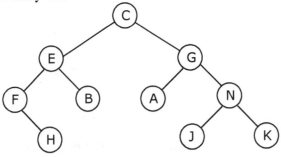

3.3 Traversing a binary tree

In many applications, we want to 'visit' the nodes of a binary tree in some
systematic way. For now, we'll think of 'visit' as simply printing the information
at the node. For a tree of *n* nodes, there are *n*! ways to visit them, assuming that
each node is visited once.

For example, for a tree with three nodes A, B and C, we can visit them in any of the following orders: ABC, ACB, BCA, BAC, CAB and CBA. Not all of these orders are useful; we will define three that are.

(1) Pre-order traversal

      (a) visit the root
      (b) traverse the left subtree in pre-order
      (c) traverse the right subtree in pre-order

Note that the traversal is defined recursively. In steps (b) and (c), we must re-apply the definition of pre-order traversal which says "vist the root, etc".

The pre-order traversal of

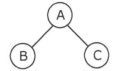

is A B C.

The pre-order traversal of

is C E F H B G A N J K.

(2) In-order traversal

      (a) traverse the left subtree in in-order
      (b) visit the root
      (c) traverse the right subtree in in-order

Here we traverse the left subtree first, then the root, then the right subtree.

The in-order traversal of

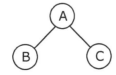

is B A C.

The in-order traversal of

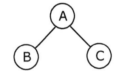

is **F H E B C A G J N K**.

(3) Post-order traversal

        (a) traverse the left subtree in post-order
        (b) traverse the right subtree in post-order
        (c) visit the root

Here we traverse the left and right subtrees *before* visiting the root.

The post-order traversal of

is **B C A**.

The post-order traversal of

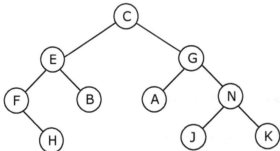

is **H F B E A J K N G C**.

Note that the traversals derive their names from the place where we visit the root relative to the traversal of the left and right subtrees. As another example, consider a binary tree which can represent the arithmetic expression

        (54 + 37) / (72 - 5 * 13)

Here is the tree:

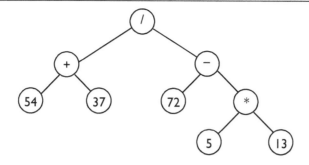

The leaves of the tree contain the operands and the branch nodes contain the operators. Given a node containing an operator, the left subtree represents the first operand and the right subtree represents the second operand.

The pre-order traversal is: / + 54 37 – 72 * 5 13

The in-order traversal is: 54 + 37 / 72 – 5 * 13

The post-order traversal is: 54 37 + 72 5 13 * – /

The post-order traversal can be used, in conjunction with a stack, to evaluate the expression. The algorithm is as follows:

```
initialize a stack, S, to empty
while we have not reached the end of the traversal
  get the next item, x
  if x is an operand, push it onto S
  if x is an operator, pop its operands from S, apply the operator and
        push the result onto S
endwhile
pop S; // this is the value of the expression
```

Consider the post-order traversal: 54 37 + 72 5 13 * – /. It is evaluated as follows:

- the next item is 54; push 54 onto S; S contains 54
- the next item is 37; push 37 onto S; S contains 54 37 (the top is on the right)
- the next item is +; pop 37 and 54 from S; apply + to 54 and 37, giving 91; push 91 onto S; S contains 91
- the next item is 72; push 72 onto S; S contains 91 72
- the next items are 5 and 13; these are pushed onto S; S contains 91 72 5 13
- the next item is *; pop 13 and 5 from S; apply * to 5 and 13, giving 65; push 65 onto S; S contains 91 72 65
- the next item is –; pop 65 and 72 from S; apply – to 72 and 65, giving 7; push 7 onto S; S contains 91 7
- the next item is /; pop 7 and 91 from S; apply / to 91and 7, giving 13; push 13 onto S; S contains 13

- we have reached the end of the traversal; we pop **S**, getting 13—the result of the expression.

Note that when operands are popped from the stack, the first one popped is the second operand and the second one popped is the first operand. This does not matter for addition and multiplication, but is important for subtraction and division.

3.4 How to represent a binary tree

As a minimum, each node of a binary tree consists of three fields: a field containing the data at the node, a pointer to the left subtree and a pointer to the right subtree. For example, suppose the data to be stored at each node is a word. We can begin by writing a class (**TreeNode**, say) with three instance variables and a constructor which creates a **TreeNode** object:

```
class TreeNode {
  NodeData data;
  TreeNode left, right;

  TreeNode(NodeData d) {
    data = d;
    left = right = null;
  }
}
```

To keep our options open, we have defined **TreeNode** in terms of a general data type which we call **NodeData**. Any program which wants to use **TreeNode** must provide its own definition of **NodeData**.

For example, if the data at a node is an integer, **NodeData** could be defined as:

```
class NodeData {
  int num;

  public NodeData(int n) {
    num = n;
  }
} //end class NodeData
```

A similar definition can be used if the data is a character. But we are not restricted to single-field data. Any number of fields can be used. Later, we will write a program to do a frequency count of words in a passage. Each node will contain a word and its frequency count. For that program, **NodeData** will contain the following, among other things:

```
class NodeData {
   String word;
   int freq;

   public NodeData(String w) {
      word = w;
      freq = 0;
   }
} //end class NodeData
```

In addition to the nodes of the tree, we will need to know the root of the tree. Keep in mind that once we know the root, we have access to all the nodes in the tree via the left and right pointers. Thus a binary tree is defined solely by its root. We will develop a **BinaryTree** class to work with binary trees. The only instance variable will be **root**. The class will start as follows:

```
class BinaryTree {
   TreeNode root;      // the only field in this class

   BinaryTree() {
      root = null;
   }
   //methods in the class
} //end class BinaryTree
```

The constructor is not really necessary since Java will set **root** to **null** when a **BinaryTree** object is created. However, we include it to emphasize that, in an empty binary tree, **root** is **null**.

If you wish, you can put the **TreeNode** class in its own file, **TreeNode.java**, and declare it **public**. However, in our programs, we will put the **TreeNode** class in the same file as **BinaryTree** since it is used only by **BinaryTree**. To do so, we must omit the word **public** and write **class TreeNode**, etc.

Building a binary tree

Let us expand our **BinaryTree** class by first writing a little method to build a binary tree. Suppose we want to build a tree consisting of a single node, thus:

The data will be supplied as: A @ @

Each @ denotes the position of a null pointer. To build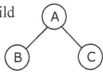

we will supply the data as: A B @ @ C @ @

Each node is immediately followed by its left subtree, then its right subtree.

By comparison, to build

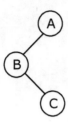

we will supply the data as: **A B @ C @ @ @**

The two @s after **C** denote its left and right subtrees (null) and the last @ denotes the right subtree of **A** (null). And to build

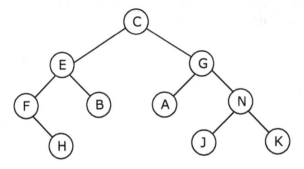

we supply the data as: C E F @ H @ @ B @ @ G A @ @ N J @ @ K @ @

Given data in this format, the following function will build the tree and return a pointer to its root:

```
static TreeNode buildTree(Scanner in) {
    String str = in.next();
    if (str.equals("@")) return null;
    TreeNode p = new TreeNode(new NodeData(str));
    p.left = buildTree(in);
    p.right = buildTree(in);
    return p;
} //end buildTree
```

The method will read data from the input stream associated with the **Scanner in**. It uses the following definition of **NodeData**:

```
class NodeData {
    String word;

    public NodeData(String w) {
        word = w;
    }
} //end class NodeData
```

We will call **buildTree** from the following constructor:

```
public BinaryTree(Scanner in) {
  root = buildTree(in);
}
```

Suppose a user class has its tree data stored in the file **btree.in**. It can create a binary tree, **bt**, with the following code:

```
Scanner in = new Scanner(new FileReader("btree.in"));
BinaryTree bt = new BinaryTree(in);
```

Suppose we wish to print the nodes of **bt** in pre-order. To use a statement such as:

```
bt.preOrder();
```

we would need to write an instance method **preOrder** in **BinaryTree** to do the job. The method is shown in the following listing of the **BinaryTree** class. It also includes the methods, **inOrder** and **postOrder**. We also retain the no-arg constructor so the user can start with an empty binary tree, if desired.

```
import java.util.*;
public class BinaryTree {
  TreeNode root;

  public BinaryTree() {
    root = null;
  }
  public BinaryTree(Scanner in) {
    root = buildTree(in);
  }
  public static TreeNode buildTree(Scanner in) {
    String str = in.next();
    if (str.equals("@")) return null;
    TreeNode p = new TreeNode(new NodeData(str));
    p.left = buildTree(in);
    p.right = buildTree(in);
    return p;
  } //end buildTree

  public void preOrder() {
    preOrderTraversal(root);
  }
  public void preOrderTraversal(TreeNode node) {
    if (node!= null) {
      node.data.visit();
      preOrderTraversal(node.left);
      preOrderTraversal(node.right);
    }
```

```
      } //end preOrderTraversal
      public void inOrder() {
         inOrderTraversal(root);
      }
      public void inOrderTraversal(TreeNode node) {
         if (node!= null) {
            inOrderTraversal(node.left);
            node.data.visit();
            inOrderTraversal(node.right);
         }
      } //end inOrderTraversal
      public void postOrder() {
         postOrderTraversal(root);
      }
      public void postOrderTraversal(TreeNode node) {
         if (node!= null) {
            postOrderTraversal(node.left);
            postOrderTraversal(node.right);
            node.data.visit();
         }
      } //end postOrderTraversal
   } //end class BinaryTree
```

The traversals all use the statement **node.data.visit();**. Since node.**data** is a **NodeData** object, the **NodeData** class should contain the method **visit**. In this example, we just print the value at the node, so we write **visit** as

```
      public void visit() {
         System.out.printf("%s ", word);
      }
```

Program P3.1 (next page) builds a binary tree and prints the nodes in pre-order, in-order and post-order. It includes the updated version of **NodeData**.

If **btree.in** contains: C E F @ H @ @ B @ @ G A @ @ N J @ @ K @ @
the program builds the tree on page 68 and prints:

```
The pre-order traversal is: C E F H B G A N J K
The in-order traversal is: F H E B C A G J N K
The post-order traversal is: H F B E A J K N G C
```

The **buildTree** method is not restricted to single-character data; any string (not containing whitespace) can be used.

Program P3.1

```
import java.io.*;
import java.util.*;
public class BinaryTreeTest {
  public static void main(String[] args) throws IOException {

    Scanner in = new Scanner(new FileReader("btree.in"));

    BinaryTree bt = new BinaryTree(in);
    System.out.printf("\nThe pre-order traversal is: ");
    bt.preOrder();
    System.out.printf("\n\nThe in-order traversal is: ");
    bt.inOrder();
    System.out.printf("\n\nThe post-order traversal is: ");
    bt.postOrder();
    System.out.printf("\n\n");
    in.close();
  } // end main

} //end class BinaryTreeTest

class NodeData {
  String word;

  public NodeData(String w) {
    word = w;
  }

  public void visit() {
    System.out.printf("%s ", word);
  }
} //end class NodeData
```

For example, if **btree.in** contains:

    hat din bun @ @ fan @ @ rum kit @ @ win @ @

P3.1 prints

```
The pre-order traversal is: hat din bun fan rum kit win

The in-order traversal is: bun din fan hat kit rum win

The post-order traversal is: bun fan din kit win rum hat
```

As an exercise, draw the tree and verify that these results are correct.

In passing, note that the in-order and pre-order traversals of a binary tree uniquely define that tree. Similarly for in-order and post-order. However, pre-order and post-order do not uniquely define the tree. In other words, it is possible to have two different trees A and B where the pre-order and post-order traversals of A are the same as the pre-order and post-order traversals of B, respectively. As an exercise, give an example of such a tree.

3.5 Binary search trees

Consider one possible binary tree built with the following three-letter words:

mac tee ode era ria lea vim

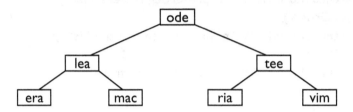

This is a special kind of binary tree. It has the property that, given *any* node, a word in the left subtree is 'smaller' and a word in the right subtree is 'greater' than the word at the node. (Here, 'smaller' and 'greater' refer to alphabetical order.)

Such a tree is called a *binary search tree* (BST). It facilitates the search for a given key using a method of searching very similar to a binary search of an array.

Consider the search for **ria**. Starting at the root, **ria** is compared with **ode**. Since **ria** is greater (in alphabetical order) than **ode**, we can conclude that if it is in the tree, it must be in the right subtree. It must be so since all the nodes in the left subtree are smaller than **ode**.

Following the right subtree of **ode**, we next compare **ria** with **tee**. Since **ria** is smaller than **tee**, we follow the left subtree of **tee**. We then compare **ria** with **ria**, and the search ends successfully.

But what if we were searching for **fun**?

- **fun** is smaller than **ode**, so we go left;
- **fun** is smaller than **lea**, so we go left again;
- **fun** is greater than **era**, so we must go right;

But since the right subtree of **era** is empty, we can conclude that **fun** is not in the tree. If it is necessary to add **fun** to the tree, note that we have also found the place where it must be added. It must be added as the right subtree of **era**, as shown on the next page:

Thus the binary search tree not only facilitates searching, but if an item is not found, it can be easily inserted. It combines the speed advantage of a binary search with the easy insertion of a linked list.

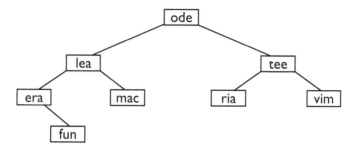

The tree drawn on the previous page is the optimal binary search tree for the seven given words. This means that it is the 'best possible' tree for these words in the sense that no 'shallower' binary tree can be built from these words. It gives the same 'number of comparisons' to find a key as a binary search on a linear array containing these words.

But this is not the only possible search tree for these words. Suppose the words came in one at a time and, as each word came in, it was added to the tree in such a way that the tree remained a binary search tree. The final tree built will depend on the order in which the words came in. For example, suppose the words came in the order:

mac tee ode era ria lea vim

Initially the tree is empty. When **mac** comes in, it becomes the root of the tree.

- **tee** comes next and is compared with **mac**. Since **tee** is greater, it is inserted as the right subtree of **mac**.
- **ode** comes next and is greater than **mac**, so we go right; **ode** is smaller than **tee** so it inserted as the left subtree of **tee**.
- **era** is next and is smaller than **mac**, so it is inserted as the left subtree of **mac**.

The tree built so far is

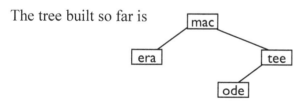

- **ria** is next and is greater than **mac**, so we go right; it is smaller than **tee**, so we go left; it is greater than **ode** so it is inserted as the right subtree of **ode**.

Following this procedure, **lea** is inserted as the right subtree of **era**, and **vim** is inserted as the right subtree of **tee**, giving the final tree:

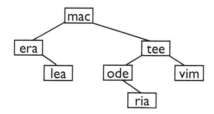

Note that the tree obtained is quite different from the optimal search tree. The number of comparisons required to find a given word has also changed. For instance, **ria** now requires four comparisons—it required three previously; and **lea** now requires three as opposed to two previously. But it's not all bad news; **era** now requires two as compared to three previously.

It can be proved that if the words come in random order, then the average search time for a given word is approximately 1.4 times the average for the optimal search tree, that is, $1.4\log_2 n$, for a tree of n nodes.

But what about the worst case? If the words come in alphabetical order, then the tree built will be:

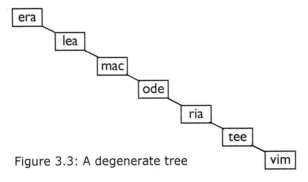

Figure 3.3: A degenerate tree

Searching such a tree is reduced to a sequential search of a linked list. This kind of tree is called a *degenerate* tree. Certain orders of the words will give some very unbalanced trees. As an exercise, draw the trees obtained for the following orders of the words:

- vim tee ria ode mac lea era
- era vim lea tee mac ria ode
- vim era lea tee ria mac ode
- lea mac vim tee era ria ode

Building a binary search tree

We now write a method to find or insert an item in a binary search tree. Assuming the previous definitions of **TreeNode** and **BinaryTree**, we can add the method **findOrInsert** (next page) to **BinaryTree**. The method searches the tree for a **NodeData** item, **d**. If it is found, it returns a pointer to the node. If it is not found, the item is inserted in the tree in its appropriate place and the method returns a pointer to the new node.

In the **while** condition, we use the expression **d.compareTo(curr.data)**. This suggests that we need to write a **compareTo** method in the **NodeData** class to compare two **NodeData** objects. The method is shown here:

```
public TreeNode findOrInsert(NodeData d) {
    if (root == null) return root = new TreeNode(d);
    TreeNode curr = root;
    int cmp;
    while ((cmp = d.compareTo(curr.data)) != 0) {
      if (cmp < 0) { //try left
        if (curr.left == null) return   curr.left = new TreeNode(d);
        curr = curr.left;
      }
      else { //try right
        if (curr.right == null) return curr.right = new TreeNode(d);
        curr = curr.right;
      }
    }
    //d is in the tree; return pointer to the node
    return curr;
  } //end findOrInsert
```

```
public int compareTo(NodeData d) {
  return this.word.compareTo(d.word);
}
```

It simply calls the **compareTo** method from the **String** class since **NodeData** consists only of a **String** object. Even if there were other fields in the class, we could, if we wish, still decide that two **NodeData** objects are compared based on the **word** field or on any other field.

Example – word frequency count

We illustrate the ideas developed so far by writing a program to do a frequency count of the words in a passage. We will store the words in a binary search tree. The tree is searched for each incoming word. If the word is not found, it is added to the tree and its frequency count is set to 1. If the word is found, then its frequency count is incremented by 1. At the end of the input, an in-order traversal of the tree gives the words in alphabetical order.

First, we must define the **NodeData** structure. This will consist of two fields—a word and its frequency. Here is the definition:

```
class NodeData {
  String word;
  int freq;
  public NodeData(String w) {
    word = w;
    freq = 0;
  }
```

```
public void incrFreq() {
   ++freq;
}
public int compareTo(NodeData d) {
   return this.word.compareTo(d.word);
}
public void visit() {
   WordFrequencyBST.out.printf("%-15s %2d\n", word, freq);
}
} //end class NodeData
```

Note the method to increase the frequency by 1. In **visit**, we print the data at a node using **WordFrequencyBST.out**. We will write the class **WordFrequency BST** shortly but, for now, note that we will let it determine where the output should go and **out** specifies the output stream. If you wish, you could send the results to the standard output stream using **System.out.printf**.

The gist of the algorithm for building the search tree is as follows:

```
create empty tree; set root to NULL
while (there is another word) {
   get the word
   search for word in tree; insert if necessary and set frequency to 0
   add 1 to frequency //for an old word or a newly inserted one
}
print words and frequencies
```

For our program, we will define a word to be any consecutive sequence of letters (uppercase or lowercase). In other words, any non-letter will delimit a word. In particular, whitespace and punctuation marks will delimit a word. If **in** is a **Scanner** object, we can specify this information with the statement:

```
in.useDelimiter("[^a-zA-Z]+"); // ^ means "not"
```

The part inside the square brackets means "any character that is *not* a lowercase or uppercase letter" and the + means one or more of those characters.

Normally, **Scanner** uses whitespace to delimit the tokens read using **next()**. However, we can change that and specify whatever characters we want to be used as delimiters. For example, to use a colon as a delimiter, we write

```
in.useDelimiter(":");
```

and when we write **in.next()**, our program will return a string consisting of the characters up to, but not including, the next colon. To use a colon or a comma, say, as a delimiter, we write

```
in.useDelimiter("[:,]"); //make a set using [ and ]
```

The square brackets denote a set. To use a colon, comma, period or question mark, we write

in.useDelimiter("[:,\\.\\?]");

The period and question mark are so-called *meta* characters (used for a special purpose) so we must specify each using an escape sequence: \. and \?. Recall that, within a string, \ is specified by \\.

If we write

in.useDelimiter("[^a-z]"); // ^ denotes negation, "not"

then a delimiter is any character that is *not* a lowercase letter. The expression a-z denotes a range—from a to z.

If we add + after the right bracket, it denotes a sequence of "one or more" non-lowercase characters. So when we use

in.useDelimiter("[^a-zA-Z]+");

this says that a delimiter is a sequence of "one or more" non-letters (neither upper nor lower case). This is what we want.

We now write Program P3.2 (the class **WordFrequencyBST**) to do the frequency count of words in the file **wordFreq.in**. It simply reflects the algorithm above.

```
Program P3.2

import java.io.*;
import java.util.*;
public class WordFrequencyBST {
  static Scanner in;
  static PrintWriter out;

  public static void main(String[] args) throws IOException {
    in = new Scanner(new FileReader("wordFreq.in"));
    out = new PrintWriter(new FileWriter("wordFreq.out"));

    BinaryTree bst = new BinaryTree();

    in.useDelimiter("[^a-zA-Z]+");
    while (in.hasNext()) {
      String word = in.next().toLowerCase();
      TreeNode node = bst.findOrInsert(new NodeData(word));
      node.data.incrFreq();
    }
    out.printf("\nWords      Frequency\n\n");
    bst.inOrder();
    in.close(); out.close();
  } // end main

} //end class WordFrequencyBST
```

Note that **in** and **out** are declared as **static** class variables. This is not necessary for **in** which could have been declared in **main** since it is used only there. However, the **visit** method of the **NodeData** class (above) needs to know where to send the output so it needs access to **out**; we can give it access by declaring **out** as a class variable.

Since **findOrInsert** requires a **NodeData** object as its argument, we must create a **NodeData** object from **word** before calling it in the statement:

```
TreeNode node = bst.findOrInsert(new NodeData(word));
```

An in-order traversal of the search tree yields the words in alphabetical order.

When P3.2 was run with the following data in **wordFreq.in**:

> The quick brown fox jumps over the lazy dog. Congratulations!
> If the quick brown fox jumped over the lazy dog then
> Why did the quick brown fox jump over the lazy dog?
> Why, why, why? To recuperate! Recuperate?

it produced the following output:

```
Words              Frequency

brown              3
congratulations    1
did                1
dog                3
fox                3
if                 1
jump               1
jumped             1
jumps              1
lazy               3
over               3
quick              3
recuperate         2
the                6
then               1
to                 1
why                4
```

3.6 A cross-reference program

We now consider a slightly more difficult problem than keeping a count of word frequencies. Given a passage, we want to create a cross-reference listing of the words in the passage. More specifically, the output consists of the lines in the passage, numbered starting at 1; this is followed by an alphabetical listing of the words, and each word is followed by the line number(s) in which it appears. If it appears more than once on a given line, the line number is repeated. For example, given the following passage from *The Prophet* by Kahlil Gibran (shown here with the lines numbered, which must be done by the program):

1.   Farewell to you and the youth I have
2. spent with you.
3.   It was but yesterday we met in a dream.
4.   You have sung to me in my aloneness,
5. and I of your longings have built a tower
6. in the sky.
7.   But now our sleep has fled and our dream
8. is over, and it is no longer dawn.
9.   The noontide is upon us and our half
10. waking has turned to fuller day, and we
11. must part.
12.   If in the twilight of memory we should
13. meet once more, we shall speak again together
14. and you shall sing to me a deeper song.
15.   And if our hands should meet in another
16. dream we shall build another tower in the
17. sky.

the program must produce the following output:

Words	Line numbers
a	3, 5, 14
again	13
aloneness	4
and	1, 5, 7, 8, 9, 10, 14, 15
another	15, 16
build	16
built	5
but	3, 7
dawn	8
day	10
deeper	14
dream	3, 7, 16
farewell	1
fled	7
fuller	10
half	9
hands	15
has	7, 10
have	1, 4, 5
i	1, 5
if	12, 15
in	3, 4, 6, 12, 15, 16
is	8, 8, 9
it	3, 8
longer	8
longings	5
me	4, 14
meet	13, 15

memory	12	
met	3	
more	13	
must	11	
my	4	
no	8	
noontide	9	
now	7	
of	5, 12	
once	13	
our	7, 7, 9, 15	
over	8	
part	11	
shall	13, 14, 16	
should	12, 15	
sing	14	
sky	6, 17	
sleep	7	
song	14	
speak	13	
spent	2	
sung	4	
the	1, 6, 9, 12, 16	
to	1, 4, 10, 14	
together	13	
tower	5, 16	
turned	10	
twilight	12	
upon	9	
us	9	
waking	10	
was	3	
we	3, 10, 12, 13, 16	
with	2	
yesterday	3	
you	1, 2, 4, 14	
your	5	
youth	1	

Output from cross-reference program

We will use a binary search tree to store the words. This will facilitate searching for a word as well as printing the words in alphabetical order. Compared to the word frequency program, the new problem here is how to store the line numbers.

What complicates matters is that some words may appear on several lines while others may appear on just one or two. Our solution is to keep a linked list of line numbers for each word. Thus each node of the tree will contain a pointer to a linked list node containing the first line number in which the word occurs. The line number nodes will have the format

lineNum	next

where **next** points to the cell containing the next line number in which the word occurs (**null**, if none). To use such nodes, we declare a class **ListNode** as follows:

```
class ListNode {
  int lineNum;
  ListNode next;

  public ListNode(int n) {
    lineNum = n;
    next = null;
  }
} //end class ListNode
```

Now the 'node data' for the tree will consist of two fields, as follows:

```
class NodeData {
  String word;
  ListNode firstLine;

  public NodeData(String w) {
    word = w;
    firstLine = null;
  }
  //other methods
} //end class NodeData
```

The constructor will store the word argument and set **firstLine** to **null**.

Assuming the data is stored in the file, **passage.txt**, we create a **Scanner in**, thus:

```
Scanner in = new Scanner(new FileReader("passage.txt"));
```

We read the data, line by line, from the file using **in.nextLine()**. Before attempting to read a line, we check that there *is* one to read using **in.hasNextLine()**. The code to read the passage and number the lines is as follows:

```
while (in.hasNextLine()) {
  String line = in.nextLine();
  out.printf("%3d. %s\n", ++currentLine, line);
}
```

Having read a line of input, we write the method **getWordsOnLine** to process the words on a line. The **Scanner** class allows us to read data from a string. Here, we declare a **Scanner** to read words from the string **inputLine** with:

```
Scanner inLine = new Scanner(inputLine);
inLine.useDelimiter("[^a-zA-Z]+");
```

The following code will process the words on a line:

```
while (inLine.hasNext()) {
   String word = inLine.next().toLowerCase();
   TreeNode node = bst.findOrInsert(new NodeData(word));
   ListNode p = new ListNode(currentLine);
   p.next = node.data.firstLine;
   node.data.firstLine = p;
}
```

This fetches the next word on the line and checks for it in the binary search tree. A **ListNode** with the current line number is created and added at the *head* of the list of line numbers. Thus the line numbers are stored in reverse order. However, we will *print* them in the correct order by printing the line number list in reverse order.

The in-order traversal method in the **BinaryTree** class calls **visit()** from the **NodeData** class. This prints a word followed by its line numbers.

All the details are shown in Program P3.3. The **BinaryTree** and **TreeNode** classes must be made available to it. We can do this by putting **BinaryTree.java** in the same folder as **CrossReference.java**. We can put the **TreeNode** class in **BinaryTree.java** or put it in its own file **TreeNode.java**.

Program P3.3

```
import java.io.*;
import java.util.*;
public class CrossReference {
   static Scanner in;
   static PrintWriter out;
   static int currentLine = 0;
   public static void main(String[] args) throws IOException {

      in = new Scanner(new FileReader("xref.in"));
      out = new PrintWriter(new FileWriter("xref.out"));

      BinaryTree bst = new BinaryTree();
      while (in.hasNextLine()) {
         String line = in.nextLine();
         out.printf("%3d. %s\n", ++currentLine, line);
         getWordsOnLine(line, bst);
      }
      out.printf("\nWords            Line numbers\n\n");
      bst.inOrder();
      out.close();
   } // end main
```

```
   public static void getWordsOnLine(String inputLine, BinaryTree bst) {
      Scanner inLine = new Scanner(inputLine);
      inLine.useDelimiter("[^a-zA-Z]+"); //one or more non-letters
      while (inLine.hasNext()) {
         String word = inLine.next().toLowerCase();
         TreeNode node = bst.findOrInsert(new NodeData(word));
         ListNode p = new ListNode(currentLine);
         p.next = node.data.firstLine;
         node.data.firstLine = p;
      }
   } //end getWordsOnLine
} //end class CrossReference

//class ListNode can go here or put in a separate file

class NodeData {
   String word;
   ListNode firstLine;

   public NodeData(String w) {
      word = w;
      firstLine = null;
   }

   public int compareTo(NodeData d) {
      return this.word.compareTo(d.word);
   }

   public void visit() {
      this.printAWord();
   }

   public void printAWord() {
      CrossReference.out.printf("%-20s", word);
      printLineNumbers(firstLine.next); //print all except first
      CrossReference.out.printf("%3d\n", firstLine.lineNum); //print first
   } //end printAWord

   public void printLineNumbers(ListNode top) {
   //line numbers are in reverse order; print list reversed
      if (top != null) {
         printLineNumbers(top.next);
         CrossReference.out.printf("%3d,", top.lineNum);
      }
   } //end printLineNumbers

} //end class NodeData
```

3.7 Non-recursive traversals

So far, we have written pre-order, in-order and post-order traversals using recursive methods. We now perform these traversals using non-recursive algorithms. We start with in-order.

As we move down the tree, we will need some way to get back up the tree. One way to do this is to stack the nodes on the way down. When needed, we will take nodes off the stack to retrace our steps. The algorithm is shown below.

```
Algorithm for in-order traversal
initialize a stack S to empty
curr = root
finished = false
while (not finished) {
   while (curr != null) {
      push curr onto S
      curr = left(curr)
   }
   if (S is empty) finished = true
   else {
      pop S into curr
      visit curr
      curr = right(curr)
   }
}
```

Given the tree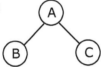

the algorithm will traverse it as follows:

We set **S** to empty, **curr** to **A** (actually a pointer to **A** but we will ignore the difference in the example) and **finished** to **false**.

- **curr** is not **null**, so we push **A** onto **S** and set **curr** to **left(A)**, that is, **B**; **S** contains **A**
- **curr** is not **null**, so we push **B** onto **S** and set **curr** to **left(B)**, that is, **null**; **S** contains **A B**
- since **curr** is **null**, we exit the **while** and check if **S** is empty; it is not, so we pop **B** into **curr** and visit **B**; we then set **curr** to **right(B)**, that is, **null**; **S** contains **A**
- control goes to the outer **while** and then to the inner **while**; since **curr** is **null**, we exit the loop immediately and check if **S** is empty; it is not, so we pop **A** into **curr** and visit **A**; we then set **curr** to **right(A)**, that is, **C**; **S** is empty

- control goes to the outer **while** and then to the inner **while**; **curr** is **C**, so we push **C** onto **S** and set **curr** to **left(C)**, that is, **null**; **S** contains **C**
- since **curr** is **null**, we exit the **while** and check if **S** is empty; it is not, so we pop **C** into **curr** and visit **C**; we then set **curr** to **right(C)**, that is, **null**; **S** is empty
- control goes to the outer **while** and then to the inner **while**; since **curr** is **null**, we exit the loop immediately and check if **S** is empty; it is, so we set **finished** to **true** and the algorithm terminates having visited the nodes in the order **B A C**.

The algorithm can be easily modified to perform a pre-order traversal. Just move **visit curr** so that it becomes the first statement in the inner while loop, which should now read:

```
while (curr != null) {
   visit curr
   push curr onto S
   curr = left(curr)
}
```

As an exercise, walk through the algorithm to do a pre-order traversal of

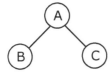

Post-order is a bit more difficult. For instance, in the above tree, we meet **A** as we go down the left and we meet **A** when we come back up from the left. However, we cannot visit **A** until we have traversed its right subtree. So **A** has to be stacked again to be met (and visited) when we come back up from the right subtree.

In other words, **A** will be taken off the stack twice and can only be visited after the second time. We need to distinguish between the first and the second time.

One solution is to push (**A, 0**) onto **S** the first time. When we pop an item, we check the second argument. If it is **0**, we replace it by **1** and push the item back onto **S**. If it is **1**, we are seeing the item for the second time so we visit it. Here is the algorithm:

```
initialize a stack S to empty
curr = root
finished = false
while (not finished) {
   while (curr != null) {
      push (curr, 0) onto S
      curr = left(curr)
   }
   if (S is empty) finished = true
   else {
      pop S into (temp, t)
```

```
        if (t == 1) visit temp
        else {
          push (temp, 1) onto S
          curr = right(temp)
        }
      } //end else
    } //end while (not finished)
```

Implementing post-order

We now write a program to perform a non-recursive post-order traversal of a binary tree. We will use the stack implementation shown on the next page. What kind of stack items would we need? As indicated in the algorithm above, each stack item consists of two fields: a **TreeNode** and an integer. We define **StackData** as follows:

```java
class StackData {
  TreeNode node;
  int n;

  public StackData(TreeNode nd, int j) {
    node = nd;
    n = j;
  }
};
```

Given these, we write **postOrderTraversal** as an instance method in our **BinaryTree** class as follows:

```java
public void postOrderTraversal() {
  Stack S = new Stack();
  TreeNode curr = root;  //root: instance variable that defines the tree
  boolean finished = false;
  while (!finished) {
    while (curr != null) {
      S.push(new StackData(curr, 0));
      curr = curr.left;
    }
    if (S.empty()) finished = true;
    else {
      StackData temp = S.pop();
      if (temp.n == 1) temp.node.data.visit();
      else {
        S.push(new StackData(temp.node, 1));
        curr = temp.node.right;
      }
} } } //end else, while (!finished), postOrderTraversal
```

```
public class Stack {
  StackNode top = null;
  public boolean empty() {
    return top == null;
  }
  public void push(StackData nd) {
    StackNode p = new StackNode(nd);
    p.next = top;
    top = p;
  } //end push
  public StackData pop() {
    if (this.empty()) {
      System.out.printf("\nAttempt to pop an empty stack\n");
      System.exit(2);
    }
    StackData hold = top.data;
    top = top.next;
    return hold;
  } //end pop
  public StackData peek() {
    if (!this.empty()) return top.data;
    return null;
  }
} //end class Stack
class StackNode {
  StackData data;
  StackNode next;
  public StackNode(StackData d) {
    data = d;
    next = null;
  }
} //end class StackNode
```

Using the **BinaryTree** constructor from page 69, we write Program P3.4 (next page) to build a tree and perform a post-order traversal.

For this program, a tree node consists of just a string so **NodeData** is defined accordingly.

If **btree.in** contains: C E F @ H @ @ B @ @ G A @ @ N J @ @ K @ @
P3.4 builds the tree on page 68 and prints:

The post-order traversal is: H F B E A J K N G C

```
                         Program P3.4
    import java.io.*;
    import java.util.*;
    public class PostOrderTest {
      public static void main(String[] args) throws IOException {

        Scanner in = new Scanner(new FileReader("btree.in"));

        BinaryTree bt = new BinaryTree(in);
        System.out.printf("\nThe post-order traversal is: ");
        bt.postOrderTraversal();
        System.out.printf("\n");
        in.close();
      } // end main
    } //end class PostOrderTest
    class NodeData {
      String word;

      public NodeData(String w) {
        word = w;
      }

      public void visit() {
        System.out.printf("%s ", word);
      }

      public int compareTo(NodeData d) {
        return this.word.compareTo(d.word);
      }
    } //end class NodeData
```

3.8 Building a binary tree with parent pointers

We have seen how to perform pre-order, in-order and post-order traversals using recursion (which is implemented using a stack) or an explicit stack. We now look at a third possibility. First, let us build the tree so that it contains "parent" pointers.

Each node now contains an additional field—a pointer to its parent. The **parent** field of the root will be null. For example, in the tree on the next page, **H**'s parent field points to **F**, **A**'s parent field points to **G** and **G**'s parent field points to **C**.

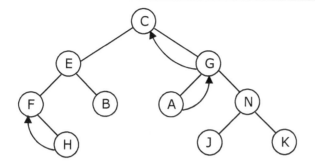

We now declare **TreeNode** with:

```
class TreeNode {
  NodeData data;
  TreeNode left, right, parent;

  public TreeNode(NodeData d) {
    data = d;
    left = right = parent = null;
  }
} //end class TreeNode
```

and rewrite **buildTree** as follows:

```
public static TreeNode buildTree(Scanner in) {
  String str = in.next();
  if (str.equals("@")) return null;
  TreeNode p = new TreeNode(new NodeData(str));
  p.left = buildTree(in);
  if (p.left != null) p.left.parent = p;
  p.right = buildTree(in);
  if (p.right != null) p.right.parent = p;
  return p;
} //end buildTree
```

After we build the left subtree of a node **p**, we check if it is **null**. If it is, there is nothing further to do. If it is not, and **q** is its root, we set **q.parent** to **p**. Similar remarks apply to the right subtree.

With parent fields, we can do traversals without needing a stack. For example, we can perform an in-order traversal as follows:

```
get the first node in in-order; call it "node"
while (node is not null) {
  visit node
  get next node in in-order
}
```

Given the non-null root of a tree, we can find the first node in in-order with:

```
TreeNode node = root;
while (node.left != null) node = node.left;
```

We go as far left as possible. When we can't go any further, we have reached the first node in in-order. Here, **node** will point to the first node in in-order.

The main problem to solve is the following: given a pointer to any node, return a pointer to its in-order successor (that is, the node which comes after it in in-order), if any. The last node in in-order will have no successor.

There are two cases to consider:

1. If the node has a non-empty right subtree, then its in-order successor is the first node in in-order of that right subtree. We can find it with the following code:

```
if (node.right != null) {
    node = node.right;
    while (node.left != null) node = node.left;
    return node;
}
```

For example, in the following tree:

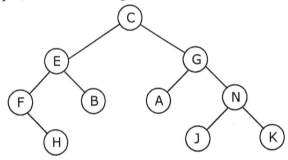

the in-order successor of G is found by going right once (to N) and then as far left as possible (to J). J is the in-order successor of G.

2. If the node has an empty right subtree, then its in-order successor is one of its ancestors. Which one? It's the lowest ancestor for which the given node is in its *left* subtree. For example, what is the in-order successor of B?

   We look at B's parent, E. Since B is in the *right* subtree of E, it is not E.

   We then look at E's parent, C. Since E (and hence, B) is in the *left* subtree of C, we conclude that C is the in-order successor of B.

   Note, however, that K, being the last node in in-order, has no successor. If we follow parent pointers from K, we never find one with K in its left subtree. In this case, our function will return **null**.

Using these ideas, we write **inOrderTraversal** as an instance method in the **BinaryTree** class and **inOrderSuccessor** as a static method called by it:

```
public void inOrderTraversal() {
    if (root == null) return;
    //find first node in in-order
    TreeNode node = root;
    while (node.left != null) node = node.left;
    while (node != null) {
        node.data.visit(); //from the NodeData class
        node = inOrderSuccessor(node);
    }
} //end inOrderTraversal

private static TreeNode inOrderSuccessor(TreeNode node) {
    if (node.right != null) {
        node = node.right;
        while (node.left != null) node = node.left;
        return node;
    }
    //node has no right subtree; search for the lowest ancestor of the
    //node for which the node is in the ancestor's left subtree
    //return null if there is no successor (node is the last in in-order)
    TreeNode parent = node.parent;
    while (parent != null && parent.right == node) {
        node = parent;
        parent = node.parent;
    }
    return parent;
} //end inOrderSuccessor
```

As an exercise, write similar functions to perform pre-order and post-order traversals. We will write a program to test these functions in the next section.

Building a binary search tree with parent pointers

We can modify the **findOrInsert** function from the **BinaryTree** class to build a search tree with parent pointers.

```
public TreeNode findOrInsert(NodeData d) {
//Searches the tree for d; if found, returns a pointer to the node.
//If not found, d is added and a pointer to the new node returned.
//The parent field of d is set to point to its parent.
    TreeNode curr, node;
    int cmp;

    if (root == null) {
        node = new TreeNode(d);
        node.parent = null;
        return root = node;
```

```
          }
          curr = root;
          while ((cmp = d.compareTo(curr.data)) != 0) {
            if (cmp < 0) { //try left
              if (curr.left == null) {
                curr.left  = new TreeNode(d);
                curr.left.parent = curr;
                return curr.left;
              }
              curr = curr.left;
            }
            else { //try right
              if (curr.right == null) {
                curr.right = new TreeNode(d);
                curr.right.parent = curr;
                return curr.right;
              }
              curr = curr.right;
            } //end else
          } //end while
          return curr;  //d is in the tree; return pointer to the node
        } //end findOrInsert
```

When we need to add a node (N, say) to the tree, if **curr** points to the node from which the new node will hang, we simply set the parent field of N to **curr**.

We can test **findOrInsert** and **inOrderTraversal** (from page 91) with Program P3.5 (next page). It simply reads words from a file **words.in**, builds the search tree and performs an in-order traversal to print the words in alphabetical order.

For example, if **words.in** contains mac tee ode era ria lea vim

P3.5 builds the binary search tree

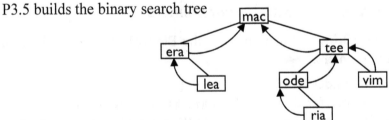

and prints

The in-order traversal is: era lea mac ode ria tee vim

3.9 Level-order traversal

In addition to pre-order, in-order and post-order, another useful order is *level-order*. Here we traverse the tree level by level, starting at the root. At each level, we traverse the nodes from left to right. For example, the level-order traversal of

```
                    Program P3.5
import java.io.*;
import java.util.*;
public class BinarySearchTreeTest {
  public static void main(String[] args) throws IOException {

    Scanner in = new Scanner(new FileReader("words.in"));

    BinaryTree bst = new BinaryTree();

    in.useDelimiter("[^a-zA-Z]+");
    while (in.hasNext()) {
      String word = in.next().toLowerCase();
      TreeNode node = bst.findOrInsert(new NodeData(word));
    }

    System.out.printf("\n\nThe in-order traversal is: ");
    bst.inOrderTraversal();
    System.out.printf("\n");
    in.close();
  } // end main

} //end class BinarySearchTreeTest

//NodeData class from P3.4 goes here
```

the tree

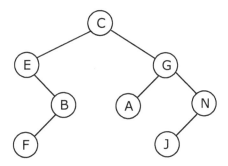

is C E G B A N F J.

To perform a level-order traversal, we will need to use a queue. The following algorithm shows how:

```
add the root to the queue, Q
while (Q is not empty) {
  remove item at the head of Q and store in p
  visit p
  if (left(p) is not null) add left(p) to Q
  if (right(p) is not null) add right(p) to Q
}
```

For the above tree, the following occurs:

- put C on **Q**;
- **Q** is not empty, so remove and visit C; add E and G to **Q** which now has E G;
- **Q** is not empty, so remove and visit E; add B to **Q** which now has G B;
- **Q** is not empty; remove and visit G; add A and N to **Q** which now has B A N;
- **Q** is not empty; remove and visit B; add F to **Q** which now has A N F;
- **Q** is not empty; remove and visit A; add nothing to **Q** which now has N F;
- **Q** is not empty; remove and visit N; add J to **Q** which now has F J;
- **Q** is not empty; remove and visit F; add nothing to **Q** which now has J;
- **Q** is not empty; remove and visit J; add nothing to **Q** which is now empty;
- **Q** is empty; the traversal ends having visited C E G B A N F J.

To use the **Queue** class shown on the next page, we will define **QueueData** as:

```
public class QueueData {
  TreeNode node;

  public QueueData(TreeNode n) {
    node = n;
  }
} //end class QueueData
```

Note that if you put **QueueData** in the same file as **Queue** or the program that uses **Queue**, you must omit the word **public**.

Using **Queue** and **QueueData**, we can write **levelOrderTraversal** in **BinaryTree** as follows:

```
public void levelOrderTraversal() {
  Queue Q = new Queue();
  Q.enqueue(new QueueData(root));
  while (!Q.empty()) {
    QueueData temp = Q.dequeue();
    temp.node.data.visit();
    if (temp.node.left != null)
      Q.enqueue(new QueueData(temp.node.left));
    if (temp.node.right != null)
      Q.enqueue(new QueueData(temp.node.right));
  }
} //end levelOrderTraversal
```

```java
public class Queue {
  QNode head = null, tail = null;

  public boolean empty() {
    return head == null;
  }
  public void enqueue(QueueData nd) {
    QNode p = new QNode(nd);
    if (this.empty()) {
      head = p;
      tail = p;
    }
    else {
      tail.next = p;
      tail = p;
    }
  } //end enqueue

  public QueueData dequeue() {
    if (this.empty()) {
      System.out.printf("\nAttempt to remove from an empty queue\n");
      System.exit(1);
    }
    QueueData hold = head.data;
    head = head.next;
    if (head == null) tail = null;
    return hold;
  } //end dequeue
} //end class Queue

class QNode {
  QueueData data;
  QNode next;

  public QNode(QueueData d) {
    data = d;
    next = null;
  }
} //end class QNode
```

3.10 Some useful binary tree functions

We now show you how to write some functions (in **BinaryTree**) which return information about a binary tree. The first counts the number of nodes in a tree:

```
public int numNodes() {
    return countNodes(root);
}

private int countNodes(TreeNode root) {
    if (root == null) return 0;
    return 1 + countNodes(root.left) + countNodes(root.right);
}
```

If **bt** is a binary tree, **bt.numNodes()** will return the number of nodes in the tree. Counting the nodes is delegated to the **private** function **countNodes**.

The next function returns the number of leaves in the tree:

```
public int numLeaves() {
    return countLeaves(root);
}

private int countLeaves(TreeNode root) {
    if (root == null) return 0;
    if (root.left == null && root.right == null) return 1;
    return countLeaves(root.left) + countLeaves(root.right);
}
```

And the next returns the height of the tree:

```
public int height() {
    return numLevels(root);
}

private int numLevels(TreeNode root) {
    if (root == null) return 0;
    return 1 + Math.max(numLevels(root.left), numLevels(root.right));
}
```

where **Math.max** returns the larger of its two arguments.

You are advised to dry-run these functions on some sample trees to verify that they do return the correct values.

3.11 Binary search tree deletion

Consider the problem of deleting a node from a binary search tree (BST) so that it remains a BST. There are 3 cases to consider:

1. the node is a leaf
2. (a) the node has no left subtree
   (b) the node has no right subtree
3. the node has non-empty left and right subtrees

We illustrate these cases using the following BST:

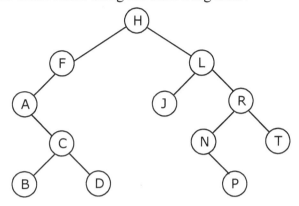

Case 1 is easy. For example, to delete P, we simply set the right subtree of N to null. Case 2 is also easy. To delete A (no left subtree), we replace it by C, its right subtree. And to delete F (no right subtree), we replace it by A, its left subtree.

Case 3 is a bit more difficult since we have to worry about what to do with 2 subtrees. For example, how do we delete L? One approach is to replace L by its in-order successor, N, which *must* have an empty left subtree. Why? Because, by definition, the in-order successor of a node is the first node (in order) in its right subtree. And this first node (in any tree) is found by going as far left as possible.

Since N has no left subtree, we will set its left link to the left subtree of L. We will set the left link of the parent of N (R in this case) to point to P, the right subtree of N. Finally, we will set the right link of N to point to the right subtree of L, giving

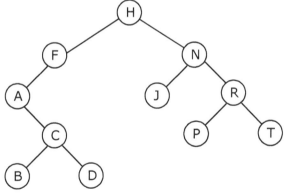

Another way to look at it is to imagine the contents of node N being copied into node L. And the left link of the parent of N is set to point to the right subtree of N.

In our algorithm, we will treat the node to be deleted as the root of a subtree. We will delete the root and return a pointer to the root of the reconstructed tree.

```
deleteNode(TreeNode T) {
    if (T == null) return null
    if (right(T) == null) return left(T)  //cases 1 and 2b
    R = right(T)
```

```
        if (left(T) == null) return R //case 2a
        if (left(R) == null) {
           left(R) == left(T)
           return R
        }
        while (left(R) != null) { //will be executed at least once
           P = R
           R = left(R)
        }
        //R is pointing to the in-order successor of T;
        //P is its parent
        left(R) = left(T)
        left(P) = right(R)
        right(R) = right(T)
        return R
     } //end deleteNode
```

Suppose we call **deleteNode** with a pointer to the node L (page 97) as argument. The function will delete L and return a pointer to the following tree:

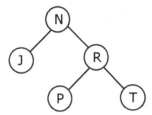

Since L was the right subtree of H, we can now set the right subtree of H to point to this tree.

3.12 Creating a 'best' binary search tree from sorted keys

We saw on page 74 that if keys come in sorted order, the binary search tree algorithm creates a degenerate tree. In this section, we show how to create a 'best' binary search tree if we *know* that the keys come in order.

Consider the following complete binary tree:

The nodes are labelled in in-order sequence. Note the following:

- the leaves are labelled with odd numbers;
- the nodes at the next level up start with 2 and the difference between their labels is 4;
- the nodes at the next level up start with 4 and the difference between their labels is 8;
- the node at the next level up is the root and is labelled 8.

For the purposes of this discussion, we consider the leaves to be at level 0 and the level increases as we go *up* the tree. Thus the root is at level 3.

Important observation: the level of a node is the highest power of two that divides its label. Thus,

- the highest power of 2 that divides odd numbers is 0; the leaves are at level 0
- the highest power of 2 that divides 2, 6, 10, 14 is 1; these nodes are at level 1
- the highest power of 2 that divides 4 and 12 is 2; these nodes are at level 2
- the highest power of 2 that divides 8 is 3; this node is at level 3

It follows that if we know the position of an item in the in-order sequence, we can calculate its level in the final tree. The following function will do this:

```
public static int getNodeLevel(int n) {
//returns the highest power of 2 that divides n
  int level = 0;
   while (n % 2 == 0) {
     level++;
      n /= 2;
   }
   return level;
}
```

In order to build the search tree, we will need to keep track of the last node processed at each level. We will use an array **lastNode** for this. We will let **MaxHeight** represent the highest tree that we will cater for; a value of 20 will let us build a tree with just over a million nodes ($2^{20} - 1 = 1,048,575$, to be exact).

Initially, we will set all the entries in **lastNode** to **null**, indicating that no nodes have been processed at any level. We will use the following algorithm to build a search tree of integers:

```
numNodes = 0
while (there is another integer) {
   read next integer, num
   TreeNode tp = new TreeNode(num)
   ++numNodes
```

```
        level = getNodeLevel(numNodes)
        //if the new node is a leaf, its left pointer is set to null (already done)
        //else its left pointer is set to the entry in lastNode one level lower
        if (level > 0) tp.left = lastNode[level – 1]
        // if lastNode[level+1] exists and has a null right link, set it to new node
        if (lastNode[level+1] != null && lastNode[level+1].right == null)
            lastNode[level+1].right = tp
        // the current node is the last node processed at this level
        lastNode[level] = tp
    } //end while
    the root of the tree is the last non-null entry in lastNode
```

Consider how this algorithm will build a search tree with the following 7 integers:

12 17 24 31 36 42 47

When 12 is read, **numNodes** is set to 1 so **level** is 0. None of the **if** conditions is true since **level** is 0 and **lastNode[1]** is null. We have a tree of 1 node:

and **lastNode[0]** is set to point to this node; we will use the notation ^12 to refer to the node containing 12. Note that when the node is created, its left and right pointers are set to null.

Next, 17 is read, **numNodes** is set to 2 so **level** is 1. Since **level** is greater than 0, the left pointer of the new node is set to **lastNode[0]**, that is, ^12.

We have a tree of 2 nodes:

lastNode[0] is ^12 and **lastNode[1]** is ^17. These are the last nodes processed at levels 0 and 1, respectively.

Next, 24 is read, **numNodes** is set to 3 so **level** is 0. Since **lastNode[1]** is not null and the right link of ^17 *is* null, we set the right link of ^17 to ^24, the new node. We have a tree of 3 nodes:

```
        17
       /  \
     12    24
```

lastNode[0] is now ^24 and **lastNode[1]** is still ^17.

Next, 31 is read, **numNodes** is set to 4 so **level** is 2. Since **level** is greater than 0, the left pointer of the new node is set to **lastNode[1]**, that is, ^17.

We have a tree of 4 nodes:

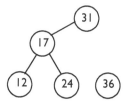

lastNode[0] is ^24, **lastNode[1]** is ^17 and **lastNode[2]** is ^31.

Next, 36 is read, **numNodes** is set to 5 so **level** is 0. Now, **lastNode[1]** is not null but its right link is *not* null, so nothing further happens. We have:

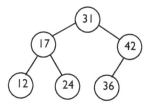

lastNode[0] is ^36, **lastNode[1]** is ^17 and **lastNode[2]** is ^31.

Next, 42 is read, **numNodes** is set to 6 so **level** is 1. Since **level** is greater than 0, the left pointer of the new node is set to **lastNode[0]**, that is, ^36. Since **lastNode[2]** is not null and the right link of ^31 *is* null, we set the right link of ^31 to ^42, the new node. We have the following:

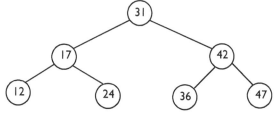

lastNode[0] is ^36, **lastNode[1]** is ^42 and **lastNode[2]** is ^31.

Finally, 47 is read, **numNodes** is set to 7 so **level** is 0. Since **lastNode[1]** is not null and the right link of ^42 *is* null, we set the right link of ^42 to ^47, the new node. We now have the tree:

lastNode[0] is ^47, **lastNode[1]** is ^42 and **lastNode[2]** is ^31.

Since there are no more numbers, the algorithm terminates with the root of the tree being set to **lastNode[2]**, the last non-null entry in **lastNode**. Thus, ^31 is properly designated as the root of the final tree.

The algorithm has built the best possible binary search tree for the 7 integers.

Building the best almost complete binary search tree

As given, the algorithm will create the best possible binary search tree if the number of nodes is exactly $2^n - 1$, for some n. In other words, we will get the best tree if the number of nodes is the right amount for creating a *complete* binary tree.

If it is not, there may be some 'hanging' nodes after the last number is processed and we will have to do some extra work to tie them into the final tree.

For example, above, after 36 is processed, we have

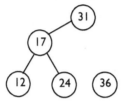

If there are no more numbers, we can complete the job by setting the right link of ^31 to ^36.

We can 'finalize' the tree after the algorithm above terminates with:

> find the highest node, n, whose right subtree is null;
> this right child is set to the highest node in lastNode
> that is not already in the left subtree of n.

In this example, 'the highest node whose right subtree is null' is ^31; it is at level 2. Since **lastNode[1]** (^17) is in the left subtree of ^31 and **lastNode[0]** (^36) is not in the left subtree of ^31, the right link of ^31 is set to ^36.

For a more involved example, consider a tree being built with 21 integers. After the last integer has been processed, we will have the following:

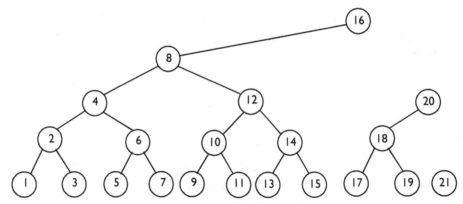

lastNode[0] is ^21, **lastNode[1]** is ^18, **lastNode[2]** is ^20, **lastNode[3]** is ^8 and **lastNode[4]** is ^16.

We will finalize this tree as follows:

- the highest node with a null right link is ^16; the highest node in **lastNode** that is not in the left subtree of ^16 is ^20; so the right link of ^16 is set to ^20.

We continue the process with node ^20, now the highest node with a null right link.

- the highest node in **lastNode** that is not in the left subtree of ^20 is ^21; so the right link of ^20 is set to ^21.

The process would normally continue with ^21 but this is a leaf so nothing further needs to be done.

The tree is now finalized with the root being ^16, the highest non-null entry in **lastNode**.

Based on the algorithm on page 99, we write the instance method **insertBestBST** in the class **BinaryTree**:

```
public void insertBestBST(int n) {
    TreeNode p = new TreeNode(new NodeData(n));
    numNodes++;
    int level = getNodeLevel(numNodes);
    // left pointer of new node is null if it is a leaf
    // else it's the entry in lastNode one level lower than new node
    if (level > 0) p.left = lastNode[level-1];
    // if lastNode[level+1] exists and has a null right link,
    // set it to the new node
    if (lastNode[level+1] != null)
      if (lastNode[level+1].right == null)
        lastNode[level+1].right = p;
    // the current node is the last node processed at this level
    lastNode[level] = p;
} //end insertBestBST
```

And, based on the discussion for finalizing the tree, we write the instance method **finalizeBestBST** in the class **BinaryTree**:

```
public void finalizeBestBST() {
    int m, n = MaxHeight - 1;
    // find the last entry in lastNode that is non-null
    // this is the root
    while (n > 0 && lastNode[n] == null) n--;
    root = lastNode[n];

    while (n > 0) {
      // find the highest node, n, whose right subtree is null;
      // this right child is set to the highest node in lastNode
      // that is not already in the left subtree of n.
      if (lastNode[n].right != null) n--;
```

```
        else {
            // need to check left(n) and all right subtrees from there
            TreeNode tn = lastNode[n].left;
            m = n - 1;
            // check if the node, tn, in left subtree is the same as
            // the last node processed at that level, lastNode[m]
            while (m >= 0 && tn == lastNode[m]) {
                tn = tn.right;
                m--;
            }
            if (m >= 0) lastNode[n].right = lastNode[m];
            n = m;
        } //end else
    } //end while
} //end finalizeBST
```

Using these methods, we write program P3.6 (next page) to read some sorted integers from a file, **bestBST.in**, and create the binary search tree based on the above discussions.

If **bestBST.in** contains

    10 15 23 32 41 46 52 59 63 71 84

P3.6 will build the following tree:

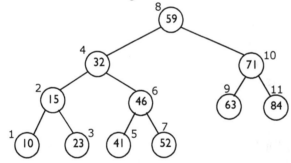

and produce the following output:

> The pre-order traversal is: 59 32 15 10 23 46 41 52 71 63 84
>
> The in-order traversal is: 10 15 23 32 41 46 52 59 63 71 84
>
> The post-order traversal is: 10 23 15 41 52 46 32 63 84 71 59

If the numbers are given in sorted order, P3.6 builds a binary *search* tree. However, if the numbers are not in order, the program still builds a tree but it will not be a search tree. It will be a tree whose in-order traversal is the same as the given order.

Program P3.6

```java
import java.io.*;
import java.util.*;
public class BestBST {
   public static void main (String[] args) throws IOException {

     Scanner in = new Scanner(new FileReader("bestBST.in"));

     BinaryTree BST = new BinaryTree();
     while (in.hasNextInt()) {
       int num = in.nextInt();
        BST.insertBestBST(num);
     }
     BST.finalizeBestBST();

     System.out.printf("\nThe pre-order traversal is: ");
     BST.preOrder();
     System.out.printf("\n\nThe in-order traversal is: ");
     BST.inOrder();
     System.out.printf("\n\nThe post-order traversal is: ");
     BST.postOrder();
     System.out.printf("\n\n");
     in.close();
   }
} // end of class BestBST
class NodeData {
  int num;

  public NodeData(int n) {
    num = n;
  }
  public void visit() {
    System.out.printf("%d ", num);
  }
} //end class NodeData
```

Building the best BST for items given in arbitrary order

Consider problem of building the best binary search tree if the data items come in arbitrary order. We can do this as follows:

- build a BST for the given order; this may or may not be a 'good' tree but it does not matter. All we want is a way to get the nodes in sorted order.

- perform an in-order traversal of this BST; this will give the nodes in sorted order. As we 'visit' each node, pass it to **insertBestBST** which will build the best tree for items which come in sorted order.
- call **finalizeBestBST** to 'finalize' the tree.

3.13 An array as a binary tree representation

A *complete* binary tree is one in which every non-leaf node has two non-empty subtrees and all leaves are at the same level. The following are all complete binary trees.

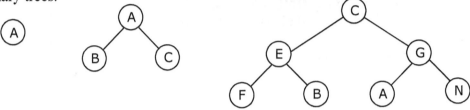

The first is a complete binary tree of height 1; the second is a complete binary tree of height 2 and the third is a complete binary tree of height 3. For a complete binary tree of height n, the number of nodes in the tree is $2^n - 1$.

Consider the third tree. Let us number the nodes as follows:

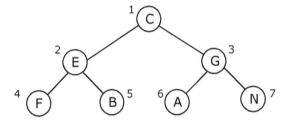

Starting from 1 at the root, we number the nodes in order from top to bottom and left to right at each level.

Observe that if a node has label n, its left subtree has label $2n$ and its right subtree has label $2n + 1$.

If the nodes are stored in an array T[1..7], thus:

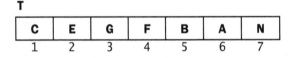

T

C	E	G	F	B	A	N
1	2	3	4	5	6	7

then

- **T[1]** is the root;
- the left subtree of **T[i]** is **T[2i]** if 2i <= 7 and null, otherwise;
- the right subtree of **T[i]** is **T[2i+1]** if 2i+1 <= 7 and null, otherwise;
- the parent of **T[i]** is **T[i/2]** (integer division).

Based on this, the array is a representation of a complete binary tree. In other words, given the array, we can easily construct the binary tree it represents.

An array represents a complete binary tree if the number of elements in the array is $2^n - 1$, for some n. If the number of elements is some other value, the array represents an *almost complete* binary tree.

An *almost complete binary tree* is one in which

(a) all levels, except possibly the lowest, are completely filled
(b) the nodes (all leaves) at the lowest level are as far left as possible

If the nodes are numbered as above, then all leaves will be labelled with consecutive numbers from **n/2 + 1** to **n**. The last non-leaf node is labelled **n/2**.

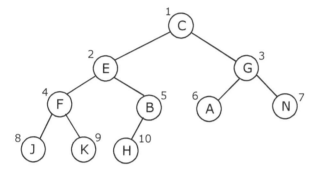

In the above tree, note that the leaves are numbered consecutively from 6 to 10. If, for instance, H were the right subtree of B instead of the left, the tree would not be "almost complete" since the leaves on the lowest level would not be "as far left as possible".

The following array of size 10 can represent this almost complete binary tree.

T

C	E	G	F	B	A	N	J	K	H
1	2	3	4	5	6	7	8	9	10

In general, if the tree is represented by an array **T[1..n]**, the following holds:

- **T[1]** is the root;
- the left subtree of **T[i]** is **T[2i]** if **2i <= n** and null, otherwise;
- the right subtree of **T[i]** is **T[2i+1]** if **2i+1 <= n** and null, otherwise;
- the parent of **T[i]** is **T[i/2]** (integer division).

Looked at another way, there is exactly one almost complete binary tree with n nodes and an array of size n represents this tree.

An almost complete binary tree has no "holes" in it—there is no room to add a node in between existing nodes. The only place to add a node is after the last one.

For instance, the following is not "almost complete" since there is a "hole" at the right subtree of **B**.

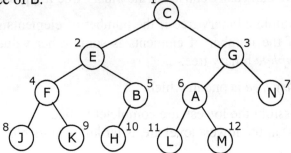

With the hole, the left subtree of **A** (in position 6) is *not* now in position 6*2 = 12 and the right subtree is not in position 6*2+1 =13. This relationship holds only when the tree is almost complete.

Given an array **T[1..n]** representing an almost complete binary tree with *n* nodes, we can perform an in-order traversal of the tree with the call **inOrder(1, n)** of the following function:

```
public static void inOrder(int j, int n) {
   if (j <= n) {
     inOrder(j * 2, n);
     visit(j); //or visit(T[j]), if you wish
     inOrder(j * 2 + 1, n);
   }
} //end inOrder
```

We can write similar functions for pre-order and post-order traversals.

By comparison to a complete binary tree, a *full binary tree* is one in which every node, except a leaf, has exactly two non-empty subtrees. For example:

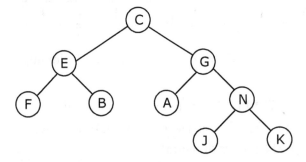

Note that a complete binary tree is always full but, as in the above tree, a full binary tree is not necessarily complete. An almost complete binary tree may or may not be full.

The following is almost complete but not full (**G** has *one* non-empty subtree):

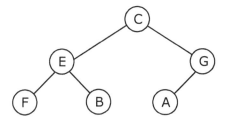

However, if node **A** is removed, the tree will be almost complete *and* full.

___

Representing an arbitrary binary tree using an array

We can use an array to represent an arbitrary binary tree if we "fill out" the tree to make it (almost) complete. Consider the following tree:

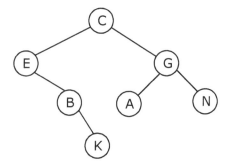

Wherever there is a null pointer we put an imaginary node, thus:

A node with an asterisk denotes an imaginary node. Note the imaginary node to the left of **E**. This, in turn, gives rise to two more in order to make the tree almost complete. The number at a node indicates the position in the array in which the node would be stored.

Normally, we would add imaginary nodes to **A** and **N** but we omit them here since these would all come at the end of the array. In other words, the last element in the array would be the last real node (**K**, in this case).

If **n** (11 in the example) is the last entry in the array **T**, we have the following:

- **T[1]** is the root;

- the left subtree of **T[i]** is **T[2i]** unless **2i > n** or **T[2i]** contains *****, in which case the left subtree is empty;
- the right subtree of **T[i]** is **T[2i+1]** unless **2i+1 > n** or **T[2i+1]** contains *****, in which case the right subtree is empty;
- for nodes in the tree, the parent of **T[i]** is **T[i/2]** (integer division).

In the example, we use 11 array locations to store a tree consisting of 7 nodes. While *some* storage is used for imaginary nodes, the representation is compact and it is easy to find the left child, the right child and the parent of a node.

Building a binary tree in an array

We now show how to build an arbitrary binary tree in an array. Given that data for the tree is in the same format as described on page 67, we write a class **BinaryTreeArray** as follows:

```java
import java.util.*;
public class BinaryTreeArray {
  int lastNode, MaxNodes;
  String[] T;

  public BinaryTreeArray(Scanner in, int max) {
    T = new String[max + 1];
    lastNode = 0;
    MaxNodes = max;
    buildTree(in, 1);
  }
  void buildTree(Scanner in, int root) {
    String str = in.next();
    if (str.equals("@")) {
      if (root <= MaxNodes) T[root] = "*";
      return;
    }
    if (root > MaxNodes) {
      System.out.printf("\nArray is too small to hold tree\n");
      System.exit(1);
    }
    if (root > lastNode) lastNode = root;
    T[root] = str;
    buildTree(in, root * 2);        //build the left subtree
    buildTree(in, root * 2 + 1);    //build the right subtree
  } //end buildTree
} //end BinaryTreeArray
```

MaxNodes is the maximum number of nodes we cater for. Its value is set when the constructor is called; the value is supplied by the user. We store the tree in **T[1]**

to **T[MaxNodes]**. When the tree is built, the variable **lastNode** holds the *last used* position in **T**. A null pointer (indicated by *****) is stored only if its position falls within **MaxNodes**. For example, if we want to build the following tree:

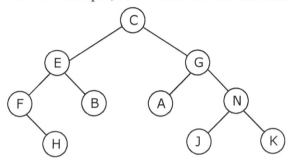

the data must be supplied as:

C E F @ H @ @ B @ @ G A @ @ N J @ @ K @ @

The function will create the following array:

T

C	E	G	F	B	A	N	*	H	*	*	*	*	J	K
1	2	3	4	5	6	7	8	9	10	11	12	13	14	15

However, if, for example, the left subtree of **G** is null (**A** is not present), **buildTree** will create:

T

C	E	G	F	B	*	N	*	H	*	*	?	?	J	K
1	2	3	4	5	6	7	8	9	10	11	12	13	14	15

T[12] and **T[13]**, which would normally hold the *children* of the left subtree of G, are undefined since no values are ever stored there. However, this is not a problem since, in *processing* the tree (for example, doing a traversal) these locations will never be accessed.

If necessary, we could write instance methods in **BinaryTreeArray** to perform the various traversals; **preOrder** is shown below:

```
public void preOrder() {
  preOrderTraversal(1);
}
void preOrderTraversal(int root) {
//tree is stored in T[1] to T[lastNode]
  if (root <= lastNode && !T[root].equals("*") ) { //if not null
    visit(root);
    preOrderTraversal(root * 2);
    preOrderTraversal(root * 2 + 1);
  }
} //end preOrderTraversal
```

```
        void visit(int node) {
            System.out.printf("%s ", T[node]);
        }
```

You are urged to write methods for the other traversals.

If the tree data is stored in a file, **btree.in**, you could test these methods by writing a class with the following statements (assume we are catering for 100 nodes):

```
        Scanner in = new Scanner(new FileReader("btree.in"));
        BinaryTreeArray bt = new BinaryTreeArray(in, 100); //MaxNodes
        System.out.printf("\nThe pre-order traversal is: ");
        bt.preOrder();
        System.out.printf("\n\n");
```

Exercises 3

1. A binary tree consists of an integer key field and pointers to the left subtree, right subtree and parent. Write the declarations required for building a tree and code to create an empty tree.

2. Each node of a binary tree has fields **left, right, key** and **parent**.

   Write a function to return the in-order successor of any given node **x**. Hint: if the right subtree of node **x** is empty and **x** has a successor **y**, then **y** is the lowest ancestor of **x** which contains **x** in its *left* subtree.

   Write a function to return the pre-order successor of any given node **x**.

   Write a function to return the post-order successor of any given node **x**.

   Using these functions, write functions to perform the in-order, pre-order and post-order traversals of a given binary tree.

3. Do exercise 2 assuming the tree is stored in an array.

4. Write functions to implement the in-order and pre-order traversals of a binary tree using the non-recursive algorithms given.

5. Write a function which, given the root of a binary search tree, deletes the smallest node and returns a pointer to the root of the reconstructed tree.

6. Write a function which, given the root of a binary search tree, deletes the largest node and returns a pointer to the root of the reconstructed tree.

7. Write a function which, given the root of a binary search tree, deletes the root and returns a pointer to the root of the reconstructed tree. Write the function replacing the root by (i) its in-order successor and (ii) its in-order predecessor.

8. Store the following integers in an array **bst[1..15]** such that **bst** represents a complete binary *search* tree: 34 23 45 46 37 78 90 2 40 20 87 53 12 15 91.

   A function **F1** outputs the in-order traversal of the above tree to a file and another function **F2** reads the numbers from the file, one at a time, and reconstructs the tree. Write **F1** and **F2**.

9. Draw a non-degenerate binary tree of 5 nodes such that the pre-order and level-order traversals produce identical results.

10. Write a function which, given the root of binary tree, returns the *width* of the tree, that is, the maximum number of nodes at any level.

11. A binary search tree contains integers. For each of the following sequences, state whether it could be the sequence of values examined in searching for the number 36. If it cannot, state why.

    7 25 42 40 33 34 39 36
    92 22 91 24 89 20 35 36
    95 20 90 24 92 27 30 36
    7 46 41 21 26 39 37 24 36

12. Draw the binary search tree (BST) obtained for the following keys assuming they are inserted in the order given: 56 30 61 39 47 35 75 13 21 64 26 73 18

    There is one almost complete BST for the above keys. Draw it.

    List the keys in an order which will produce the almost complete BST.

    Assuming that the almost complete tree is stored in a one-dimensional array **num[1..13]**, write a recursive function for printing the integers in post-order.

13. An imaginary 'external' node is attached to each null pointer of a binary tree of *n* nodes. How many external nodes are there?

    If **I** is the sum of the levels of the original tree nodes and **E** is the sum of the levels of the external nodes, prove that $E - I = 2n$. (**I** is called the *internal path length*.)

    Write a recursive function which, given the root of a binary tree, returns **I**.

    Write a non-recursive function which, given the root of a binary tree, returns **I**.

14. Draw the binary tree whose in-order and post-order traversals of the nodes are:

    In-order: G D P K E N F A T L
    Post-order: G P D K F N T A L E

15. Draw the binary tree whose in-order and pre-order traversals of the nodes are:

    In-order: G D P K E N F A T L
    Pre-order: N D G K P E T F A L

16. Draw two different binary trees such that the pre-order and post-order traversals of the one tree are identical to the pre-order and post-order traversals of the other tree.

17. Write a recursive function which, given the root of a binary tree and a key, searches for the key using (i) a pre-order (ii) an in-order (iii) a post-order traversal. If found, return the node containing the key; otherwise, return **null**.

18. Each node of a *binary search tree* contains three fields—**left**, **right** and **data**—with their usual meanings; **data** is a positive integer field. Write an *efficient* function which, given the root of the tree and **key**, returns the *smallest* number in the tree which is *greater* than **key**. If there is no such number, return -1.

19. Write a program which takes a Java program as input and outputs the program, numbering the lines, followed by an alphabetical cross-reference listing of all user identifiers; that is, a user identifier is followed by the numbers of all lines in which the identifier appears. If an identifier appears more than once in a given line, the line number must be repeated the number of times it appears.

    The cross-reference listing must *not* contain Java reserved words, words within character strings or words within comments.

4 Sorting

In this chapter, we will explain:

- how to sort a list of items using *selection sort*
- how to sort a list of items using *insertion sort*
- what is a *heap* and how to perform *heapsort*
- how a heap can be used to implement a *priority queue*
- how to sort a list of items using *quicksort*
- how to find the kth smallest item in a list
- how to sort a list of items using *mergesort*
- how to sort a list of items using *Shell (diminishing increment) sort*

In this chapter, we discuss several methods for sorting a list of items. For completeness, we start with a brief review of the 'simple' methods—selection and insertion sort. We then take a detailed look at some faster methods—heapsort, mergesort, quicksort and Shell (diminishing increment) sort.

4.1 Selection sort

Consider the following list of numbers stored in an array, **num**:

num

57	48	79	65	15	33	52
1	2	3	4	5	6	7

Sorting **num** in ascending order using *selection sort* proceeds as follows:

1st pass
- Find the smallest number in positions 1 to 7; the smallest is 15, found in position 5.
- Interchange the numbers in positions 1 and 5. This gives us:

num

15	48	79	65	57	33	52
1	2	3	4	5	6	7

2nd pass
- Find the smallest number in positions 2 to 7; the smallest is 33, found in position 6.
- Interchange the numbers in positions 2 and 6. This gives us:

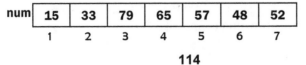

num

15	33	79	65	57	48	52
1	2	3	4	5	6	7

3rd pass

3rd pass

- Find the smallest number in positions 3 to 7; the smallest is 48, found in position 6.
- Interchange the numbers in positions 3 and 6. This gives us:

num

15	33	48	65	57	79	52
1	2	3	4	5	6	7

4th pass

- Find the smallest number in positions 4 to 7; the smallest is 52, found in position 7.
- Interchange the numbers in positions 4 and 7. This gives us:

num

15	33	48	52	57	79	65
1	2	3	4	5	6	7

5th pass

- Find the smallest number in positions 5 to 7; the smallest is 57, found in position 5.
- Interchange the numbers in positions 5 and 5. This gives us:

num

15	33	48	52	57	79	65
1	2	3	4	5	6	7

6th pass

- Find the smallest number in positions 6 to 7; the smallest is 65, found in position 6.
- Interchange the numbers in positions 6 and 7. This gives us:

num

15	33	48	52	57	65	79
1	2	3	4	5	6	7

and the array is now completely sorted.

If we let j go from 1 to 6, on each pass, we find the smallest number from positions j to 7. If the smallest number is in position s, we interchange the numbers in positions j and s. For an array of size n, we make $n - 1$ passes. In our example, we sorted 7 numbers in 6 passes. The following is an outline of the algorithm for sorting **num[1..n]**:

```
for j = 1 to n - 1
  s = position of smallest number from num[j] to num[n]
  swap num[j] and num[s]
endfor
```

We can implement this algorithm as follows, using the generic parameter, **list**:

```
//sort list[lo] to list[hi] in ascending order
public static void selectionSort(int[] list, int lo, int hi) {
   for (int j = lo; j < hi; j++) {
     int s = getSmallest(list, j, hi);
     swap(list, j, s);
   }
}
```

The two statements in the **for** loop *could* be written as:

```
swap(list, j, getSmallest(list, j, hi));
```

We can write **getSmallest** and **swap** as follows:

```
public static int getSmallest(int[] list, int lo, int hi) {
//return location of smallest from list[lo..hi]
   int small = lo;
   for (int j = lo + 1; j <= hi; j++)
     if (list[j] < list[small]) small = j;
   return small;
}

public static void swap(int[] list, int i, int j) {
//swap elements list[i] and list[j]
   int hold = list[i];
   list[i] = list[j];
   list[j] = hold;
}
```

Analysis of selection sort

In order to find the smallest of k items, we make k-1 comparisons. On the first pass, we make n-1 comparisons to find the smallest of n items. On the second pass, we make n-2 comparisons to find the smallest of n-1 items. And so on, until the last pass where we make 1 comparison to find the smaller of 2 items. In general, on the jth pass, we make n-j comparisons to find the smallest of n-j+1 items. Hence:

total number of comparisons = $1 + 2 + ... + n\text{-}1 = \frac{1}{2}\,n(n\text{-}1) \approx \frac{1}{2}\,n^2$

We say selection sort is of order $O(n^2)$ ("big O n squared"). The constant ½ is not important in "big O" notation since, as n gets very big, the constant becomes insignificant.

On each pass, we swap two items using 3 assignments. Since we make n-1 passes, we make $3(n-1)$ assignments in all. Using "big O" notation, we say that the number of assignments is $O(n)$. The constants 3 and 1 are not important as n gets large.

Does selection sort perform any better if there is order in the data? No. One way to find out is to give it a sorted list and see what it does. If you work through the algorithm, you will see that the method is oblivious to order in the data. It will make the same number of comparisons every time, regardless of the data.

As an exercise, modify the programming code so that it counts the number of comparisons and assignments made in sorting a list using selection sort.

4.2 Insertion sort

Consider the same array as before:

num

57	48	79	65	15	33	52
1	2	3	4	5	6	7

Now, think of the numbers as cards on a table and picked up one at a time in the order in which they appear in the array. Thus, we first pick up 57, then 48, then 79, and so on, until we pick up 52. However, as we pick up each new number, we add it to our hand in such a way that the numbers in our hand are all sorted.

When we pick up 57, we have just one number in our hand. We consider one number to be sorted.

When we pick up 48, we add it in front of 57 so our hand contains

    48 57

When we pick up 79, we place it after 57 so our hand contains

    48 57 79

When we pick up 65, we place it after 57 so our hand contains

    48 57 65 79

At this stage, four numbers have been picked up and our hand contains them in sorted order.

When we pick up 15, we place it before 48 so our hand contains

    15 48 57 65 79

When we pick up 33, we place it after 15 so our hand contains

    15 33 48 57 65 79

Finally, when we pick up 52, we place it after 48 so our hand contains

    15 33 48 52 57 65 79

The numbers have been sorted in ascending order.

The method described illustrates the idea behind *insertion sort*. The numbers in the array will be processed one at a time, from left to right. This is equivalent to picking up the numbers from the table, one at a time. Since the first number, by itself, is sorted, we will process the numbers in the array starting from the second.

When we come to process **num[j]**, we can assume that **num[1]** to **num[j-1]** are sorted. We then attempt to insert **num[j]** among **num[1]** to **num[j-1]** so that **num[1]** to **num[j]** are sorted. We will then go on to process **num[j+1]**. When we do so, our assumption that **num[1]** to **num[j]** are sorted will be true.

Sorting **num** in ascending order using insertion sort proceeds as follows:

1st pass

- Process **num[2]**, that is, 48. This involves placing 48 so that the first two numbers are sorted; **num[1]** and **num[2]** now contain

num

48	57
1	2

and the rest of the array remains unchanged.

2nd pass

- Process **num[3]**, that is, 79. This involves placing 79 so that the first three numbers are sorted; **num[1]** to **num[3]** now contain

num

48	57	79
1	2	3

and the rest of the array remains unchanged.

3rd pass

- Process **num[4]**, that is, 65. This involves placing 65 so that the first four numbers are sorted; **num[1]** to **num[4]** now contain

num

48	57	65	79
1	2	3	4

and the rest of the array remains unchanged.

4th pass

- Process **num[5]**, that is, 15. This involves placing 15 so that the first five numbers are sorted. To simplify the explanation, think of 15 as being taken out and stored in a simple variable (**key**, say) leaving a 'hole' in **num[5]**. We can picture this as follows:

key

15

num

48	57	65	79		33	52
1	2	3	4	5	6	7

The insertion of 15 in its correct position proceeds as follows:

- Compare 15 with 79; it is smaller so move 79 to location 5, leaving location 4 free. This gives:

key		num						
15		48	57	65		79	33	52
		1	2	3	4	5	6	7

- Compare 15 with 65; it is smaller so move 65 to location 4, leaving location 3 free. This gives:

key		num						
15		48	57		65	79	33	52
		1	2	3	4	5	6	7

- Compare 15 with 57; it is smaller so move 57 to location 3, leaving location 2 free. This gives:

key		num						
15		48		57	65	79	33	52
		1	2	3	4	5	6	7

- Compare 15 with 48; it is smaller so move 48 to location 2, leaving location 1 free. This gives:

key		num						
15			48	57	65	79	33	52
		1	2	3	4	5	6	7

- There are no more numbers to compare with 15 so it is inserted in location 1, giving

key		num						
15		15	48	57	65	79	33	52
		1	2	3	4	5	6	7

- We can express the logic of placing 15 by saying that as long as **key** is less than **num[k]**, for some **k**, we move **num[k]** to position **num[k+1]** and move on to consider **num[k-1]**, providing it exists. It won't exist when **k** is actually 1. In this case, the process stops and **key** is inserted in position 1.

5th pass

- Process **num[6]**, that is, 33. This involves placing 33 so that the first six numbers are sorted. This is done as follows:
- Store 33 in **key**, leaving location 6 free;
- Compare 33 with 79; it is smaller so move 79 to location 6, leaving location 5 free;
- Compare 33 with 65; it is smaller so move 65 to location 5, leaving location 4 free;

- Compare 33 with 57; it is smaller so move 57 to location 4, leaving location 3 free;
- Compare 33 with 48; it is smaller so move 48 to location 3, leaving location 2 free;
- Compare 33 with 15; it is bigger; insert 33 in location 2. This gives:

key		num						
33		15	33	48	57	65	79	52
		1	2	3	4	5	6	7

- We can express the logic of placing 33 by saying that as long as **key** is less than **num[k]**, for some **k**, we move **num[k]** to position **num[k+1]** and move on to consider **num[k-1]**, providing it exists. If **key** is greater than or equal to **num[k]** for some **k**, then **key** is inserted in position **k+1**. Here, 33 is greater than **num[1]** and so is inserted into **num[2]**.

6th pass

- Process **num[7]**, that is, 52. This involves placing 52 so that the first seven (all) numbers are sorted. This is done as follows:
- Store 52 in **key**, leaving location 7 free;
- Compare 52 with 79; it is smaller so move 79 to location 7, leaving location 6 free;
- Compare 52 with 65; it is smaller so move 65 to location 6, leaving location 5 free;
- Compare 52 with 57; it is smaller so move 57 to location 5, leaving location 4 free;
- Compare 52 with 48; it is bigger; insert 52 in location 4. This gives:

key		num						
52		15	33	48	52	57	65	79
		1	2	3	4	5	6	7

The array is now completely sorted.

The following algorithm will sort **num[1..n]**, using insertion sort:

```
for j = 2 to n do
   insert num[j] among num[1] to num[j-1] so that
   num[1] to num[j] are sorted
endfor
```

Using this algorithm, we write the method **insertionSort** (next page) using the parameter, **list**. This method is a bit more general in that it sorts any *portion* of the array from **list[lo]** to **list[hi]**.

The **while** statement is at the heart of the sort. It states that as long as we are within the array (**k >= lo**) and the current number (**key**) is less than the one in the array (**key < list[k]**), we move **list[k]** to the right (**list[k + 1] = list[k]**) and move on to the next number on the left (**--k**).

```
public static void insertionSort(int[] list, int lo, int hi) {
//sort list[lo] to list[hi] in ascending order
   int j, k, key;
   for (j = lo+1; j <= hi; j++) {
     key = list[j];
     k = j - 1; //start comparing with previous item
     while (k >= lo && key < list[k]) {
       list[k + 1] = list[k];
       --k;
     }
     list[k + 1] = key;
   }
} //end insertionSort
```

Analysis of insertion sort

In processing item j, we can make as few as 1 comparison (if **num[j]** is bigger than **num[j-1]**) or as many as j-1 comparisons (if **num[j]** is smaller than all the previous items). For random data, we would expect to make $\frac{1}{2}(j$-1$)$ comparisons, on average. Hence, the average total number of comparsions to sort n items is:

$$\sum_{j=2}^{n}\frac{1}{2}(j-1) = \frac{1}{2}\{1 + 2 + ...+ n\text{-}1\} = \frac{1}{4}\,n(n\text{-}1) \approx \frac{1}{4}\,n^2$$

We say insertion sort is of order $O(n^2)$ ("big O n squared"). The constant ¼ is not important as n gets large.

Each time we make a comparison, we also make an assignment. Hence the total number of assignments is also $\frac{1}{4}\,n(n$-1$) \approx \frac{1}{4}\,n^2$.

We emphasize that this is an *average* for random data. Unlike selection sort, the *actual* performance of insertion sort depends on the data supplied. If the given array is already sorted, insertion sort will quickly determine this by making n-1 comparisons. In this case, it runs in $O(n)$ time. One would expect that insertion sort *will* perform better the more order there is in the data.

If the given data is in *descending* order, insertion sort performs at its worst since each new number has to travel all the way to the beginning of the list. In this case, the number of comparisons is $\frac{1}{2}\,n(n$-1$) \approx \frac{1}{2}\,n^2$. The number of assignments is also $\frac{1}{2}\,n(n$-1$) \approx \frac{1}{2}\,n^2$.

Thus, the number of comparisons made by insertion sort ranges from n-1 (best), to $\frac{1}{4}\,n^2$ (average) to $\frac{1}{2}\,n^2$ (worst). The number of assignments is always the same as the number of comparisons.

As an exercise, modify the programming code so that it counts the number of comparisons and assignments made in sorting a list using insertion sort.

4.3 Heapsort

In this section, we describe a method of sorting (called *heapsort*) which *interprets* the elements in an array as an almost complete binary tree. Consider the following array which is to be sorted in ascending order:

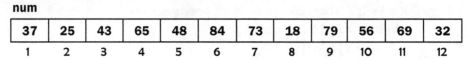

num

37	25	43	65	48	84	73	18	79	56	69	32
1	2	3	4	5	6	7	8	9	10	11	12

We can think of this array as an almost complete binary tree with 12 nodes:

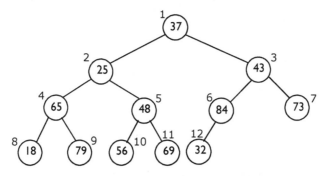

Suppose we now require that the value at each node must be greater than or equal to the values in its left and right subtrees, if present. As it is, only node 6 and the leaves have this property. Shortly, we will see how to rearrange the nodes so that *all* nodes satisfy this condition. But, first, we give it a name:

A *heap* is an almost complete binary tree such that the value at the root is greater than or equal to the values at the left and right children and the left and right subtrees are also heaps.

An immediate consequence of this definition is that the largest value is at the root. Such a heap is referred to as a *max-heap*. We also define a *min-heap* with the word 'greater' replaced by 'smaller'. For a min-heap, the *smallest* value is at the root.

We now show how to convert the above binary tree into a max-heap.

First, we observe that all the leaves are heaps since they have no children.

Starting at the last non-leaf node (6, in the example) we convert the tree rooted there into a max-heap. If the value at the node is greater than its children, there is nothing to do. This is the case with node 6, since 84 is bigger than 32.

Next, we move on to node 5. The value here, 48, is smaller than at least one child (both, in this case, 56 and 69). We first find the larger child (69) and interchange it with node 5. Thus 69 ends up in node 5 and 48 ends up in node 11.

Next, we go to node 4. The larger child, 79, is moved to node 4 and 65 is moved to node 9. At this stage, the tree looks like this:

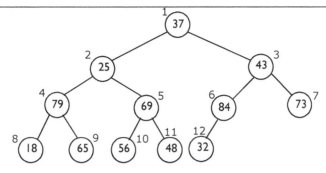

Continuing at node 3, 43 must be moved. The larger child is 84, so we interchange the values at nodes 3 and 6. The value now at node 6 (43) is bigger than its child (32) so there is nothing more to do. Note, however, that if the value at node 6 were 28, say, it would have had to be exchanged with 32.

Moving to node 2, 25 is exchanged with its larger child, 79. But 25 now in node 4 is smaller than 65, its right child in node 9. Thus, these two values must be exchanged.

Finally, at node 1, 37 is exchanged with its larger child 84. It is further exchanged with its (new) larger child, 73, giving the following tree, which is now a heap:

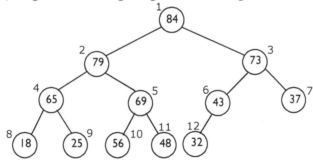

Note that the largest value, 84, is at the root of the tree. Now that the values in the array form a heap, we can sort them in ascending order as follows:

Store the last item, 32, in a temporary location. Next, move 84 to the last position (node 12), freeing node 1. Then, imagine 32 is in node 1 and move it so that items 1 to 11 become a heap. This will be done as follows:

32 is exchanged with its bigger child, 79, which now moves into node 1. 32 is further exchanged with its (new) bigger child, 69, which moves into node 2. Finally, 32 is exchanged with 56, giving:

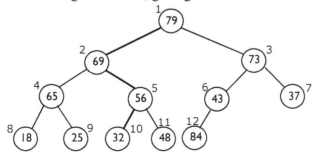

At this stage, the second largest number, 79, is in node 1. This is placed in node 11 and 48 "sifted down" from node 1 until items 1 to 10 form a heap. Now, the third largest number, 73, will be at the root. This is placed in node 10, and so on. The process is repeated until the array is sorted.

After the initial heap is built, the sorting process can be described with:

```
for k = n downto 2 do
   item = num[k]      //extract current last item
   num[k] = num[1]    //move top of heap to current last node
   siftDown(item, num, 1, k-1) //restore heap properties from 1 to k-1
end for
```

where **siftDown(item, num, 1, k-1)** is based on the following conditions:

- **num[1]** is empty;
- **num[2]** to **num[k-1]** form a heap;
- starting at position 1, **item** is inserted so that **num[1]** to **num[k-1]** form a heap.

In the algorithm above, each time through the loop, the value in the current last position (**k**) is stored in **item**. The value at node 1 is moved to postion **k**; node 1 becomes empty (available) and nodes 2 to **k-1** all satisfy the heap property.

The call **siftDown(item, num, 1, k-1)** will add **item** so that **num[1]** to **num[k-1]** contain a heap. This ensures that the next highest number is at node 1.

The nice thing about **siftDown** (when we write it) is that it can be used to create the initial heap from the given array. Recall the process of creating a heap on page 122. At each node (**j**, say), we "sifted the value down" so that we formed a heap rooted at **j**. To use **siftDown** in this situation, we generalize it as follows:

```
void siftDown(int key, int[] num, int root, int last)
```

This assumes that

- **num[root]** is empty;
- **num[root+1]** to **num[last]** form a heap;
- starting at **root**, **key** is inserted so that **num[root]** to **num[last]** form a heap.

Given an array of values **num[1]** to **num[n]**, we could build the heap with:

```
for j = n/2 downto 1 do       // n/2 is the last non-leaf node
   siftDown(num[j], num, j, n)
```

We now show how to write **siftDown**.

Consider the following:

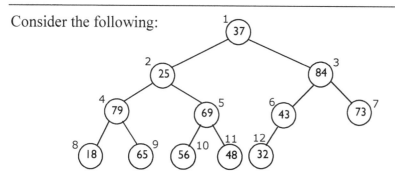

Except for nodes 1 and 2, all the other nodes satisfy the "heap property" that they are bigger than or equal to their children. Suppose we want to make node 2 the root of a heap. As it is, the value 25 is smaller than its children (79 and 69). We want to write **siftDown** so that the call **siftDown(25, num, 2, 12)** will do the job. Here, 25 is the **key**, **num** is the array, 2 is the root and 12 is the position of the last node.

After this, each of nodes 2 to 12 will be the root of a heap and the call **siftDown(37, num, 1, 12)** will ensure that the entire array contains a heap.

The gist of **siftDown** is as follows:

```
find the larger child of num[root]; //suppose it is in node m
if (key >= num[m]) we are done; put key in num[root]
//key is smaller than the bigger child
store num[m] in num[root]  //promote bigger child
set root to m
```

The process is repeated until the value at **root** is bigger than its children or there are no children. Here is **siftDown**:

```
public static void siftDown(int key, int[] num, int root, int last) {
   int bigger = 2 * root;
   while (bigger <= last) { //while there is at least one child
     if (bigger < last) //there is a right child as well; find the bigger
       if (num[bigger+1] > num[bigger]) bigger++;
     //'bigger' holds the index of the bigger child
     if (key >= num[bigger]) break;
     //key is smaller; promote num[bigger]
     num[root] = num[bigger];
     root = bigger;
     bigger = 2 * root;
   }
   num[root] = key;
} //end siftDown
```

We can now write **heapSort** as follows:

```
public static void heapSort(int[] num, int n) {
//sort num[1] to num[n]
  //convert the array to a heap
  for (int k = n / 2; k >= 1; k--) siftDown(num[k], num, k, n);

  for (int k = n; k > 1; k--) {
    int item = num[k]; //extract current last item
    num[k] = num[1];  //move top of heap to current last node
    siftDown(item, num, 1, k-1); //restore heap properties from 1 to k-1
  }
} //end heapSort
```

and test it with:

```
int[] num = {0, 37, 25, 43, 65, 48, 84, 73, 18, 79, 56, 69, 32};
int j, n = 12;
heapSort(num, n);
for (j = 1; j <= n; j++) System.out.printf("%d ", num[j]);
System.out.printf("\n");
```

This produces the following output (**num[1]** to **num[12]** sorted):

18 25 32 37 43 48 56 65 69 73 79 84

Programming note: as written, **heapSort** sorts an array assuming that n elements are stored from subscripts 1 to **n**. If they are stored from 0 to **n-1**, appropriate adjustments would have to be made. They would be based mainly on the following observations:

- the root is stored in **num[0]**;
- the left child of node **j** is node **2j + 1** if **2j + 1 < n**;
- the right child of node **j** is node **2j + 2** if **2j + 2 < n**;
- the parent of node **j** is node **(j − 1) / 2** (integer division);
- the last non-leaf node is **(n − 2) / 2** (integer division);

You can verify these observations using the following tree (n = 12):

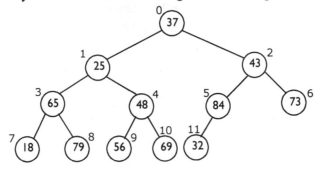

You are urged to rewrite **heapSort** so that it sorts an array **num[0..n-1]**. For instance, the only change required in **siftDown** is in the calculation of **bigger**. Instead of **2 * root**, we now use **2 * root + 1**.

4.4 Building a heap using 'sift-up'

Consider the problem of adding a new node to an existing heap. Specifically, suppose **num[1]** to **num[n]** contain a heap. We wish to add a new number, **newKey**, so that **num[1]** to **num[n+1]** contain a heap which includes **newKey**. We assume the array has room for the new key.

For example, suppose we have the following heap:

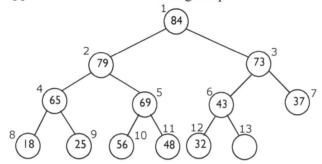

and we want to add 40 to the heap. When the new number is added, the heap will contain 13 elements. We imagine 40 is placed in **num[13]** (but do not store it there, as yet) and compare it with its parent 43 in **num[6]**. Since 40 is smaller, the heap property is satisfied; we place 40 in **num[13]** and the process ends.

But suppose we want to add 80 to the heap. We imagine 80 is placed in **num[13]** (but do not actually store it there, as yet) and compare it with its parent 43 in **num[6]**. Since 80 is bigger, we move 43 to **num[13]** and imagine 80 being placed in **num[6]**.

Next, we compare 80 with its parent 73 in **num[3]**. It is bigger, so we move 73 to **num[6]** and imagine 80 being placed in **num[3]**.

We then compare 80 with its parent 84 in **num[1]**. It is smaller, so we place 80 in **num[3]** and the process ends.

Note that if we were adding 90 to the heap, 84 would be moved to **num[3]** and 90 would be inserted in **num[1]**. It is now the largest number in the heap.

The following shows the heap after 80 is added:

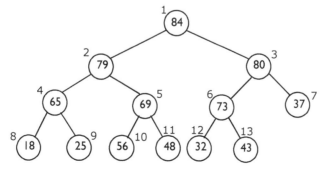

The following algorithm adds **newKey** to a heap stored in **num[1]** to **num[n]**:

```
child = n + 1;
parent = child / 2;
while (parent > 0) {
    if (newKey <= num[parent]) break;
    num[child] = num[parent]; //move down parent
    child = parent;
    parent = child / 2;
}
num[child] = newKey;
n = n + 1;
```

The process described is usually referred to as "sifting up". We can rewrite the above algorithm as a function **siftUp**. We assume that **siftUp** is given an array **heap[1..n]** such that **heap[1..n-1]** contains a heap and **heap[n]** is to be sifted up so that **heap[1..n]** contains a heap. In other words, **heap[n]** plays the role of **newKey** in the above algorithm.

We show **siftUp** as part of Program P4.1 (next page) which creates a heap out of numbers stored in a file, **heap.in**.

If **heap.in** contains

       37 25 43 65 48 84 73 18 79 56 69 32

P4.1 will build the heap (described next) and print:

       84 79 73 48 69 37 65 18 25 43 56 32

After 37, 25 and 43 are read, we will have:

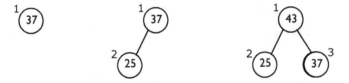

After 65, 48, 84 and 73 are read, we will have:

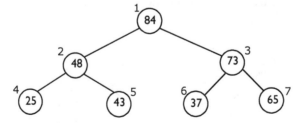

And after 18, 79, 56, 69 and 32 are read,

Program P4.1

```java
import java.io.*;
import java.util.*;
public class SiftUpTest {
    final static int MaxHeapSize = 100;
    public static void main (String[] args) throws IOException {
        Scanner in = new Scanner(new FileReader("heap.in"));
        int[] num = new int[MaxHeapSize + 1];
        int j, n = 0, number;

        while (in.hasNextInt()) {
            number = in.nextInt();
            if (n < MaxHeapSize) { //check if array has room
                num[++n] = number;
                siftUp(num, n);
            }
        }
        for (j = 1; j <= n; j++) System.out.printf("%d ", num[j]);
        System.out.printf("\n");
        in.close();
    } //end main

    public static void siftUp(int[] heap, int n) {
    //sifts up the value in heap[n] so that heap[1..n] contains a heap
        int siftItem = heap[n];
        int child = n;
        int parent = child / 2;
        while (parent > 0) {
            if (siftItem <= heap[parent]) break;
            heap[child] = heap[parent]; //move down parent
            child = parent;
            parent = child / 2;
        }
        heap[child] = siftItem;
    } //end siftUp
} //end class SiftUpTest
```

we will have the final heap:

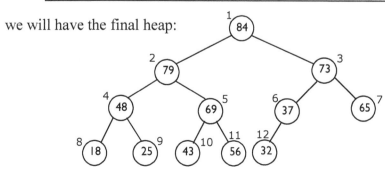

Note that this heap is different from that on page 123 even though they are formed from the same numbers. What hasn't changed is that the largest value, 84, is at the root.

If the values are already stored in an array **num[1..n]**, we can create the heap with:

```
for (int k = 2; k <= n; k++) siftUp(num, k);
```

4.5 Analysis of heapsort

Is **siftUp** or **siftDown** better for creating a heap? Keep in mind that the most times any node will ever have to move is $\log_2 n$.

In **siftDown**, we process $n/2$ nodes and, at each step, we make 2 comparisons: one to find the bigger child and one to compare the node value with the bigger child. In a simplistic analysis, in the worst case, we will need to make $2*n/2*\log_2 n = n\log_2 n$ comparisons. However, a more careful analysis will show that we need make, at most, only $4n$ comparisons.

In **siftUp**, we process n-1 nodes. At each step, we make one comparison: the node with its parent. In a simplistic analysis, in the worst case, we make $(n$-1$)\log_2 n$ comparisons. However, it is possible that all the leaves may have to travel all the way to the top of the tree. In this case, we have $n/2$ nodes having to travel a distance of $\log_2 n$, giving a total of $(n/2)\log_2 n$ comparisons. And that's only for the leaves. In the end, a more careful analysis still gives us approximately $n\log_2 n$ comparisons for **siftUp**.

The difference in performance is hinged on the following: in **siftDown**, there is no work to do for half the nodes (the leaves); **siftUp** has the most work to do for these very nodes.

Whichever method we use for creating the initial heap, heapsort will sort an array of size n making at most $2n\log_2 n$ comparisons and $n\log_2 n$ assignments. This is very fast. In addition, heapsort is *stable* in the sense that its performance is always at worst $2n\log_2 n$, regardless of the order of the items in the given array.

To give an idea how fast heapsort (and all sorting methds which are of order $O(n\log_2 n)$ e.g. quicksort, mergesort) is, let us compare it with selection sort which makes roughly $\frac{1}{2} n^2$ comparisons to sort n items.

n	selection(comp)	heap(comp)	select(sec)	heap(sec)
100	5,000	1,329	0.005	0.001
1,000	500,000	19,932	0.5	0.020
10,000	50,000,000	265,754	50	0.266
100,000	5,000,000,000	3,321,928	5000	3.322
1,000,000	500,000,000,000	39,863,137	500000	39.863

The second and third columns show the number of comparisons that each method makes. The last two columns show the running time of each method (in seconds) assuming that the computer can process one million comparisons per second. For example, to sort one million items, selection sort will take 500000 seconds (almost 6 days!) whereas heapsort will do it in less than 40 seconds.

4.6 Heaps and priority queues

A priority queue is one in which each item is assigned some 'priority' and its position in the queue is based on this priority. The item with 'top' priority is placed at the head of the queue. The following are some typical operations which may be performed on a priority queue:

- remove (serve) the item with the highest priority
- add an item with a given priority
- remove (delete without serving) an item from the queue
- change the priority of an item, adjusting its position based on its new priority

We can think of 'priority' as an integer—the bigger the integer, the higher the priority.

Immediately, we can surmise that if we implement the queue as a max-heap, the item with the highest priority will be at the root, so it can be easily removed. Re-organizing the heap will simply involve 'sifting down' the last item from the root.

Adding an item will involve placing the item in the postion after the current last one, and sifting it up until it finds its correct position.

To delete an arbitrary item from the queue, we will need to know its position. Deleting it will involve replacing it with the current last item and sifting it up or down to find its correct position. The heap will shrink by one item.

If we change the priority of an item, we may need to sift it either up or down to find its correct position. Of course, it may also remain in its original position, depending on the change.

In many situations (e.g. a job queue on a multi-tasking computer) the priority of a job may increase over time so that it eventually gets served. In these situations, a job moves closer to the top of the heap with each change; thus, only 'sift up' is required.

In a typical situation, information about the items in a priority queue is held in another structure which can be quickly searched e.g. a binary search tree. One field in the node will contain the index of the item in the array used to implement the priority queue.

Using the job queue example, suppose we want to add an item to the queue. We can search the tree by job number, say, and add the item to the tree. Its priority number is used to determine its position in the queue. This position is stored in the tree node.

If, later, the priority changes, the item's position in the queue is adjusted and this new position is stored in the tree node. Note that adjusting this item may also involve changing the position of other items (as they move up or down the heap) and the tree will have to be updated for these items as well.

In Chapter 5, we will show how a priority queue is used in the implementation of two graph algorithms—Prim's and Dijkstra's.

4.7 Quicksort

At the heart of quicksort is the notion of *partitioning* the list with respect to one of the values called a *pivot*. For example, given the following list to be sorted:

num

53	12	98	63	18	32	80	46	72	21
1	2	3	4	5	6	7	8	9	10

we can *partition* it with respect to the first value, 53. This means placing 53 in such a position that all values to the left of it are smaller and all values to the right are greater than or equal to it. Shortly, we will describe an algorithm which will partition the above as:

num

21	12	18	32	46	53	80	98	72	63
1	2	3	4	5	6	7	8	9	10

The value 53 is used as the *pivot*. It is placed in position 6. All values to the left of 53 are smaller than 53 and all values to the right are greater. The location in which the pivot is placed is called the *division point* (**dp**, say). By definition, 53 is in its final sorted position.

If we can sort **num[1..dp-1]** and **num[dp+1..n]**, we would have sorted the entire list. But we can use the same process to sort *these* pieces, indicating that a recursive procedure is appropriate.

Assuming a function **partition** is available which partitions a given section of an array and returns the division point, we can write **quicksort** as follows:

```
public static void quicksort(int[] A, int lo, int hi) {
//sorts A[lo] to A[hi] in ascending order
  if (lo < hi) {
    int dp = partition(A, lo, hi);
    quicksort(A, lo, dp-1);
    quicksort(A, dp+1, hi);
  }
} //end quicksort
```

The call **quicksort(num, 1, n)** will sort **num[1..n]** in ascending order.

We now look at how **partition** may be written. Consider the array:

num

53	12	98	63	18	32	80	46	72	21
1	2	3	4	5	6	7	8	9	10

We will partition it with respect to **num[1]**, 53 (the pivot) by making one pass through the array. We will look at each number, in turn. If it is bigger than the pivot, we do nothing. If it is smaller, we move it to the left side of the array. Initially, we set the variable **lastSmall** to 1; as the method proceeds, **lastSmall** will be the index of the last item that is known to be smaller than the pivot. We partition **num** as follows:

- compare 12 with 53; it is smaller, so add 1 to **lastSmall** (making it 2) and swap **num[2]** with itself;
- compare 98 with 53; it is bigger, so move on;
- compare 63 with 53; it is bigger, so move on;
- compare 18 with 53; it is smaller, so add 1 to **lastSmall** (making it 3) and swap **num[3]**, 98, with 18;

At this stage, we have:

num

53	12	18	63	98	32	80	46	72	21
1	2	3	4	5	6	7	8	9	10

- compare 32 with 53; it is smaller, so add 1 to **lastSmall** (making it 4) and swap **num[4]**, 63, with 32;
- compare 80 with 53; it is bigger, so move on;
- compare 46 with 53; it is smaller, so add 1 to **lastSmall** (making it 5) and swap **num[5]**, 98, with 46;

At this stage, we have:

num

53	12	18	32	46	63	80	98	72	21
1	2	3	4	5	6	7	8	9	10

- compare 72 with 53; it is bigger, so move on;
- compare 21 with 53; it is smaller, so add 1 to **lastSmall** (making it 6) and swap **num[6]**, 63, with 21;
- we have come to the end of the array; swap **num[1]** and **num[lastSmall]**; this moves the pivot into its final position.

We end up with:

num

21	12	18	32	46	53	80	98	72	63
1	2	3	4	5	6	7	8	9	10

and the division point is denoted by **lastSmall** (6).

We can express the above procedure as a function **partition1**:

```
public static int partition1(int[] A, int lo, int hi) {
//partition A[lo] to A[hi] using A[lo] as the pivot
  int pivot = A[lo];
  int lastSmall = lo;
  for (int j = lo + 1; j <= hi; j++)
    if (A[j] < pivot) {
      ++lastSmall;
      swap(A, lastSmall, j);
    }
  //end for
  swap(A, lo, lastSmall);
  return lastSmall;  //return the division point
} //end partition1

public static void swap(int[] list, int i, int j) {
//swap list[i] and list[j]
  int hold = list[i];
  list[i] = list[j];
  list[j] = hold;
}
```

Quicksort is one of those methods whose performance can range from very fast to very slow. Typically, it is of order $O(n\log_2 n)$ and, for random data, the number of comparisons varies between $n\log_2 n$ and $3n\log_2 n$. However, things can get worse.

The idea behind partitioning is to break up the given portion into two fairly equal pieces. Whether or not this happens depends, to a large extent, on the value that is chosen as the pivot.

In the function, we choose the first element as the pivot. This will work well in most cases, especially for random data. However, if the first element happens to be the smallest, the partitioning operation becomes almost useless since the division point will simply be the first position. The 'left' piece will be empty and the 'right' piece will be only one element smaller than the given sublist. Similar remarks apply if the pivot is the largest element.

While the algorithm will still work, it will be slowed considerably. For example, if the given array is sorted, quicksort will become as slow as selection sort.

One way to avoid this problem is to choose a random element as the pivot, not merely the first one. While it is still possible that this method will choose the smallest (or the largest), that choice will not be systematic but merely 'by chance'.

Yet another method is to choose the median of the first (**A[lo]**), last (**A[hi]**) and middle (**A[(lo+hi)/2]**) items as the pivot. You are advised to experiment with various ways of choosing the pivot.

Our experiments showed that choosing a random element as the pivot was simple and effective, even for sorted data. In fact, in many cases, the method ran faster with sorted data than with random data, an unusual result for quicksort.

Another way to partition

There are many ways to achieve the goal of partitioning—splitting the list into two parts such that the elements in the left part are smaller than the elements in the right part. Our first method, above, placed the pivot in its final position. For variety, we look at another way to partition. While this method still partitions with respect to a pivot, it does *not* place the pivot in its final sorted position. As we will see, this is not a problem.

Consider, again, the array **num[1..n]** where **n** = 10:

num

53	12	98	63	18	32	80	46	72	21
1	2	3	4	5	6	7	8	9	10

We choose 53 as the pivot. The general idea is to scan from the right looking for a key that is smaller than, or equal to, the pivot. We then scan from the left for a key that is greater than, or equal to, the pivot. We swap these two values; this process effectively puts smaller values to the left and bigger values to the right.

We use two variables, **lo** and **hi**, to mark our positions on the left and right. Initially, we set **lo** to 0 and **hi** to 11 (**n+1**). We then loop as follows:

- subtract 1 from **hi** (making it 10);
- compare **num[hi]**, 21, with 53; it is smaller, so stop scanning from the right with **hi** = 10;
- add 1 to **lo** (making it 1);
- compare **num[lo]**, 53, with 53; it is not smaller, so stop scanning from the left with **lo** = 1;
- **lo** (1) is less than **hi** (10), so swap **num[lo]** and **num[hi]**;
- subtract 1 from **hi** (making it 9);
- compare **num[hi]**, 72, with 53; it is bigger, so decrease **hi** (making it 8) and compare **num[hi]**, 46, with 53; it is smaller, so stop scanning from the right with **hi** = 8;
- add 1 to **lo** (making it 2);
- compare **num[lo]**, 12, with 53; it is smaller, so add 1 to **lo** (making it 3) and compare **num[lo]**, 98, with 53; it is bigger, so stop scanning from the left with **lo** = 3;

- **lo** (3) is less than **hi** (8), so swap **num[lo]** and **num[hi]**;

At this stage, we have **lo** = 3, **hi** = 8 and **num** as follows:

num

21	12	46	63	18	32	80	98	72	53
1	2	3	4	5	6	7	8	9	10

- subtract 1 from **hi** (making it 7);
- compare **num[hi]**, 80, with 53; it is bigger, so decrease **hi** (making it 6) and compare **num[hi]**, 32, with 53; it is smaller, so stop scanning from the right with **hi** = 6;
- add 1 to **lo** (making it 4);
- compare **num[lo]**, 63, with 53; it is bigger, so stop scanning from the left with **lo** = 4;
- **lo** (4) is less than **hi** (6), so swap **num[lo]** and **num[hi]**, giving:

num

21	12	46	32	18	63	80	98	72	53
1	2	3	4	5	6	7	8	9	10

- subtract 1 from **hi** (making it 5);
- compare **num[hi]**, 18, with 53; it is smaller, so stop scanning from the right with **hi** = 5;
- add 1 to **lo** (making it 5);
- compare **num[lo]**, 18, with 53; it is smaller, so add 1 to **lo** (making it 6) and compare **num[lo]**, 63, with 53; it is bigger, so stop scanning from the left with **lo** = 6;
- **lo** (6) is *not* less than **hi** (5), so the algorithm ends.

The value of **hi** is such that the values in **num[1..hi]** are smaller than those in **num[hi+1..n]**. Here, the values in **num[1..5]** are smaller than those in **num[6..10]**. Note that 53 is not in its final sorted position. However, this is not a problem since, to sort the array, all we need to do is sort **num[1..hi]** and **num[hi+1..n]**.

We can write the above procedure as **partition2**:

```
public static int partition2(int[] A, int lo, int hi) {
//return dp such that A[lo..dp] <= A[dp+1..hi]
  int pivot = A[lo];
  --lo; ++hi;
  while (lo < hi) {
    do --hi; while (A[hi] > pivot);
    do ++lo; while (A[lo] < pivot);
    if (lo < hi) swap(A, lo, hi);
  }
  return hi;
} //end partition2
```

With *this* version of partition, we can write **quicksort2** as follows:

```
public static void quicksort2(int[] A, int lo, int hi) {
//sorts A[lo] to A[hi] in ascending order
   if (lo < hi) {
      int dp = partition2(A, lo, hi);
      quicksort2(A, lo, dp);
      quicksort2(A, dp+1, hi);
   }
}
```

In **partition2**, we choose the first element as the pivot. However, as discussed, choosing a random element will give better results. We can do this with:

```
swap(A, lo, random(lo, hi));
int pivot = A[lo];
```

where **random** can be written as:

```
public static int random(int m, int n) {
//returns a random integer from m to n, inclusive
   return (int) (Math.random() * (n - m + 1)) + m;
}
```

4.7.1 Non-recursive quicksort

In the versions of **quicksort**, above, after a sublist is partitioned, we call **quicksort** with the left part followed by the right part. For most cases, this will work fine. However, it is possible that, for large **n**, the number of pending recursive calls can get so large so as to generate a "recursive stack overflow" error.

In our experiments, this occurred with **n** = 7000 if the given data was already sorted and the first element was chosen as the pivot. However, there was no problem even for **n** = 100000 if a random element was chosen as the pivot.

Another approach is to write **quicksort** non-recursively. This would require us to stack the pieces of the list that remain to be sorted. It can be shown that when a sublist is subdivided, if we process the *smaller* sublist first, the number of stack elements will be restricted to at most $\log_2 n$.

For example, suppose we are sorting **A[1..99]** and the first division point is 40. Assume we are using **partition2** which does not put the pivot in its final sorted position. Thus, we must sort **A[1..40]** and **A[41..99]** to complete the sort. We will stack (41, 99) and deal with **A[1..40]** (the shorter sublist) first.

Suppose the division point for **A[1..40]** is 25. We will stack (1, 25) and process **A[26..40]** first. At this stage we have two sublists—(41, 99) and (1, 25)—on the stack which remain to be sorted. Attempting to sort **A[26..40]** will cause another sublist to be added to the stack, and so on. In our implementation, we will also

Data structures in Java

add the shorter sublist to the stack, but this will be taken off immediately and processed.

The result mentioned above assures us that there will never be more than $\log_2 99 = 7$ (rounded up) elements on the stack at any given time. Even for $n = 1,000,000$, we are guaranteed that the number of stack items will not exceed 20.

Of course, we will have to manipulate the stack ourselves. Each stack element will consist of two integers (**left** and **right**, say) meaning that the portion of the list from **left** to **right** remains to be sorted. We define **StackData** as:

```
class StackData {
    int left, right;

    public StackData(int a, int b) {
        left = a;
        right = b;
    }
} //end class StackData
```

and use the stack implementation from page 87. We now write **quicksort3** based on the above discussion.

```
public static void quicksort3(int[] A, int lo, int hi) {
    Stack S = new Stack();
    S.push(new StackData(lo, hi));
    int stackItems = 1, maxStackItems = 1;
    while (!S.empty()) {
        --stackItems;
        StackData d = S.pop();
        if (d.left < d.right) { //if the sublist is > 1 element
            int dp = partition2(A, d.left, d.right);
            if (dp - d.left + 1 < d.right - dp) {  //compare lengths of sublists
                S.push(new StackData(dp+1, d.right));
                S.push(new StackData(d.left, dp));
            }
            else {
                S.push(new StackData(d.left, dp));
                S.push(new StackData(dp+1, d.right));
            }
            stackItems += 2;        //two items added to stack
        } //end if
        if (stackItems > maxStackItems) maxStackItems = stackItems;
    } //end while
    System.out.printf("Max stack items: %d\n\n", maxStackItems);
} //end quicksort3
```

138

When **partition2** returns, the lengths of the two sublists are compared and the longer one is placed on the stack first followed by the shorter one. This ensures that the shorter one will be taken off first and processed before the longer one.

We also added statements to **quicksort3** to keep track of the maximum number of items on the stack at any given time. When used to sort 100000 integers, the maximum number of stack items was 13; this is less than $\log_2 100000 = 17$, rounded up.

As written, even if a sublist consists of 2 items only, the method will go through the whole process of calling partition, checking the lengths of the sublists and stacking the two sublists. This seems an awful lot of work to sort 2 items.

We can make quicksort more efficient by using a simple method (insertion sort, say) to sort sublists which are shorter than some pre-defined length (8, say). You are urged to write quicksort with this change and experiment with different values of the pre-defined length.

4.7.2 Finding the kth smallest number

Consider the problem of finding the kth smallest number in a list of n numbers. One way to do this is to sort the n numbers and pick out the kth one. If the numbers are stored in an array **A[1..n]**, we simply retrieve **A[k]** after sorting.

Another, more efficient, way is to use the idea of partitioning. We will use that version of **partition** which places the pivot in its final sorted position. Consider an array **A[1..99]** and suppose a call to **partition** returns a division point of 40. This means that the pivot has been placed in **A[40]** with smaller numbers to the left and bigger numbers to the right. In other words, the 40th smallest number has been placed in **A[40]**. So if k is 40, we have our answer immediately.

What if k were 59? We know that the 40 smallest numbers occupy A[1..40]. So the 59th must be in A[41..99] and we can confine our search to this part of the array. In other words, with one call to **partition**, we can eliminate 40 numbers from consideration. The idea is similar to *binary search*.

Suppose the next call to **partition** returns 65. We now know the 65th smallest number and the 59th will be in **A[41..64]**; we have eliminated **A[66..99]** from consideration. We repeat this process each time reducing the size of the part that contains the 59th smallest number. Eventually, **partition** will return 59 and we will have our answer.

The following is one way to write **kthSmall**; it uses **partition1**.

```
public static int kthSmall(int[] A, int k, int lo, int hi) {
//returns the kth smallest from A[lo] to A[hi]
  int kShift = lo + k - 1; //shift k to the given portion, A[lo..hi]
  if (kShift < lo || kShift > hi) return -9999;
  int dp = partition1(A, lo, hi);
```

```
        while (dp != kShift) {
            if (kShift < dp) hi = dp - 1;      //kth smallest is in the left part
            else lo = dp + 1;                  //kth smallest is in the right part
            dp = partition1(A, lo, hi);
        }
        return A[dp];
    } //end kthSmall
```

For instance, the call **kthSmall(num, 59, 1, 99)** will return the 59th smallest number from **num[1..99]**. Note, however, that the call **kthSmall(num, 10, 30, 75)** will return the 10th smallest number from **num[30..75]**.

As an exercise, write the recursive version of **kthSmall**.

4.8 Mergesort

Mergesort uses an idea similar to quicksort—the idea of splitting the list in two. We can express it as follows:

```
sort a list {
    sort the first half of the list
    sort the second half of the list
    merge the sorted halves
}
```

In quicksort, partitioning breaks up the given sublist into two parts which can be quite different in size. Mergesort breaks up the list into two equal parts, sorts the parts and then merges them into one sorted list.

Of course, the question arises: how do we sort the first half (and the second half)? Well, we use the same method! To sort the first half, we break it up into two equal pieces, sort the pieces and merge the pieces into one sorted list. And we repeat the process for each piece. We stop breaking up a piece when it is a single element which, by definition, is sorted.

We can write **mergeSort** as follows:

```
public static void mergeSort(int[] A, int lo, int hi) {
    if (lo < hi) { //list contains at least 2 elements
        int mid = (lo + hi) / 2; //get the mid-point subscript
        mergeSort(A, lo, mid); //sort first half
        mergeSort(A, mid + 1, hi); //sort second half
        merge(A, lo, mid, hi); //merge sorted halves
    }
} //end mergeSort
```

where **merge(A, lo, mid, hi)** merges the sorted pieces **A[lo..mid]** and **A[mid+1..hi]** into one sorted piece **A[lo..hi]**. Here is **merge**:

```
public static void merge(int[] A, int lo, int mid, int hi) {
//A[lo..mid] and A[mid+1..hi] are sorted;
//merge the pieces so that A[lo..hi] are sorted
   int[] T = new int[hi - lo + 1];
   int i = lo;
   int j = mid + 1;
   int k = 0;
   while (i <= mid || j <= hi) {
      if (i > mid) T[k++] = A[j++];          //A[lo..mid] completely processed
      else if (j > hi) T[k++] = A[i++];      // A[mid+1..hi] completely processed
      else if (A[i] < A[j]) T[k++] = A[i++]; //neither part completed
      else T[k++] = A[j++];
      else T[k++] = A[j++];
   }
   for (j = 0; j < hi-lo+1; j++) A[lo + j] = T[j];
} //end merge
```

It is not possible to merge the pieces "in place" without overwriting some of the numbers. So the pieces are merged into a temporary array **T** and, at the end, copied back into **A**. This need for extra storage is one disadvantage of mergesort; the maximum size of **T** is the same as **A**. The time taken to copy elements is also a minor drawback.

However, mergesort is fast; its running time is of order $O(n\log_2 n)$, on par with heapsort and quicksort.

4.9 Shell (diminishing increment) sort

Shell sort (named after Donald Shell) uses a series of *increments* to govern the sorting process. For example, to sort the following array:

num

67	90	28	84	29	58	25	32	16	64	13	71	82	10	51	57
1	2	3	4	5	6	7	8	9	10	11	12	13	14	15	16

we use 3 increments—8, 3 and 1. The increments decrease in size (hence the term *diminishing increment sort*) with the last one being 1.

Using increment 8, we 8-sort the array. This means that we sort the elements that are 8-apart. We sort elements 1 and 9, 2 and 10, 3 and 11, 4 and 12, 5 and 13, 6 and 14, 7 and 15, 8 and 16. This will transform **num** into:

num

16	64	13	71	29	10	25	32	67	90	28	84	82	58	51	57
1	2	3	4	5	6	7	8	9	10	11	12	13	14	15	16

Next, we 3-sort the array, that is, we sort elements that are 3-apart. We sort elements (1, 4, 7, 10, 13, 16), (2, 5, 8, 11, 14) and (3, 6, 9, 12, 15). This gives us:

141

num

16	28	10	25	29	13	57	32	51	71	58	67	82	64	84	90
1	2	3	4	5	6	7	8	9	10	11	12	13	14	15	16

Note that, at each step, the array is a little closer to being sorted. Finally, we perform a 1-sort, sorting the entire list, giving:

num

10	13	16	25	28	29	32	51	57	58	64	67	71	82	84	90
1	2	3	4	5	6	7	8	9	10	11	12	13	14	15	16

You may ask, why didn't we just do a 1-sort from the beginning and sort the entire list? The idea here is that, when we reach the stage of doing a 1-sort, the array is more or less in order and if we use a method that works better with partially ordered data (e.g. insertion sort) then the sort can proceed quickly.

When the increment is large, the pieces to sort are small. In the example, when the increment is 8, each piece consists of two elements only. Presumably, we can sort a small list quickly. When the increment is small, the pieces to sort are bigger. However, by the time we get to the small increments, the data is partially sorted and we can sort the pieces quickly if we use a method which takes advantage of order in the data.

We will use a slightly modified version of insertion sort to sort elements that are *h*-apart rather than 1-apart.

Recall that, in insertion sort, when we come to process **num[j]**, we assume that **num[1..j-1]** are sorted and insert **num[j]** among the previous items so that **num[1..j]** are sorted.

Suppose the increment is **h** and consider how we might process **num[j]** where **j** is any valid subscript. Remember, our goal is to sort items that are **h**-apart. So we must sort **num[j]** with respect to **num[j-h]**, **num[j-2h]**, **num[j-3h]**, etc. provided these elements fall within the array. When we come to process **num[j]**, if the previous items that are **h**-apart are sorted among themselves, we must simply insert **num[j]** among those items so that the sublist ending at **num[j]** is sorted.

To illustrate, suppose **h** = 3 and **j** = 4. There is only one element before **num[4]** that is 3 away, that is, **num[1]**. So when we come to process **num[4]**, we can assume that **num[1]**, by itself, is sorted. We insert **num[4]** relative to **num[1]** so that **num[1]** and **num[4]** are sorted.

Similarly, there is only one element before **num[5]** that is 3 away, that is, **num[2]**. So when we come to process **num[5]**, we can assume that **num[2]**, by itself, is sorted. We insert **num[5]** relative to **num[2]** so that **num[2]** and **num[5]** are sorted. Similar remarks apply to **num[3]** and **num[6]**.

When we get to **num[7]**, the two items before **num[7]** (**num[1]** and **num[4]**) are sorted. We insert **num[7]** such that **num[1]**, **num[4]** and **num[7]** are sorted.

When we get to **num[8]**, the two items before **num[8]** (**num[2]** and **num[5]**) are sorted. We insert **num[8]** such that **num[2]**, **num[5]** and **num[8]** are sorted.

When we get to **num[9]**, the two items before **num[9]** (**num[3]** and **num[6]**) are sorted. We insert **num[9]** such that **num[3]**, **num[6]** and **num[9]** are sorted.

When we get to **num[10]**, the three items before **num[10]** (**num[1]**, **num[4]** and **num[7]**) are sorted. We insert **num[10]** such that **num[1]**, **num[4]**, **num[7]** and **num[10]** are sorted.

And so on. Starting at **h+1**, we step through the array processing each item with respect to previous items which are multiples of **h** away.

In the example, when **h** = 3, we said we must sort elements (1, 4, 7, 10, 13, 16), (2, 5, 8, 11, 14) and (3, 6, 9, 12, 15). This is true but our algorithm will not sort items (1, 4, 7, 10, 13, 16), followed by items (2, 5, 8, 11, 14) followed by items (3, 6, 9, 12, 15).

Rather, it will sort them in parallel by sorting the pieces in the following order: (1, 4), (2, 5), (3, 6), (1, 4, 7), (2, 5, 8), (3, 6, 9), (1, 4, 7, 10), (2, 5, 8, 11), (3, 6, 9, 12), (1, 4, 7, 10, 13), (2, 5, 8, 11, 14), (3, 6, 9, 12, 15) and finally (1, 4, 7, 10, 13, 16).

The following will perform an **h**-sort on **A[1..n]**:

```
public static void hsort(int[] A, int n, int h) {
  for (int j = h + 1; j <= n; j++) {
    int k = j - h;
    int key = A[j];
    while (k > 0 && key < A[k]) {
      A[k + h] = A[k];
      k = k - h;
    }
    A[k + h] = key;
  }
} //end hsort
```

The alert reader will realise that if we set **h** to 1, this becomes insertion sort.

Programming note: To sort **A[0..n-1]**, we must change the **for** statement to

```
for (j = h; j < n; j++)
```

and use **k >= 0** in the **while** statement.

Given a series of increments h_t, h_{t-1},..., h_1 = 1, we simply call **hsort** with each increment, from largest to smallest, to effect the sort.

But how do we decide which increments to use for a given **n**? Many methods have been proposed; the following gives reasonable results:

```
let h₁ = 1
generate hₛ₊₁ = 3hₛ + 1, for s = 1, 2, 3,...
and stop with hₜ when hₜ₊₂ ≥ n
```

For example, if **n** = 100, we generate $h_1 = 1$, $h_2 = 4$, $h_3 = 13$, $h_4 = 40$, $h_5 = 121$. Since $h_5 > 100$, we use h_1, h_2 and h_3 as the increments to sort 100 items.

The performance of Shell sort lies somewhere between the simple $O(n^2)$ methods (insertion, selection) and the $O(n\log_2 n)$ methods (heapsort, quicksort, mergesort). Its order is approximately $O(n^{1.3})$ for *n* in a practical range tending to $O(n(\log_2 n)^2)$ as *n* tends to infinity.

As an exercise, write programming code to sort a list using Shell sort, counting the number of comparisons and assignments made in sorting the list.

Exercises 4

1. Write a program to compare the performance of the sorting methods discussed in this chapter with respect to "number of comparisons" and "number of assignments". For quicksort, compare the performance of choosing the first element as the pivot with choosing a random element.

   Run the program to (i) sort 10, 100, 1000, 10000 and 100000 elements supplied in random order and (ii) sort 10, 100, 1000, 10000 and 100000 elements which are already sorted.

2. A function **makeHeap** is passed an integer array **A**. If **A[0]** contains **n**, then **A[1]** to **A[n]** contain numbers in arbitrary order. Write **makeHeap** such that **A[1]** to **A[n]** contain a max-heap (*largest* value at the root). Your function must create the heap by processing the elements in the order **A[2]**, **A[3]**,...,**A[n]**.

3. A heap is stored in a one-dimensional integer array **num[1..n]** with the *largest* value in position 1. Give an efficient algorithm which deletes the root and rearranges the other elements so that the heap now occupies **num[1]** to **num[n-1]**.

4. A heap is stored in a one-dimensional integer array **A[0..max]** with the *largest* value in position 1. **A[0]** specifies the number of elements in the heap at any time. Write a function to add a new value **v** to the heap. Your function should work if the heap is initially empty and should print a message if there is no room to store **v**.

5. Write code to read a set of positive integers (terminated by 0) and create a heap in an array **H** with the *smallest* value at the top of the heap. As each integer is read, it is inserted among the existing items such that the heap properties are maintained. At any time, if *n* numbers have been read then **H[1..n]** must contain a heap. Assume that **H** is large enough to hold all the integers.

   Given the data: **51 26 32 45 38 89 29 58 34 23 0**

   show the contents of **H** after each number has been read and processed.

6. A function is given an integer array **A** and two subscripts **m** and **n**. The function must rearrange the elements **A[m]** to **A[n]** and return a subscript **d** such that all elements to the left of **d** are less than or equal to **A[d]** and all elements to the right of **d** are greater than **A[d]**.

7. Write a function which, given an integer array **num** and an integer **n**, sorts the elements **num[1]** to **num[n]** using Shell sort. The function must return the number of key comparisons made in performing the sort. You may use any reasonable method for determining increments.

8. An *integer* max-heap is stored in an array (**A**, say) such that the size of the heap (**n**, say) is stored in **A[0]** and **A[1]** to **A[n]** contain the elements of the heap with the *largest* value in **A[1]**.

   Write a function **deleteMax** which, given an array like **A**, deletes the largest element and reorganizes the array so that it remains a heap.

   Given two arrays **A** and **B** containing heaps as described above, write programming code to merge the elements of **A** and **B** into another array **C** such that **C** is in ascending order. Your method must proceed by comparing an element of **A** with one in **B**. You may assume that **deleteMax** is available.

9. A single integer array **A[1..n]** contains the following: **A[1..k]** contains a min-heap and **A[k+1..n]** contains arbitrary values. Write efficient code to merge the two portions so that **A[1..n]** contains one min-heap. Do *not* use any other array.

10. Write a recursive function for finding the kth smallest number in an array of *n* numbers, without sorting the array.

11. Write insertion sort using a binary search to determine the position in which **A[j]** will be inserted among the sorted sublist **A[1..j-1]**.

12. A sorting algorithm is said to be *stable* if equal keys retain their original relative order after sorting. Which of the sorting methods discussed are stable?

13. You are given a list of *n* numbers. Write efficient algorithms to find (i) the smallest (ii) the largest (iii) the mean (iv) the median (the middle value) and (v) the mode (the value that appears most often).

    Write an efficient algorithm to find all five values.

14. It is known that every number in a list of *n distinct* numbers is between 100 and 9999. Devise an efficient method for sorting the numbers.

    Modify the method to sort the list if it may contain duplicate numbers.

15. Modify mergesort and quicksort so that if a sublist to be sorted is smaller than some pre-defined size, it is sorted using insertion sort.

16. You are given a list of *n* numbers and another number **x**. You must find the smallest number in the list that is greater than or equal to **x**. You must then delete this number from the list and replace it by a new number **y**, retaining the list structure. Devise ways of solving this problem using (i) unsorted array (ii) sorted array (iii) sorted linked list (iv) binary search tree (v) heap.

    Which of these is the most efficient?

17. You are given a (long) list of English words. Write a program to determine which of those words are anagrams of each other. Output consists of each group of anagrams (two or more words) followed by a blank line. Two words are anagrams if they consist of the same letters, e.g. (teacher, cheater), (sister, resist).

18. Each value in **A[1..n]** is either 1, 2 or 3. You are required to find the *minimal* number of *exchanges* to sort the array. For example, the array

2	2	1	3	3	3	2	3	1
1	2	3	4	5	6	7	8	9

can be sorted with 4 exchanges, in order: (1, 3) (4, 7) (2, 9) (5, 9). Another solution is (1, 3) (2, 9) (4, 7) (5, 9). The array cannot be sorted with less than 4 exchanges.

5 Graphs

In this chapter, we will explain:

- some graph terminology
- how to perform *depth-first* and *breadth-first* traversals of a graph
- how to represent a graph in a computer program
- how to build a graph representation from given data
- how to classify the edges in a graph
- how to perform a *topological sort* of a graph
- how to derive minimum-cost paths from a source node to all other nodes using Dijkstra's algorithm (edge weights must be non-negative)
- how to derive minimum-cost paths from a source node to all other nodes using the Bellman-Ford algorithm (edge weights can be negative)
- how to construct a minimum-cost spanning tree using Prim's algorithm
- how to construct a minimum-cost spanning tree using Kruskal's algorithm

I n this chapter, we discuss a general-purpose data structure—the graph. We have seen how useful trees can be but a tree is just a special case of a graph. We should expect that, with a graph, we can model much more complex situations than we can with a tree.

5.1 Graph terminology

A *graph* G is a pair $(\mathcal{V}, \mathcal{E})$ where $\mathcal{V}$ is a finite set and $\mathcal{E}$ is a binary relation on $\mathcal{V}$. Each element of $\mathcal{V}$ is called a *vertex* or *node* and each element of $\mathcal{E}$ is called an *edge*. $\mathcal{V}$ is called the *vertex set* and $\mathcal{E}$ is called the *edge set*. The number of vertices is denoted by $|\mathcal{V}|$ and the number of edges by $|\mathcal{E}|$.

For example, if $\mathcal{V}$ is the set {A, B, H, K, N} and $\mathcal{E}$ is the set {(A, H), (H, B), (B, K), (B, A), (N, H), (N, B)}, we have a graph with 5 vertices (nodes) and 6 edges which we can draw as follows:

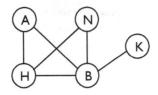

Figure 5.1: A graph (undirected) with 5 nodes and 6 edges

If *𝓔* consists of *unordered* pairs of vertices, the graph is *undirected*. Given the edge (**u**, **v**) ε *𝓔*, we simply say there is an edge connecting **u** and **v**. We consider that the edge goes *from* **u** to **v** or *from* **v** to **u**, so an undirected edge is sometimes called *bidirectional*.

If *𝓔* consists of *ordered* pairs of vertices, the graph is *directed*. We call it a directed graph or *digraph*. Given the directed edge (**u**, **v**) ε *𝓔*, we say there is an edge *from* **u** *to* **v** (depicted as **u** → **v**). We sometimes refer to **u** as the *parent* and **v** as the *child*. There is *no* implication that there is automatically an edge from **v** to **u**; there will be an edge from **v** to **u** only if the edge (**v**, **u**) is also in *𝓔*.

In the above graph, suppose the same set of edges were directed. That is, suppose *𝓔* = {(A, H), (H, B), (B, K), (B, A), (N, H), (N, B)} where (**u**, **v**) ε *𝓔* means that there is an edge from **u** to **v** but not vice versa. We can draw *this* graph as follows:

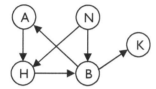

Figure 5.2: A directed graph with 5 nodes and 6 edges

To represent a directed edge (**u**, **v**), we draw an arrowed line from **u** to **v**. If, in addition, there is a directed edge (K, B), we could draw the graph as follows:

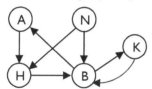

Figure 5.3: Graph with 2 edges connecting the same nodes

If (**u**, **v**) ε *𝓔* is a directed edge, we say that vertex **v** is *adjacent* to vertex **u**. If the graph is undirected, then **u** is also adjacent to **v**. In Figure 5.3, A is adjacent to B (but not vice versa); B is adjacent to K *and* K is adjacent to B.

If (**u**, **v**) is directed, we say that (**u**, **v**) is *incident from* or *leaves* vertex **u** and is *incident to* or *enters* vertex **v**. If it is undirected, we say that (**u**, **v**) is *incident on* vertices **u** and **v**. In either case, we say that **u** and **v** are *neighbours*. Thus, two vertices are neighbours if they are connected by an edge, directed or undirected.

In Figure 5.3, the edge (B, A) leaves vertex B and enters vertex A. B is a neighbour of A (and vice versa) even though B is not adjacent to A.

If a graph is directed, the *in-degree* of a vertex is the number of edges *entering* it. The *out-degree* of a vertex is the number of edges *leaving* it. The *degree* of a vertex is the sum of its in-degree and out-degree. This is the same as the number of neighbours of the vertex.

In Figure 5.3, the in-degree of B is 3 and its out-degree is 2; its degree is 5. For A, its in-degree and out-degree are both 1 and its degree is 2. And we have in-degree(N) = 0, out-degree(N) = 2, degree(N) = 2. A vertex with an in-degree of 0 is said to be *isolated*. Thus, N is an isolated vertex.

If a graph is undirected, the *degree* of a vertex is the number of edges incident on it. As in the directed case, this is simply the number of neighbours of the vertex. In Figure 5.1, degree(A) = 2 and degree(B) = 4.

We say there is a *path* from vertex u to vertex v if it is possible to get from u to v by following edges in the graph. More formally, there is a path of length n from u to v if there exists a sequence of vertices u $= v_0, v_1, v_2,...,v_n =$ v such that (v_{i-1}, v_i) ε $\mathcal{E}$, for $i = 1, 2, ..., n$. The length of the path is the number of edges in the path. If there is a path from u to v, we say that v is *reachable* from u. A path is *simple* if all the vertices in the path are distinct.

In Figure 5.3, the path N → H → B → A from N to A is simple and of length 3. The path N → B → K → B is of length 3 but not simple (B is repeated).

The path $v_0 \to v_1 \to v_2,... \to v_n$ is a *cycle* if $v_0 = v_n$ and there are at least two edges in the path. (Here, we do not include a cycle created by a self-loop, an edge from a vertex to itself.) In other words, a cycle is a path that begins and ends at the same vertex. The cycle is *simple* if $v_1, v_2,...,v_n$ are distinct.

In Figure 5.3, the path A → H → B → A is a simple cycle. On the other hand, the path A → H → B → K → B → A is a cycle (first and last nodes are the same) but it is not simple (B is repeated).

An *acyclic* graph is one with no cycles. A *directed acyclic graph* is commonly referred to as a *dag*.

An undirected graph is *connected* if there is at least one path between any two vertices. A directed graph is *strongly connected* if there is at least one path between any two vertices. In other words, 'connected' and 'strongly connected' imply that every vertex is reachable from every other vertex.

The undirected graph in Figure 5.1 is connected. However, the directed graph in Figure 5.3 is not strongly connected since, for instance, N is not reachable from any of the other vertices. However, if we omit N and the edges leaving it, the *subgraph* that remains is strongly connected. We say the subgraph is a *strongly connected component* of the original graph.

A *(free) tree* is a connected, acyclic, undirected graph. Figure 5.4 shows a free tree. A free tree with n vertices will necessarily have n-1 edges. We use the term 'free tree' as opposed to a 'rooted tree', the kind we discussed in Chapter 3. We could re-draw Figure 5.4 as a rooted tree (with root A) shown in Figure 5.5. If we wish, we could designate *any* vertex as the root.

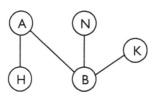

Figure 5.4: A free tree   Figure 5.5: A rooted tree

A *weighted* graph is one in which each edge has an associated *weight* or *cost*. For example, each vertex might represent a town and each edge represents a road between two towns. The weight of an edge is the distance between the two towns connected by the edge. The 'weight' can also be the normal time to drive between two towns or the bus fare from one town to the other. As we shall see, weighted graphs are among the most useful kinds of graphs.

5.2 How to represent a graph

Consider a graph G(V, E) with $|V| = n$ vertices and $|E| = p$ edges. To represent G, we must find a way to store the n vertices and the p edges, including their weights, if any. The two most common ways to represent G are (i) using an **n** × **n** *adjacency matrix* and (ii) using **n** *adjacency lists*. For example, the following graph has 7 vertices:

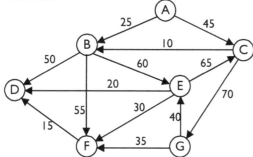

We can represent it using a 7 × 7 adjacency matrix, **G**, thus:

	1	2	3	4	5	6	7
1	0	25	45	∞	∞	∞	∞
2	∞	0	∞	50	60	55	∞
3	∞	10	0	∞	∞	∞	70
4	∞	∞	∞	0	∞	∞	∞
5	∞	∞	65	20	0	30	∞
6	∞	∞	∞	15	∞	0	∞
7	∞	∞	∞	∞	40	35	0

Adjacency matrix, G

We assign each vertex a unique number from 1 to 7. Here, we assign 1 to A, 2 to B, 3 to C, 4 to D, 5 to E, 6 to F and 7 to G. First, we set **G[u, u]** to 0 for all **u**.

Then, if there is an edge of weight **w** from node **u** to node **v**, we set **G[u, v]** to **w**. For example, since there is an edge of weight 60 from B to E, we set G[2, 5] = 60. And we set G[6, 4] to 15 since there is an edge of weight 15 from F to D. If there is no edge from **u** to **v**, we set **G[u, v]** = ∞.

In the adjacency list representation, from each vertex **u**, we keep a linked list of the edges leaving **u**. For the above graph, we get the following:

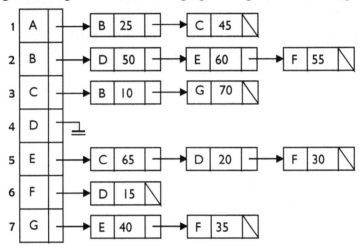

The vertices are shown stored in an array, but any other structure, such as a hash table (next chapter) or a binary search tree, may be used. Each edge-list node consists of three fields: the child vertex, the weight of the edge and a pointer to the next edge node.

Note, for instance, that the edge-list of **D** is empty since there are no edges leaving **D**. The nodes of an edge-list can be in any order; we have put them in alphabetical order.

In the edge-list, we have used the *name* of the child vertex for simplicity and clarity. However, in practice, it is usually best to use the *location* of the vertex in whatever data structure is used to hold the vertices. This will give us access to all the other information which may be stored in a vertex, not just the name. We will see more of this later. For now, we store the edge-list by replacing the name of the vertex with its location in the array, giving the representation on the next page.

As we shall see shortly, this representation is more flexible.

Which representation is better? Adjacency matrix or adjacency list? It depends on the number of edges and the kinds of operations which may need to be performed on the structure.

If there is an edge from each vertex to every other vertex, there will be $n(n-1)$ edges, roughly n^2 edges. If there is a large number of edges (closer to n^2), we say

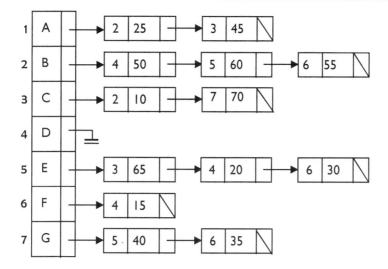

the graph is *dense*. If there are relatively few edges (closer to *n*, or a small multiple of *n*), we say the graph is *sparse*.

For a dense graph, the matrix representation would be more space-efficient since most of the n^2 entries in the matrix would be non-∞. For a sparse graph, the matrix representation would be inefficient since most of the entries would be ∞. However, the list representation would be better since only the relatively few edges would be stored.

As an exercise, decide which representation is better for each of the following:

- Given two vertices, is there an edge between them?
- Given a vertex, what are the edges leaving the vertex?
- Given a vertex, what are the edges entering the vertex?
- Add a vertex (and associated egdes) to the graph.
- Delete a vertex (and associated edges) from the graph.
- Add an edge to the graph.
- Delete an edge from the graph.
- Change the weight of an edge.
- Process all the edges of a graph.
- Produce a sorted list, by weight, of the edges of the graph.

There are some situations (mainly when the graph is dense) and some operations (such as determining if an edge connects two given vertices) where the matrix representation is decidedly superior. However, for the most part, we will use the list representation since it is generally more space-efficient and allows efficient implementation of the most common operations.

5.3 Building a graph

We can *describe* the graph above with the following data:

```
7
A B C D E F G
A 2 B 25 C 45
B 3 D 50 E 60 F 55
C 2 B 10 G 70
D 0
E 3 C 65 D 20 F 30
F 1 D 15
G 2 E 40 F 35
```

The first line says there are 7 vertices. The next line gives the names or labels of the vertices. This is followed by 7 more lines, each of which describes the edges leaving a vertex. The first item is the name of a vertex; this is followed by the number of edges, *k*, leaving the vertex. Next are *k* pairs of values; each pair describes an edge. For example, the line

```
A 2 B 25 C 45
```

says that vertex A has 2 edges leaving it. They go to B (with a weight of 25) and C (with a weight of 45).

We wish to write a program to read graph data in the above format and build the adjacency list representation of the graph. We will build the representation shown on the previous page.

As shown, each vertex has at least two fields—the name of the vertex and a pointer to the first edge node. Each edge node has three fields—the *location* of the child vertex, the weight of the edge and a pointer to the next edge.

We will need to create two classes—one for the graph vertices and the other for edge nodes. First, we define the class **GVertex**:

```
class GVertex {
    String id;
    char colour;
    int parent, cost, discover, finish, inDegree;
    GEdge firstEdge;

    public GVertex (String label) {
        id = label;
        firstEdge = null;
    }
}
```

The **id** field will hold the name of the vertex and **firstEdge** will point to the first edge node (of type **GEdge**, to be defined next). The other fields shown will be used in various ways. We will show how to use them as the need arises.

Next, we define the class **GEdge**:

```
class GEdge {
  int child, weight; //'child' is the location of the child vertex
  GEdge nextEdge;

  public GEdge (int c, int w) {
    child = c;
    weight = w;
    nextEdge = null;
  }
}
```

With **GVertex** and **GEdge**, we can start to write a **Graph** class in which we will construct graphs and manipulate them in various ways.

As mentioned, we will store the graph vertices in an array—a **GVertex** array. We will call the array **vertex**. We will need a field (**numV**, say) to hold the number of vertices in the graph. As we develop our graph routines, some will need to print output. We will define the field **out** (of type **PrintWriter**) as the place to send output. It will be set when the **Graph** constructor is called. Here is **Graph**, so far:

```
public class Graph {
  GVertex[] vertex;
  int numV;
  PrintWriter out;

  public Graph(PrintWriter fout, int n) {
    numV = n;
    vertex = new GVertex[n+1];
    vertex[0] = new GVertex("#");
    out = fout;
  }
} //end class Graph
```

The number of vertices, *n*, is passed to the constructor. This is used to declare **vertex**. We will use **vertex[1]** to **vertex[n]** to hold information for the *n* vertices. In rare situations, it will be useful to use **vertex[0]**; we will see these as they arise. For now, just note that we set the **id** field of **vertex[0]** to "#".

Consider how the **Graph** class might be used. Here is a class **GraphTest** which shows how (it assumes the graph data is stored in the file, **graph.in**):

```
import java.io.*;
import java.util.*;
public class GraphTest {

  public static void main (String[] args) throws IOException {
    Scanner in = new Scanner(new FileReader("graph.in"));
    PrintWriter out = new PrintWriter(new FileWriter("graph.out"));
    int numVertices = in.nextInt();
```

```
                Graph G = new Graph(out, numVertices);
                G.buildGraph(in);
                G.printGraph();
            } //end main
        } //end class GraphTest
```

This reads the number of vertices in the graph. It passes this value to the **Graph** constructor which will allocate storage for the graph vertices. It then calls **buildGraph** to build the graph and **printGraph** to print it.

Here is **buildGraph**:

```
        public void buildGraph(Scanner in) {
            for (int j = 1; j <= numV; j++)  vertex[j] = new GVertex(in.next());
            for (int j = 1; j <= numV; j++) {
                String vertexID = in.next();
                int numEdges = in.nextInt();
                for (int k = 1; k <= numEdges; k++) {
                    String adjID = in.next();
                    int weight = in.nextInt();
                    addEdge(vertexID, adjID, weight);
                }
            }
        } //end buildGraph
```

The constructor would have set **numV**. The first **for** loop reads the names of the vertices and stores them in **GVertex** objects. The next **for** loop does the following, using, for example: C 2 B 10 G 70

- Each pass through the loop processes edge data for one vertex.
- The vertex name, **vertexID**, is read. This is the parent node, **C**.
- The number of edges, **numEdges**, is read; this is 2.
- The inner **for** loop reads one pair of values—a vertex name (the adjacent or child vertex) and a weight—on each pass. It passes the edge information— parent, child and weight—to **addEdge** which adds it to the appropriate list of edges.

Here is **addEdge**:

```
        private void addEdge(String X, String Y, int weight) {
            //add an edge X -> Y with a given weight
            int j, k;
            //find X in the list of nodes; its location is j
            for (j = 1; j <= numV; j++) if (X.equals(vertex[j].id)) break;

            //find Y in the list of nodes; its location is k
            for (k = 1; k <= numV; k++) if (Y.equals(vertex[k].id)) break;
            if (j > numV || k > numV) {
```

```
            System.out.printf("No such edge: %s to %s\n", X, Y);
            System.exit(1);
        }
        GEdge ge = new GEdge(k, weight); //create edge vertex
        // add it to the list of edges, possible empty, from X;
        // it is added so that the list is in order by vertex id
        GEdge prev, curr;
        prev = curr = vertex[j].firstEdge;
        while (curr != null && Y.compareTo(vertex[curr.child].id) > 0) {
            prev = curr;
            curr = curr.nextEdge;
        }
        if (prev == curr) {
          ge.nextEdge = vertex[j].firstEdge;
           vertex[j].firstEdge = ge;
        }
        else {
          ge.nextEdge = curr;
          prev.nextEdge = ge;
        }
    } //end addEdge()
```

This method first searches for the parent vertex, **X**, in the list of vertices. It then searches for the child vertex, **Y**, in the list; suppose its location is **k**. Recall that **k**, not **Y**, will be stored in the edge node. A new edge node containing **k** and the weight of the edge is created. It is then added to the edge list of **X** so that the edge list is in order by vertex name.

Because of the way **addEdge** is written, there is some flexibility in the way edge data for the graph is provided. In the sample data on page 152, the edge data was given in the same order the vertices were given, that is, A B C D E F G. And the edge data for a given vertex was given in ascending order by child vertex name (e.g. the edges from B are given in the order D, E, F).

But this is not necessary. The vertices' data can be given in any order and the edge data for a given vertex can be supplied in any order; **addEdge** will put them in order. So the sample data *could* have been provided as:

```
7
A B C D E F G
B 3 F 55 D 50 E 60
G 2 F 35 E 40
D 0
A 2 B 25 C 45
F 1 D 15
C 2 B 10 G 70
E 3 D 20 F 30 C 65
```

Whichever way the data is supplied, **buildGraph** will build the same graph.

Once the graph is built, we call **printGraph** to verify that the graph built is indeed the correct one. Here is **printGraph**:

```
void printGraph() {
    for (int j = 1; j <= numV; j++) {
        out.printf("%s: ", vertex[j].id);
        GEdge p = vertex[j].firstEdge;
        while (p != null) {
            out.printf("%s %d ", vertex[p.child].id, p.weight);
            p = p.nextEdge;
        }
        out.printf("\n");
    }
    out.printf("\n");
} //end printGraph
```

When run with the above data, **printGraph** prints:

```
A: B 25 C 45
B: D 50 E 60 F 55
C: B 10 G 70
D:
E: C 65 D 20 F 30
F: D 15
G: E 40 F 35
```

The vertices are printed in the order they were given (on the second line of data) and the edge list for a given vertex is in alphabetical order.

5.4 Traversing a graph

Consider the problem of traversing a graph by visiting the vertices in some systematic way. We would need to choose one vertex from which to start. Given the following graph, suppose we start from A.

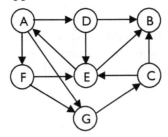

Figure 5.6: A sample graph

One immediate problem is which vertex should we visit next, D or F? In general, if there are several adjacent vertices from which to choose, which one do we choose? The choice is usually arbitrary. Sometimes the choice is forced by the representation of the graph. For example, if the graph is stored using adjacency lists, adjacent vertices will be visited in the order they appear in the edge list. In this graph, we can choose to visit adjacent vertices in alphabetical order.

Suppose we choose D. We would need to remember that F is on hold and we must get back to it at some later time. From D, we must choose B or E. Suppose we choose B. Again, we will need to remember that E is on hold until later. There are no edges leaving B so we have reached a dead-end.

Our traversal method must define how to proceed on reaching a dead-end. One way is to *backtrack* to the vertex from which we came (D, in this case) and try the next adjacent vertex, if any. Here, we would try E. If there were no 'next' vertex, we backtrack again, and try the next adjacent vertex, if any. If we backtrack all the way to the start and there is no 'next' vertex to try, the traversal ends.

Suppose we had visited A D B E, in that order. Where do we go from E? Proceeding as before, we will choose the first edge, A. But now we have a problem. We have already visited A so our method must recognize this. If not, we will end up going around in circles with no way out.

One solution is to 'mark' a vertex when it is visited. If traversing an edge would take us to a marked vertex, that edge is not followed. So A will not be chosen. The next adjacent vertex B is also marked (since it has been visited), so B is not chosen. In this case, we backtrack to D and then to A, and try the next vertex from A. This is F, which is unmarked, so it is visited. A common way to mark a vertex is to set some field (**visited**, say) to **false** before the vertex is visited and **true** after it is visited.

In our algorithms, we will use a **colour** field to mark a vertex. This will give us a little more flexibility, in working with graphs generally, than the two-valued **visited** field. We will set **colour** to **white** before a vertex is visited. After it is visited, its colour can be **gray** or **black**, depending on the particular algorithm. A non-white value will mean the vertex has already been seen.

We will see how these three issues—multiple adjacent vertices, reaching a dead-end and not getting caught in a cycle—are handled by the depth-first and breadth-first traversal algorithms.

5.5 Depth-first traversal

Consider one way of traversing the sample graph of Figure 5.6, starting from A (we assume vertices are marked as they are visited):

- visit A
- follow the first (in alphabetical order) edge and visit D
- follow the first edge from D and visit B
- we have reached a dead-end; backtrack to D and follow the next edge to visit E
- from E, follow the first edge to A; A is marked, so follow the next edge to B; B is also marked and there are no more edges from E; backtrack to D

- there are no more edges from D; backtrack to A
- from A, follow the next edge to visit F
- from F, follow the first edge to E; E is marked, so follow the next edge to G
- G is unmarked so visit G and follow its first (and only) edge to C; C is unmarked so visit C
- from C, follow the first edge to B; B is marked, so follow the next edge to E; E is also marked and there are no more edges from C; backtrack to G
- there are no more edges from G; backtrack to F
- there are no more edges from F; backtrack to A
- from A, follow the next edge to G; G is marked and there are no more edges leaving A; the algorithm ends having visited the vertices in the order: A D B E F G C.

What we have done is visited the vertices in a *depth-first* manner, starting from A. But consider what will happen is we start the traversal from B. We won't go anywhere since there are no edges leaving B. We will visit only B. When we do the traversal of a graph, we will have to arrange things so that all the vertices get visited. One way is to start a new traversal from a vertex that has not yet been visited.

Given a vertex, **v**, we can do a depth-first traversal starting from **v** with:

```
void dfTraverse(v) {
  print v.id
  v.colour = gray
  for each edge (v, x)
    if (x.colour == white) dfTraverse(x)
  v.colour = black
}
```

When **dfTraverse(v)** is called, the colour of **v** is **white**. Its colour is set to **gray** to indicate that it has been seen. We then process all the edges leaving **v**. When that is done, its colour is set to **black**. So **white** means "not seen", **gray** means "being processed" and **black** means "completely processed".

Note that when we look at an edge (**v**, **x**), if **x** is not **white**, nothing happens and we simply move on to the next edge, if any.

To ensure that we cover all the vertices in the graph, we can use:

```
void depthFirstTraversal(G(V, E)) {
  for each vertex v ε V
    v.colour = white
  for each vertex v ε V
    if (v.colour == white) dfTraverse(v)
}
```

We first set all the vertices to **white**. We then call **dfTraverse** with the first vertex in $\mathcal{V}$ since it is **white**. When this call returns, we check if any vertex is still **white**. If we find one, we call **dfTraverse** with this vertex. This process is repeated until all the vertices in the graph are covered.

In the sample graph, suppose B is designated as the first vertex and A is designated as the second. The call **dfTraverse(B)** will print B only. On return, the vertex A will still be **white** so the call **dfTraverse(A)** is made. This will print A D E F G C. On return, no **white** vertices remain so the traversal ends. The complete traversal is B A D E F G C.

A depth-first traversal of a graph *defines* a depth-first tree. Consider, again, the depth-first traversal of the graph

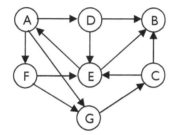

starting at A and let us identify the edges we followed to visit each of the other vertices D B E F G C in depth-first order:

- to vist D, we followed the edge A → D, so A → D is a tree edge;
- to vist B, we followed the edge D → B, so D → B is a tree edge;
- to vist E, we followed the edge D → E, so D → E is a tree edge;
- to vist F, we followed the edge A → F, so A → F is a tree edge;
- to vist G, we followed the edge F → G, so F → G is a tree edge;
- to vist C, we followed the edge G → C, so G → C is a tree edge;

Those 6 edges define a tree, rooted at A, which connects the 7 vertices. On the left of Figure 5.7, we show only the tree edges. On the right, we draw the tree in the conventional manner. The order of the subtrees (from left to right) is the order in which they are visited.

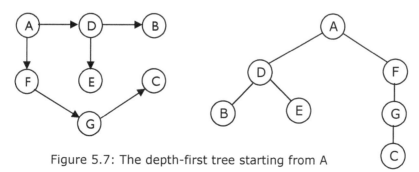

Figure 5.7: The depth-first tree starting from A

But what kind of tree will we get if we started the traversal at B? In this case, we will get 2 trees—a depth-first *forest*. The first tree consists of B only and the second consists of the edges A → D, D → E, A → F, F → G and G → C. This is illustrated in Figure 5.8:

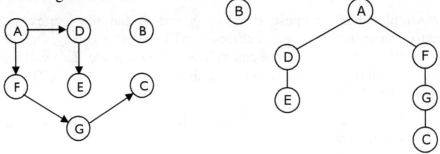

Figure 5.8: The depth-first forest starting from B

In general, a depth-first traversal of a graph will produce a depth-first forest.

Classifying edges based on depth-first traversal

Consider, again, the edges in the depth-first tree (drawn conventionally on the right) defined by the depth-traversal of the graph (on the left) starting from A:

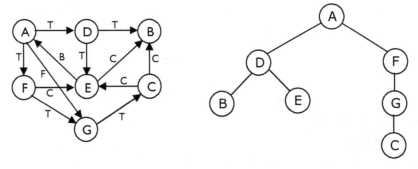

We call these *tree* edges (label **T**). We now classify the other edges in the graph.

A → G: in the depth-first tree, this edge connects a vertex, A, to a *descendant*, G, that is not a child. We call such an edge a *forward* edge (label **F**). For example, if there were an edge A → E, it would also be a forward edge.

E → A: in the depth-first tree, this edge connects a vertex, E, to an *ancestor*, A. We call such an edge a *back* edge (label **B**). For example, if there were edges B → D or C → F, these would also be back edges.

E → B: in the depth-first tree, this edge connects a vertex, E, to a *sibling*, B. We call such an edge a *cross* edge (label **C**). Any edge that is neither tree, forward nor back is a cross edge.

F → E: in the depth-first tree, this edge connects a vertex, F, to an unrelated[3] (neither ancestor nor descendant) vertex, E. This is a *cross* edge.

---

[3] We *could* call E a nephew (niece) of F

C → B, **C → E**: these connect a vertex to an unrelated vertex (in the depth-first tree) and are *cross* edges.

We can easily modify our depth-first traversal algorithm (page 158) to classify the edges of a graph. In processing the edge **v → x**:

>if **x** is **white**, then **v → x** is a tree edge;
>if **x** is **gray**, then **v → x** is a back edge;
>if **x** is **black**, then **v → x** is either a forward or a cross edge;

As you see, tree and back edges are easy to classify. But how do we distinguish between a forward and a cross edge?

To show how, we introduce the notion of *discovery* and *finish* times of a vertex. The discovery time is when the vertex is first encountered. The finish time is when all the edges leaving the vertex have been processed. Remember that **dfTraverse(v)** is called when **v** is first encountered:

```
void dfTraverse(v) {
  print v.id
  v.colour = gray
  for each edge (v, x)
    if (x.colour == white) dfTraverse(x)
  v.colour = black
}
```

So we should set its **discover** value when we set its **colour** to **gray**. Similarly, we should set its **finish** value when we set its **colour** to **black** (just after processing all its edges). We will initialize a **time** variable to 0 and increment it each time we need to set a **discover** or **finish** time for a vertex. The changes are shown below:

```
void dfTraverse(v) {
  print v.id
  v.colour = gray
  v.discover = ++time;
  for each edge (v, x)
    if (x.colour == white) dfTraverse(x)
  v.colour = black
  v.finish = ++time;
}
```

Now we can distinguish between forward and cross edges:

```
if x is black, then
  if (v.discover < x.discover) v → x is a forward edge
  else v → x is a cross edge
endif
```

Here is **dfTraverse** with all the above changes incorporated:

```
void dfTraverse(v) {
  print v.id
  v.colour = gray
  v.discover = ++time
  for each edge (v, x)
    if (x.colour == white) {
      (v, x) is a tree edge
      dfTraverse(x)
    }
    else if (x.colour == gray) (v, x) is a back edge
    else if (v.discover < x.discover) (v, x) is a forward edge
        else (v, x) is a cross edge
  endfor
  v.colour = black
  v.finish = ++time
}
```

When run on the sample graph, starting from A, we get the results shown in Figure 5.9. We show the discover/finish times separately from the classification of the edges, to reduce the clutter in one diagram:

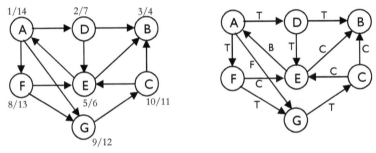

Figure 5.9: Graph with discover/finish times and classified edges

We now trace the call **dfTraverse(A)** to show how we arrive at these diagrams.

- set A.**discover** to 1 and A.**colour** to **gray**;
- follow the first (in alphabetical order) edge to D; D is **white**, set D.**discover** to 2 and D.**colour** to **gray**
- follow the first edge from D to B; B is **white**, set B.**discover** to 3 and B.**colour** to **gray**
- there are no edges leaving B; set B.**finish** to 4, B.**colour** to **black** and backtrack to D
- from D, follow the next edge to E; E is **white**, set E.**discover** to 5 and E.**colour** to **gray**
- from E, follow the first edge to A; A is **gray** so (E, A) is a back edge and we follow the next edge to B; B is **black** and E.**discover** (5) > B.**discover** (3) so (E, B) is a cross edge; there are no more edges from E so set E.**finish** to 6, E.**colour** to **black** and backtrack to D

- there are no more edges from D; set D.**finish** to 7, D.**colour** to **black** and backtrack to A
- from A, follow the next edge to F; F is **white**, set F.**discover** to 8 and F.**colour** to **gray**
- from F, follow the first edge to E; E is **black** and F.**discover** (8) > E.**discover** (5) so (F, E) is a cross edge; follow the next edge to G;
- G is **white**, set G.**discover** to 9, G.**colour** to **gray** and follow its first (and only) edge to C; C is **white**, set C.**discover** to 10 and C.**colour** to **gray**
- from C, follow the first edge to B; B is **black** and C.**discover** (10) > B.**discover** (3) so (C, B) is a cross edge; follow the next edge to E; E is **black** and C.**discover** (10) > E.**discover** (5) so (C, E) is a cross edge; there are no more edges from C so set C.**finish** to 11, C.**colour** to **black** and backtrack to G
- there are no more edges from G; set G.**finish** to 12, G.**colour** to **black** and backtrack to F
- there are no more edges from F; set F.**finish** to 13, F.**colour** to **black** and backtrack to A
- from A, follow the next edge to G; G is **black** and A.**discover** (1) < G.**discover** (9) so (A, G) is a forward edge; there are no more edges leaving A; set A.**finish** to 14, A.**colour** to **black** and **dfTraverse(A)** returns.

Implementing depth-first traversal

We now expand our **Graph** class to perform a depth-first traversal. We add the following class variables:

```
final static char White = 'w';
final static char Gray = 'g';
final static char Black = 'b';
static int time = 0;
```

We write the traversal to compute the discover/finish but not to classify the edges. If required, this can be easily added.

```
public void depthFirstTraversal(int s) {
//do a depth first traversal starting from vertex s
  for (int j = 1; j <= numV; j++) {
    vertex[j].colour = White;
     vertex[j].parent = 0;
  }
  time = 0;
  dfTraverse(s);
  for (int j = 1; j <= numV; j++)
    if (vertex[j].colour == White) dfTraverse(j);
  out.printf("\n");
} //end depthFirstTraversal()
```

```
private void dfTraverse(int s) {
  out.printf("%s ", vertex[s].id);
  vertex[s].colour = Gray;
  vertex[s].discover = ++time;
  GEdge edge = vertex[s].firstEdge;
  while (edge != null) {
    if (vertex[edge.child].colour == White) {
      vertex[edge.child].parent = s;
      dfTraverse(edge.child);
    }
    edge = edge.nextEdge;
  }
  vertex[s].colour = Black;
  vertex[s].finish = ++time;
} //end dfTraverse
```

We also keep track of the path to a vertex in the depth-first tree by storing 'parent' information. Initially (in **depthFirstTraversal**), we set all the **parent** fields to 0. In **dfTraverse**, when a white vertex is discovered, its parent field is set. For example, if we follow the edge $D \rightarrow E$ and E is **white,** then (D, E) is a tree edge; we set E.**parent** to D.

Assuming the **parent** fields have been set, we can print the path to any destination vertex, **D**, given its string **id**, with **printPath**:

```
public void printPath(String D) {
  int j;
  for (j = 1; j <= numV; j++) //find D in the list of nodes (location j)
    if (D.equals(vertex[j].id)) break;
  if (j > numV) out.printf("\nNo such node %s\n", D);
  else {
    out.printf("\nPath to %s: ", D);
    followPath(j);
    out.printf("\n");
  }
}
private void followPath(int c) {
  if (c != 0) {
    followPath(vertex[c].parent);
    out.printf("%s " , vertex[c].id);
  }
}
```

The **parent** fields link the vertices on the path in reverse order. For example, the path to C from A is: $A \rightarrow F \rightarrow G \rightarrow C$ but the **parent** fields point the other way, that is: C → G → F → A (the parent of C is G whose parent is F whose parent is A whose parent is none).

Given the destination vertex, **followPath** simply prints the linked list of vertices in reverse order. The call **printPath("C")** will print

        Path to C: A F G C

Programming note: For **buildGraph** (page 154) to create the representation of the sample graph, you will need to supply the data as follows:

```
7
A B C D E F G
A 3 D 1 F 1 G 1
B 0
C 2 B 1 E 1
D 2 B 1 E 1
E 2 A 1 B 1
F 2 E 1 G 1
G 1 C 1
```

Since **buildGraph** expects the weight of the edges to be given, we have used 1 for all the weights. The following code in **main** can be used to test our methods:

```
int numVertices = in.nextInt();
Graph G = new Graph(out, numVertices);
G.buildGraph(in);
G.printGraph();
out.printf("\nDepth-first traversal\n");
G.depthFirstTraversal(1);
G.printPath("C");
```

5.6 Topological sorting

There are many situations in which several tasks have to be done and some of these tasks can be done only after others have been completed. For example, in assembling a vehicle, certain parts must be assembled before others can be worked on. The engine cannot be assembled before the parts that go inside it. In teaching a course, several topics may have to be taught and some can be taught only after others have been covered.

In the latter case, we would like to arrange the topics in such an order that if topic A is needed to understand topic B, then A will be taught before B. We will need to do a *topological sort* of the topics.

The topological sorting problem can be stated as follows: given n items, numbered 1 to n, and m requirements of the form $j \to k$, meaning item j must come before item k, arrange the items in an order such that all requirements are satisfied or determine that no solution is possible.

For example, suppose $n = 9$ and $m = 10$ with the following requirements:

$3 \to 7$	$4 \to 2$	$8 \to 6$	$9 \to 5$	$1 \to 2$
$6 \to 5$	$2 \to 5$	$7 \to 8$	$8 \to 1$	$1 \to 9$

Two of the many solutions are:

4 3 7 8 6 1 9 2 5

3 7 8 6 1 9 4 2 5

If, in addition to the above requirements, we have $5 \to 8$, then there is no solution since $8 \to 6$, $6 \to 5$, $5 \to 8$ imply that 8 must come before 5 *and* 5 must come before 8, both of which cannot be satisfied. In this case, we say the requirements are *circular*.

We can solve the 'topological sort' problem by modelling it using a graph. The graph will have n vertices, one for each item. Each requirement $j \to k$ is represented by a directed edge from vertex j to vertex k. The 10 requirements above will be represented by the following graph:

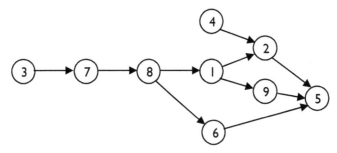

If the graph is acyclic (no cycles) then there is at least one solution to the problem. However, if the graph contains a cycle, there is no solution since this means that the requirements are circular. For example, if there is an edge $5 \to 8$, then the edges $(8, 6)$, $(6, 5)$ and $(5, 8)$ form a cycle.

We can produce the topological sorted order by doing the following:

perform a depth-first traversal of the graph
as each vertex is finished, push it onto a stack, S
when the traversal is done, pop S, and print each item as it is popped

For example, starting at vertex 1, the discover/finish times are shown here:

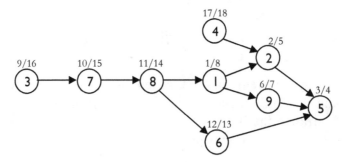

Vertex 5 is the first to finish, so it goes on the stack first. Vertex 4 is the last to finish so it goes on the stack last. In general, vertices go on the stack in the order in which they finish. The topological sort is obtained by listing the vertices in *decreasing order by finish time*. Here, we get the order 4 3 7 8 6 1 9 2 5, the first solution above.

As an exercise, find the solution starting the traversal at vertex 4. Also find solutions starting at any of the other vertices.

This exercise should make it clear that it does not really matter which vertex we start from; if the problem has a solution, one will be found. However, it is customary to start the traversal from a vertex whose *indegree* is 0. If a vertex A has an indegree of 0, it means that there is no edge leading into it. This, in turn, means that there is no requirement that any other item come before it. So we might as well start with A.

We now write **topologicalSort** which performs a depth-first traversal starting from whichever vertex is designated as the first when the graph is built. For the sample problem above, the graph data *could* be supplied as:

```
9
1 2 3 4 5 6 7 8 9
3 1 7 1
7 1 8 1
8 2 1 1 6 1
6 1 5 1
1 2 2 1 9 1
4 1 2 1
2 1 5 1
9 1 5 1
5 0
```

The edge weights, which are not important for solving the problem, are set to 1. Since 1 is designated as the first vertex in the vertex list (line 2 of the data), the traversal will start from 1.

A stack will be required for pushing vertices as they are finished. Each stack item will simply be the index of a vertex. For this problem, we define **StackData** as:

```
class StackData {
   int n; //index of a graph vertex
   public StackData(int j) {
      n = j;
   }
};
```

We now write **topologicalSort**.

```
        public void topologicalSort() {
            Stack S = new Stack();
            for (int j = 1; j <= numV; j++) vertex[j].colour = White;
            for (int j = 1; j <= numV; j++)
                if (vertex[j].colour == White) dfTopSort(S, j);
            out.printf("\nTopological sort: ");
            while (!S.empty()) out.printf("%s ", vertex[S.pop().n].id);
            out.printf("\n");
        } //end topologicalSort

        private void dfTopSort(Stack S, int s) {
            vertex[s].colour = Gray;
            GEdge edge = vertex[s].firstEdge;
            while (edge != null) {
              if (vertex[edge.child].colour == Gray) {
                  out.printf("\nGraph has a cycle: cannot sort\n");
                  out.flush();
                  System.exit(1);
              }
              if (vertex[edge.child].colour == White) dfTopSort(S, edge.child);
              edge = edge.nextEdge;
            }
            vertex[s].colour = Black;
            S.push(new StackData(s));
        } //end dfTopSort
```

Most of the work is done in **dfTopSort**. This is the usual depth-first traversal except that it checks for back edges. Recall that if the edge (v, x) is being processed and **x.colour** is **Gray**, then (v, x) is a back edge. This can only happen if there is a cycle in the graph and, hence, there is no solution.

Note that it is not necessary to record the discover/finish times. As soon as a vertex is finished (after processing all its edges), it is pushed onto the stack. So the vertices go on the stack in *increasing* order by finish time. When we take them off, they will be in *decreasing* order by finish time.

We can perform a topological sort on a graph **G** with the statement:

```
        G.topologicalSort();
```

5.7 Breadth-first traversal

We now look at the other common way of traversing a graph—breadth-first traversal. This is similar to level-order traversal for a (binary) tree. Given the graph:

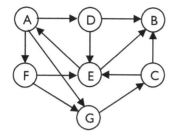

we perform a breadth-first traversal starting from A, as follows, assuming that edges of a vertex are processed in alphabetical order:

- from A, there are edges to D, F and G and these will be visited in that order
- from D, there are edges to B and E and these will be visited in that order
- from F, there are edges to E and G; these have already been seen so there is nothing to do
- from G, there is an edge to C and this is visited
- from B, there is no edge so there is nothing to do
- from E, there are edges to A and B; these have already been seen so there is nothing to do
- from C, there are edges to B and E; these have already been seen so there is nothing to do

There are no more vertices to process so the traversal ends, having visited the vertices in the order A D F G B E C.

The traversal may be easier to follow if we draw the graph in a tree-like manner:

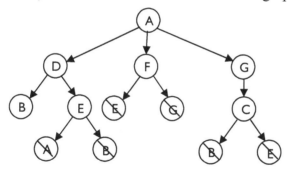

Using this diagram, the breadth-first traversal is a little more obvious. Essentially, it reduces to a level-order traversal: traverse vertices from left to right, from top to bottom. If you meet a vertex that has already been seen, ignore it. This is indicated by a line across the vertex.

Like the level-order traversal of a tree, we can perform a breadth-first traversal of a graph using a queue. The gist of the algorithm is as follows:

```
initialize a queue, Q
set the colour of all vertices to White and parent fields to 0
enqueue the start vertex, s
s.colour = gray
```

```
        while (Q is not empty) {
          let p = Q.dequeue
          visit p
          for each edge (p, x)
            if (x.colour is white) {
              x.colour = gray
              x.parent = p
              enqueue x
            }
          endfor
          p.colour = black
        }
```

We trace the algorithm with the sample graph starting from A. Vertices are visited as they are taken off the queue.

- A is put on Q with A.**colour** set to **gray** and we enter **while** loop
- Q is not empty; **p** is set to A; we process the edges (A, D), (A, F) and (A, G); the colour of D, F and G is set to **gray**, their **parent** is set to A and they are put on Q; Q now contains D F G (D at the head, G at the tail)
- A.**colour** is set to **black** and we go back to the top of the **while** loop
- Q is not empty; **p** is set to D; we process the edges (D, B) and (D, E); the colour of B and E is set to **gray**, their **parent** is set to D and they are put on Q; Q now contains F G B E
- D.**colour** is set to **black** and we go back to the top of the **while** loop
- Q is not empty; **p** is set to F; we process the edges (F, E) and (F, G); the colour of E and G is not **white** so there is nothing to do; Q contains G B E
- F.**colour** is set to **black** and we go back to the top of the **while** loop
- Q is not empty; **p** is set to G; we process the edge (G, C); the colour of C is set to **gray**, its **parent** is set to G and it is put on Q; Q contains B E C
- G.**colour** is set to **black** and we go back to the top of the **while** loop
- Q is not empty; **p** is set to B; there are no edges leaving B so there is nothing to do; Q contains E C
- B.**colour** is set to **black** and we go back to the top of the **while** loop
- Q is not empty; **p** is set to E; we process the edges (E, A) and (E, B); the colour of A and B is not **white** so there is nothing to do; Q contains C
- E.**colour** is set to **black** and we go back to the top of the **while** loop
- Q is not empty; **p** is set to C; we process the edges (C, B) and (C, E); the colour of B and E is not **white** so there is nothing to do; Q is empty
- C.**colour** is set to **black** and we go back to the top of the **while** loop
- Q is empty so the algorithm terminates

We can implement breadth-first traversal with a method in the **Graph** class. Each queue item is just the index of a vertex. We will need the following:

```
class QueueData {
  int n;
  public QueueData(int j) {
    n = j;
  }
} //end class QueueData
```

Here is **breadthFirstTraversal**; it prints the vertices in breadth-first order:

```
public void breadthFirstTraversal(int s) {
//do a breadth first traversal starting from vertex[s]
  for (int j = 1; j <= numV; j++) {
    vertex[j].colour = White;
    vertex[j].parent = 0;
  }
  vertex[s].colour = Gray;
  vertex[s].parent = 0;
  Queue Q = new Queue();
  Q.enqueue(new QueueData(s));

  while (!Q.empty()) {
    int aParent = Q.dequeue().n;
    out.printf("%s ", vertex[aParent].id);
    GEdge edge = vertex[aParent].firstEdge;
    while (edge != null) {
      if (vertex[edge.child].colour == White) {
        vertex[edge.child].colour = Gray;
        vertex[edge.child].parent = aParent;
        Q.enqueue(new QueueData(edge.child));
      }
      edge = edge.nextEdge;
    }
    vertex[aParent].colour = Black;
  }
  out.printf("\n");
} //end breadthFirstTraversal()
```

Suppose we wish to get from one vertex, S, to another vertex, D, by following the *fewest number of edges*. We could do a breadth-first traversal from S and stop when D is first encountered. We could then reconstruct the path using the **parent** fields as in **printPath** (page 164).

5.8 Single-source shortest paths: Dijkstra's algorithm

In what we have done so far (traversals and topological sort), we did not need to usc the weights of edges in the graph. Now we consider the problem of finding the shortest path from a source node, S, to a destination node, D, where 'shortest' is defined as the lowest sum of weights of the edges on a path from S to D. We use the terms *least-cost* path, *minimum-weight* path and *shortest* path to mean the same thing.

Consider the graph:

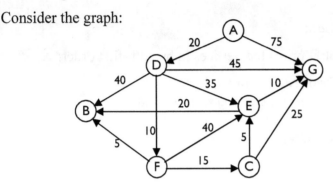

Suppose we wish to find the shortest path from A to E. There are several ways to get to E: A → D → E (with a cost of 20 + 35 = 55), A → D → F → E (with a cost of 20 + 10 + 40 = 70) and A → D → F → C → E (with a cost of 20 + 10 + 15 + 5 = 50). Of these, the last is the least-cost path.

While we may be interested in finding the shortest path from one vertex to another specific vertex, it turns out that it is no easier to solve this problem than to find the shortest paths from the source vertex to *all* other vertices. We will find these shortest paths using an algorithm due to E. W. Dijkstra.

This algorithm assumes that *the edge weights are non-negative*. We will see the need for this condition shortly. We will first show how Dijkstra's algorithm finds the shortest paths from vertex A to all other vertices in the above graph. We assume that

- V.**cost** holds the current cost of a path from A to a vertex V
- V.**parent** holds the parent of V on the current shortest path from A to V

Initially, we set all the parent fields to **nil** (meaning "no parent") and the cost fields to infinity (∞), indicating that no path to the vertex has yet been found.

vertex	A	B	C	D	E	F	G
parent	**nil**	nil	nil	nil	nil	nil	nil
cost	**0**	∞	∞	∞	∞	∞	∞

We will also need a priority queue, Q, which holds the vertices based on their current cost. Initially, we will put all the vertices on Q. Vertex A, with a cost of 0, will be at the head:

$$Q: \quad A_0 \ B_\infty \ C_\infty \ D_\infty \ E_\infty \ F_\infty \ G_\infty \text{ (head is on the left)}$$

- We take A off the queue and look at the edges leaving A. We will process edges in alphabetical order but any order will work. The edge (A, D) gives us a path to D at a cost of 20. This is lower than the current cost to D (∞) so we update the cost to 20, set the parent of D to A and adjust D's position in Q. The edge (A, G) gives us a path to G at a cost of 75. This is lower than the current cost to G (∞) so we update the cost to 75, set the parent of G to A and adjust G's position in Q. We have:

vertex	**A**	B	C	**D**	E	F	G
parent	**nil**	nil	nil	**A**	nil	nil	A
cost	**0**	∞	∞	**20**	∞	∞	75

Q: D_{20} G_{75} B_∞ C_∞ E_∞ F_∞

- We take D off the queue. Whenever we take a vertex off the queue, we have found the shortest path to that vertex. So we can conclude that the mininum cost to D (from A) is 20. Why is this so? Well, if there were a shorter path to D, it will have to go through G (there is no other edge leaving A). But the cost to G is 75. The only way to get a shorter path to D via G is for edges to have negative weights (for example, if there was an edge G → D with weight -60). Since we do not allow negative weights, this cannot happen.

- We process the edges leaving D. The edge (D, B) gives us a path to B at a cost of 20 + 40 = 60 (the cost to D plus the weight of (D, B)). This is lower than the current cost to B (∞) so we update the cost to 60, set the parent of B to D and adjust B's position in Q.

  The edge (D, E) gives us a path to E at a cost of 20 + 35 = 55 (the cost to D plus the weight of (D, E)). This is lower than the current cost to E (∞) so we update the cost to 55, set the parent of E to D and adjust E's position in Q.

  The edge (D, F) gives us a path to F at a cost of 20 + 10 = 30 (the cost to D plus the weight of (D, F)). This is lower than the current cost to F (∞) so we update the cost to 30, set the parent of F to D and adjust F's position in Q.

  The edge (D, G) gives us a path to G at a cost of 20 + 45 = 65 (the cost to D plus the weight of (D, G)). This is lower than the current cost to G (75) so we update the cost to 65, change G's parent to D and adjust G's position in Q. We have:

vertex	**A**	B	C	**D**	E	**F**	G
parent	**nil**	D	nil	**A**	D	**D**	D
cost	**0**	60	∞	**20**	55	**30**	65

Q: F_{30} E_{55} B_{60} G_{65} C_∞

- We take F off the queue and process the edges leaving F. The edge (F, B) gives us a path to B at a cost of 30 + 5 = 35 (the cost to F plus the weight of (F, B)). This is lower than the current cost to B (60) so we update the cost to 35, change B's parent to F and adjust B's position in Q.

The edge (F, C) gives us a path to C at a cost of 30 + 15 = 45 (the cost to F plus the weight of (F, C)). This is lower than the current cost to C (∞) so we update the cost to 45, change C's parent to F and adjust C's position in Q.

The edge (F, E) gives us a path to E at a cost of 30 + 40 = 70 (the cost to F plus the weight of (F, E)). This is higher than the current cost to E (55) so we leave E as it is. We now have:

vertex	A	B	C	D	E	F	G
parent	nil	F	F	A	D	D	D
cost	0	35	45	20	55	30	65

Q: B_{35} C_{45} E_{55} G_{65}

- We take B off the queue and process the edges leaving B. But there are none, so nothing changes except Q, which is now:

    Q: C_{45} E_{55} G_{65}

- We take C off the queue and process the edges leaving C. The edge (C, E) gives us a path to E at a cost of 45 + 5 = 50 (the cost to C plus the weight of (C, E)). This is lower than the current cost to E (55) so we update the cost to 50, change E's parent to C and adjust E's position in Q.

- The edge (C, G) gives us a path to G at a cost of 45 + 25 = 70 (the cost to C plus the weight of (C, G)). This is higher than the current cost to G (65) so we leave G as it is. We now have:

vertex	A	B	C	D	E	F	G
parent	nil	F	F	A	C	D	D
cost	0	35	45	20	50	30	65

Q: E_{50} G_{65}

- We take E off the queue and process the only edge leaving E. The edge (E, G) gives us a path to G at a cost of 50 + 10 = 60 (the cost to E plus the weight of (E, G)). This is lower than the current cost to G (65) so we update the cost to 60, change G's parent to E and adjust G's position in Q. We have:

vertex	A	B	C	D	E	F	G
parent	nil	F	F	A	C	D	E
cost	0	35	45	20	50	30	60

Q: G_{60}

- We take G off the queue and process the edges leaving G. But there are none, so nothing changes except Q, which is now empty.
- Since Q is empty, the algorithm terminates, with the following results:

    Cost to B: 35, Path: A → D → F → B

Cost to C: 45, Path: A → D → F → C
Cost to D: 20, Path: A → D
Cost to E: 50, Path: A → D → F → C → E
Cost to F: 30, Path: A → D → F
Cost to G: 60, Path: A → D → F → C → E → G

The path to any vertex can be found by following the parent pointers. For example, the parent of B is F, the parent of F is D and the parent of D is A. So the path from A to B is A D F B.

We can formulate Dijkstra's algorithm as follows:

```
Dijkstra(G, W, s)
//find minimum-cost paths from s to every other vertex
//assumes that W(p, x), the weight of the edge (p, x), >= 0
// Q is a priority queue

  initSingleSource(G, s)  //see below
  add all the vertices of G to Q
  while not empty(Q) do
    p = Q.extract-min()
    if (p.cost == ∞) break; //no paths to remaining vertices
    for each edge (p, x)      //for each edge leaving p
      if (p.cost + W(p, x) < x.cost) then // better path found
        x.cost = p.cost + W(p, x)
        x.parent = p
        adjust x's position in Q
      endif
    endfor
  endwhile
  for each vertex v in G
    print v.cost and the path to get to v from s
end Dijkstra
```

where we write **initSingleSource** as:

```
initSingleSource(G, s)
  for each vertex v in G
    v.cost = ∞
    v.parent = nil
  endfor
  s.cost = 0
end initSingleSource
```

Implementing Dijkstra's algorithm

We can implement Dijkstra's algorithm as an instance method in the **Graph** class in a fairly straightforward manner, as shown on the next page:

```java
public void Dijkstra(int s) {
    final int Infinity = 999999;
    int[] heap = new int[numV+1];
    int[] heapLoc = new int[numV+1];
    //heapLoc[j] gives the position in heap of vertex j
    //if heapLoc[j] = k, then heap[k] contains j

    initSingleSource(s);
    for (int j = 1; j <= numV; j++) heap[j] = heapLoc[j] = j;
    heap[1] = s; heap[s] = 1; heapLoc[s] = 1; heapLoc[1] = s;
    int heapSize = numV;
    while (heapSize > 0) {
        int u = heap[1];
        if (vertex[u].cost == Infinity) break; //no paths to remaining vertices
        //reorganize heap after removing top item
        siftDown(heap[heapSize], heap, 1, heapSize-1, heapLoc);
        GEdge p = vertex[u].firstEdge;
        while (p != null) {
            if (vertex[u].cost + p.weight < vertex[p.child].cost) {
                vertex[p.child].cost = vertex[u].cost + p.weight;
                vertex[p.child].parent = u;
                siftUp(heap, heapLoc[p.child], heapLoc);
            }
            p = p.nextEdge;
        }
        --heapSize;
    } //end while

    printCostPath();
} //end Dijkstra

private void initSingleSource(int s) {
    for (int j = 1; j <= numV; j++) {
        vertex[j].cost = Infinity;
        vertex[j].parent = 0;
    }
    vertex[s].cost = 0;
} //end initSingleSource

private void printCostPath() {
    for (int j = 1; j <= numV; j++) {
        out.printf("Cost to %s: %d, Path: ", vertex[j].id, vertex[j].cost);
        followPath(j);
        out.printf("\n");
    }
} //end printCostPath
```

If **G** is a **Graph** object, we call the method with **G.Dijkstra(s)** where **s** is the *index* of the source vertex in the order that the vertices were supplied when the graph was built. For example, if the order was A B C D E F G, then **G.Dijkstra(1)** will find minimum-cost paths from A and **G.Dijkstra(6)** will find minimum-cost paths from F.

The code closely follows the algorithm above. The priority queue is implemented using a min-heap (item with the *lowest* cost is at the root). The items in the array **heap** are simply the vertex numbers (1, 2, 3, etc.). So, for instance, if vertex 4 has the current lowest cost then **heap[1]** will contain 4.

We will need to keep track of where a vertex is in the heap. This is necessary to be able to adjust the position of a vertex in the heap when its path cost is lowered. For example, suppose **vertex[2].cost** is 60 and **heap[3]** = 2 (meaning that vertex 2 is stored in location 3). If **vertex[2].cost** changes to 35, we will have to adjust the postion of vertex 2 in the heap based on its new cost. But we can only do so if we know where it is.

We use the array **heapLoc** to keep track of the location of a vertex in **heap**. In this example, we will have **heapLoc[2]** = 3, meaning that vertex 2 is stored in **heap[3]**. Suppose, as a result of its cost changing to 35, vertex 2 must be moved to **heap[1]**. This would also mean that whatever was in **heap[1]** (vertex 5, say) must be moved to **heap[3]**. These changes would be reflected in **heapLoc**. So **heapLoc[2]** will become 1 (meaning that vertex 2 is in **heap[1]**) and **heapLoc[5]** will become 3 (meaning that vertex 5 is in **heap[3]**).

The statements

```
for (int j = 1; j <= numV; j++) heap[j] = heapLoc[j] = j;
heap[1] = s; heap[s] = 1; heapLoc[s] = 1; heapLoc[1] = s;
```

initialize the heap. The **for** loop puts vertex **j** in **heap[j]**. The other statements ensure that the source vertex **s** is placed at the root of the heap, by swapping it with vertex 1. Of course, if the start vertex *is* 1, these statements have no effect.

Reorganizing the heap is done using slightly modified versions of **siftDown** and **siftUp** from Chapter 4:

```
private void siftDown(int key, int[] heap, int root, int last, int[] heapLoc) {
   int smaller = 2 * root;
   while (smaller <= last) { //while there is at least one child
      if (smaller < last) //there is a right child as well; find the smaller
        if (vertex[heap[smaller+1]].cost < vertex[heap[smaller]].cost)
           smaller++;
      //'smaller' holds the index of the smaller child
      if (vertex[key].cost <= vertex[heap[smaller]].cost) break;
      //cost[key] is bigger; promote heap[smaller]
      heap[root] = heap[smaller];
```

```
        heapLoc[heap[smaller]] = root;
        root = smaller;
        smaller = 2 * root;
     } //end while
     heap[root] = key;
     heapLoc[key] = root;
  } //end siftDown
  private void siftUp(int heap[], int n, int[] heapLoc) {
  //sifts up heap[n] so that heap[1..n] contains a heap based on cost
     int siftItem = heap[n];
     int child = n;
     int parent = child / 2;
     while (parent > 0) {
        if (vertex[siftItem].cost >= vertex[heap[parent]].cost) break;
        heap[child] = heap[parent]; //move down parent
        heapLoc[heap[parent]] = child;
        child = parent;
        parent = child / 2;
     }
     heap[child] = siftItem;
     heapLoc[siftItem] = child;
  } //end siftUp
```

5.9 Single-source shortest paths: Bellman-Ford algorithm

The Bellman-Ford algorithm finds the shortest paths from a given source vertex to all other vertices. However, it does not require that the weights of the edges be non-negative, as in Dijkstra's algorithm. It will find shortest paths for graphs with negative-weight edges. However, if the graph contains a *negative-weight cycle*, then there is no solution and the algorithm detects this.

To illustrate the last point, consider:

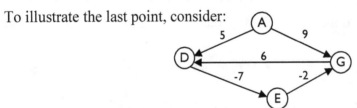

What is the cost of a path from A to G? The path A → G gives a cost of 9. But the path A → G → D → E → G gives a cost of 6. Further, each time we traverse the path G → D → E → G we reduce the cost by 3 since G → D → E → G is a *negative-weight cycle* with a cost of -3. In other words, we can reduce the cost of the path from A to G to any value we wish by traversing the cycle an appropriate number of times. Hence, there is no "minimum-cost" to the path.

On the other hand, if the weight of D → E were -3, say, there would be no negative-weight cycle and the minimum cost from A to G would be 9. So negative-weight *edges* are not a problem but a negative-weight *cycle* is.

Suppose the graph has *n* vertices. Bellman-Ford will first make *n*-1 passes over *all* the edges. Given an edge **p → x**, it checks to see if there is a better path to **x** via **p**. If there is no path to **p** as yet (its cost is infinite) there is nothing to do for this edge. If **p.cost** is finite, the cost to **x** via **p** is **p.cost + weight(p → x)**; if *this* cost is less than the current cost to **x** (**x.cost**), the algorithm updates **x.cost** to this new value and sets **x.parent** to **p**. This 'processing' is sometimes called *relaxing the edge*. We can express this as follows:

```
relax(W, p, x)
  if (p.cost != ∞ && p.cost + W(p, x) < x.cost) {
    x.cost = p.cost + W(p, x)
    x.parent = p
  endif
end relax
```

After the first *n*-1 passes, a final pass is made. If the cost to any vertex can be further reduced, then the graph contains a negative-weight cycle and there is no solution. Otherwise, the **v.cost** gives the minimum cost to **v** for all vertices **v** and the **parent** fields define the paths. We express these ideas as follows:

```
boolean Bellman-Ford(G, W, s)
//find minimum-cost paths from s to every other node
//W(p, x) is the weight of the edge p → x
//return false if there is no solution; true, otherwise
  initSingleSource(G, s)
  for pass = 1 to n – 1        //n is the number of vertices
    for each edge p → x
      relax(W, p, x)
  endfor
  //make a final pass to check for negative-weight cycles
  for each edge p → x
    if (p.cost != ∞ && p.cost + W(p, x) < x.cost) {
      print "Graph contains a negative-weight cycle: no solution"
      return false
    endif
  endfor
  for each vertex v in G
    print v.cost and the path to get to v from s
  return true
end Bellman-Ford
```

We illustrate how the algorithm works by finding minimum-cost paths from A in the following graph:

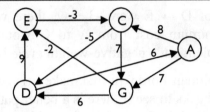

Initially, we have:

vertex	A	C	D	E	G
parent	**nil**	nil	nil	nil	nil
cost	**0**	∞	∞	∞	∞

We will relax the edges in the order (A, C), (A, G), (C, D), (C, G), (D, A), (D, E), (E, C), (G, D) and (G, E). We note that *any* order will give the same result after all the passes.

- relaxing (A, C) changes **C.cost** to 8 and **C.parent** to A; relaxing (A, G) changes **G.cost** to 7 and **G.parent** to A; relaxing (C, D) changes **D.cost** to 3 and **D.parent** to C; relaxing (C, G) changes nothing; relaxing (D, A) does nothing; relaxing (D, E) changes **E.cost** to 12 and **E.parent** to D; since **E.cost** is now 12, relaxing (E, C) does nothing since **C.cost** is 8; relaxing (G, D) changes nothing; relaxing (G, E) changes **E.cost** to 5 and **E.parent** to G. We have

vertex	A	C	D	E	G
parent	**nil**	A	C	G	A
cost	**0**	8	3	5	7

- 2nd pass: relaxing (A, C), (A, G), (C, D), (C, G), (D, A) and (D, E) changes nothing; relaxing (E, C) changes **C.cost** to 2 and **C.parent** to E; relaxing (G, D) and (G, E) changes nothing. We have

vertex	A	C	D	E	G
parent	**nil**	E	C	G	A
cost	**0**	2	3	5	7

- 3rd pass: relaxing (A, C) and (A, G) does nothing; relaxing (C, D) changes **D.cost** to -3 and its parent remains C; relaxing (C, G), (D, A), (D, E), (E, C), (G, D) and (G, E) changes nothing. We have

vertex	A	C	D	E	G
parent	**nil**	E	C	G	A
cost	**0**	2	-3	5	7

- 4th pass: nothing changes on this pass; all the costs remain the same from the third pass.

- final pass: as we would expect, nothing changes here; no vertex cost is reduced, so we have a solution, as follows:

  Cost to A: 0, Path: A
  Cost to C: 2, Path: A → G → E → C
  Cost to D: -3, Path: A → G → E → C → D
  Cost to E: 5, Path: A → G → E
  Cost to G: 7, Path: A → G

As an exercise, run the Bellman-Ford algorithm on the following graph, with A as the source vertex. Try processing the edges in different orders.

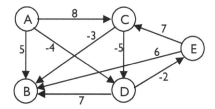

Implementing the Bellman-Ford algorithm

We can implement the Bellman-Ford algorithm as an instance method in the **Graph** class as shown on the next page.

There is no need for **relax** to check if **vertex[u].cost** is **Infinity** since this is done before calling **relax**.

If **G** is a **Graph** object, we call the method with **G.BellmanFord(s)** where **s** is the *index* of the source vertex in the order that the vertices were supplied when the graph was built. For example, if the order was A B C D E F G, then **G.BellmanFord(1)** will find minimum-cost paths from A and **G.BellmanFord(4)** will find minimum-cost paths from D.

The edges are processed in the order in which they appear in the adjacency-list representation. The order of the vertices is the order given when the graph was built. And, for each vertex, the children are processed in ascending order.

5.10 Minimum-cost spanning trees

Given an undirected graph, G, a *spanning tree* of G is a subgraph of G containing all the vertices but only those edges of G that are necessary to form a (free) tree. For example, given the graph:

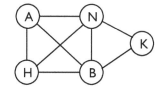

```java
public boolean BellmanFord(int s) {
  final int Infinity = 999999;
  int j, u, v, pass;

  initSingleSource(s);
  for (pass = 1; pass < numV; pass++) {
    for (j = 1; j <= numV; j++) {
      if (vertex[j].cost != Infinity) {
        GEdge p = vertex[j].firstEdge;
        while (p != null) {
          relax(j, p.child, p.weight);
          p = p.nextEdge;
        }
      } //end if
    } //end for j
  } //end for pass
  //make final pass to check for negative weight cycles
  for (j = 1; j <= numV; j++) {
    GEdge p = vertex[j].firstEdge;
    while (p != null) {
      if (vertex[j].cost + p.weight < vertex[p.child].cost) {
        out.printf("\nNo solution: graph has negative weight cycle\n");
        return false;
      }
      p = p.nextEdge;
    } //end while
  } //end for
  printCostPath();
  return true;
} //end BellmanFord

private void relax(int u, int v, int weight) {
//relax the edge (vertex[u], vertex[v])
  if (vertex[u].cost + weight < vertex[v].cost) {
    vertex[v].cost = vertex[u].cost + weight;
    vertex[v].parent = u;
  }
} //end relax
```

the following are two possible spanning trees for it:

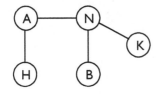
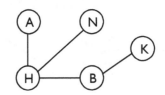

Recall that a tree of *n* vertices will necessarily have *n*-1 edges.

If the graph is *weighted*, the *cost* of a spanning tree is the sum of the weights of its edges. For example, given the graph:

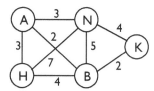

the cost of the spanning tree

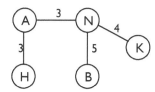

is 3 + 3 + 4 + 5 = 15.

The cost of

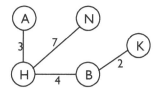

is 2 + 3 + 4 + 7 = 16.

A *minimum-cost spanning tree* (MST) is one with the lowest cost of all possible spanning trees. There may be more than one MST for a given graph. The MST for the above graph is:

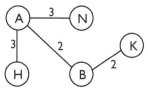

Its cost is 10.

Minimum-cost spanning trees have useful applications. For example, it may be required to connect several computers using a minimum of cabling. If we model the network using a graph where the computers are the vertices and the weight of an edge (P, X) is the length of cable required to connect computers P and X, then an MST of the graph gives the required answer.

Finding a minimum-cost spanning tree: Prim's algorithm

Prim's algorithm starts off with any vertex as the first vertex in the tree and grows the tree one vertex at a time. We illustrate the method using the following graph:

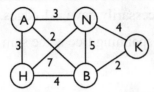

Suppose we start with H. We look at the neighbours of H and note the connection cost of each neighbour. Here, the cost of connecting A is 3, the cost of connecting B is 4 and the cost of connecting N is 7. These neighbours are placed in a priority queue. We can record this information as follows:

vertex	A	B	**H**	K	N
parent	H	H	**nil**	nil	H
cost	3	4	**0**	∞	7

Q: A_3 B_4 N_7

Next, we remove the item at the head of the queue and 'process' it. Here, we remove A and add it to the growing MST which now consists of H and A connected by an edge of weight 3.

We process A by looking at its neighbours which are *not* in the MST. The first is B. The cost of connecting B to the tree via A is 2. The current connection cost of B is 4. We have a better connection for B so we set its cost to 2 and its parent to A.

The next neighbour of A is H but H is in the MST. The next neighbour is N. The cost of connecting N to the tree via A is 3. The current connection cost of N is 7. We have a better connection for N so we set its cost to 3 and its parent to A. At this stage, we have (items in bold are in the MST):

vertex	**A**	B	**H**	K	N
parent	**H**	A	**nil**	nil	A
cost	**3**	2	**0**	∞	3

Q: B_2 N_3

Next, we remove B from the queue and process it by looking at its neighbours not in the MST. Neighbours A and H are in the MST so we look at the next neighbour N. The cost of connecting N to the tree via B is 5. The current connection cost of N is 3 which is better so we leave things as they are.

The next neighbour is K. The cost of connecting K to the tree via B is 2. The current connection cost of K is ∞. We have a better connection for K so we set its cost to 2 and its parent to B. At this stage, we have (items in bold are in the MST):

vertex	A	B	H	K	N
parent	H	A	nil	B	A
cost	3	2	0	2	3

Q: K_2 N_3

Next, we remove K from the queue and process it by looking at its neighbours not in the MST. The only such neighbour is N. The cost of connecting N to the tree via K is 4. The current connection cost of N is 3 which is better so we leave things as they are. At this stage, we have (items in bold are in the MST):

vertex	A	B	H	K	N
parent	H	A	nil	B	A
cost	3	2	0	2	3

Q: N_3

Finally, we remove N from the queue. All its neighbours are already in the MST so nothing further happens. The algorithm ends and the parent fields define the minimum-cost spanning tree.

It's easy to see that the cost fields add up to 10 and that the edges (H, A), (A, B), (B, K) and (A, N) form the tree.

As an exercise, work through the algorithm using K as the starting vertex.

The alert reader will recognize that Prim's algorithm is very similar in nature to Dijkstra's. In both algorithms, we keep track of the "current cost" of a vertex which determines its position in a priority queue. In both algorithms, when we take a vertex off the queue, that vertex is "finished"—either the minimum cost to get to it from the source vertex has been found or it is added to the MST.

We then process the neighbours of the "finished" vertex, P. In Dijkstra's, we ask what is the cost of the *path to a neighbour* via P. In Prim's, we ask what is the cost of *connecting a neighbour* to the spanning tree via P. We should expect that the implementation of Prim's would be similar to that of Dijkstra's.

In processing the neighbours of a vertex, Prim's algorithm needs to know if a neighbour is already in the MST. We will use the **colour** property of a vertex for this. All vertices are set to **White**, initially. When one is added to the MST, its **colour** is set to **Black**. We can formulate Prim's algorithm as follows:

```
Prim(G, W, s)
//construct minimum-cost spanning tree starting with vertex s
// Q is a priority queue

   initPrim(G, s) //see below
   add all the vertices of G to Q
```

```
                while not empty(Q) do
                  p = Q.extract-min()
                  if (p.cost ==  ∞) break; //remaining vertices unreachable
                  p.colour = Black //this vertex is added to the MST
                  for each edge (p, x)        //for each edge leaving p
                    if (W(p, x) < x.cost) then // lower connection cost found
                      x.cost = W(p, x)
                      x.parent = p
                      adjust x's position in Q
                    endif
                  endfor
                endwhile
                for each vertex v in G
                  if (v != s) print edge (v.parent, v) and v.cost
              end Prim
```

where we write **initPrim** as:

```
              initPrim(G, s)
                for each vertex v in G
                  v.cost = ∞
                  v.parent = nil
                  v.colour = White
                endfor
                s.cost = 0
              end initPrim
```

Implementing Prim's algorithm

We implement Prim's algorithm as an instance method in the **Graph** class. The code is fairly straightforward. For instance, we write **initPrim** as:

```java
              private void initPrim(int s) {
                for (int j = 1; j <= numV; j++) {
                  vertex[j].cost = Infinity;
                  vertex[j].parent = 0;
                  vertex[j].colour = White; //to Black when vertex is added to MST
                }
                vertex[s].cost = 0;
              } //end initPrim
```

And here is method **Prim**:

```java
              public void Prim(int s) {
              //perform Prim's algorithm starting with vertex s
                final int Infinity = 999999;
                int[] heap = new int[numV+1];
```

```
        int[] heapLoc = new int[numV+1];

        initPrim(s);
        for (int j = 1; j <= numV; j++) heap[j] = heapLoc[j] = j;
        heap[1] = s; heap[s] = 1; heapLoc[s] = 1; heapLoc[1] = s;
        int heapSize = numV;
        while (heapSize > 0) {
          int u = heap[1];
          if (vertex[u].cost == Infinity) break;
          vertex[u].colour = Black;
          //reorganize heap after removing top item
          siftDown(heap[heapSize], heap, 1, heapSize-1, heapLoc);
          GEdge p = vertex[u].firstEdge;
          while (p != null) {
            if (vertex[p.child].colour == White && p.weight < vertex[p.child].cost)
            {
              vertex[p.child].cost = p.weight;
              vertex[p.child].parent = u;
              siftUp(heap, heapLoc[p.child], heapLoc);
            }
            p = p.nextEdge;
          }
          --heapSize;
        } //end while

      printMST(s);
    } //end Prim
```

The methods **siftDown** and **siftUp** are the same as for Dijkstra's. We print the MST using **printMST**:

```
    private void printMST(int s) {
      out.printf("\nThe edges/weights in the MST are\n");
      int costMST = 0;
      for (int j = 1; j <= numV; j++)
        if (j != s) {
          out.printf("(%s, %s): %d\n", vertex[vertex[j].parent].id,
              vertex[j].id, vertex[j].cost);
          costMST += vertex[j].cost;
        }
      out.printf("\nCost of tree: %d\n", costMST);
    } //end printMST
```

For the sample graph,

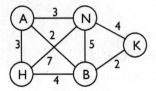

we must provide the data as:

```
5
A B H K N
A 3 B 2 H 3 N 3
B 4 A 2 H 4 K 2 N 5
H 3 A 3 B 4 N 7
N 4 A 3 B 5 H 7 K 4
K 2 B 2 N 4
```

Note that the edges must be repeated to reflect that they go in both directions.

The statements:

```
int numVertices = in.nextInt();
Graph G = new Graph(out, numVertices);
G.buildGraph(in);
G.Prim(3);
```

will read the data, build the graph and construct the minimum-spanning tree starting with vertex 3, H. The output produced is:

```
The edges/weights in the MST are
(H, A): 3
(A, B): 2
(B, K): 2
(A, N): 3

Cost of tree: 10
```

As an exercise, construct the MST for the following graph:

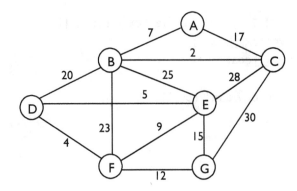

Finding a minimum-cost spanning tree: Kruskal's algorithm

Kruskal's algorithm for constructing an MST is one of those algorithms that is easy to describe but not so easy to implement. First, the description:

```
Kruskal's algorithm for G(V, E)
    for each v in V, create a tree consisting of v only
    sort the edges of E by non-decreasing weight
    for each edge (u, v) in E, in order by non-decreasing weight
        if u and v belong to different trees, connect them with the edge (u, v)
end Kruskal
```

We illustrate the method with the following graph:

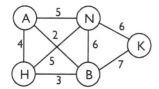

First, we create 5 trees consisting of one vertex each:

Next, we sort the edges in order by weight, giving:

```
(A, B, 2)
(B, H, 3)
(A, H, 4)
(A, N, 5)
(H, N, 5)
(B, N, 6)
(K, N, 6)
(B, K, 7)
```

If two or more edges have the same weight, their relative order does not matter. We now 'step through' the edges, in order:

- (A, B, 2): A and B are in different trees, so we connect them with this edge and we have the following trees:

- (B, H, 3): B and H are in different trees, so we connect them with this edge:

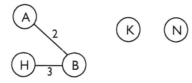

- (A, H, 4): A and H are in the same tree, so we disregard this edge.
- (A, N, 5): A and N are in different trees, so we connect them with this edge:

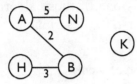

- (H, N, 5): H and N are in the same tree, so we disregard this edge.
- (B, N, 6): B and N are in the same tree, so we disregard this edge.
- (K, N, 6): K and N are in different trees, so we connect them with this edge:

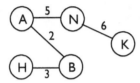

- (B, K, 7): B and K are in the same tree, so we disregard this edge.

All the edges have been processed and we have a minimum-cost spanning tree with a cost of 16. This is not the only one. The following is another MST with a cost of 16.

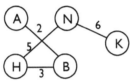

Here, we processed *all* the edges. However, we could keep track of how many edges have been used to join trees and stop when *n*-1 edges have been used (if there are *n* vertices).

Implementing Kruskal's algorithm

A key issue in implementing Kruskal's algorithm is how to determine if two vertices are in different trees and, if they are, how to join the two trees. The fact that the vertices are in *trees* is not important. All we need to know is whether two vertices are in the same *set* and, if they are not, how to join the two sets. For now, we will discuss a very simplistic method.

Suppose there are 8 vertices numbered 1, 2, 3, 4, 5, 6, 7, 8. Initially, each vertex is in its own set. We use an array **P[1..8]** and represent this information as follows:

P	0	0	0	0	0	0	0	0
	1	2	3	4	5	6	7	8

Now suppose we want to join {2} and {5}. We can do this by setting P[2] to 5 (or by setting P[5] to 2). If we then want to join {2, 5} and {7}, we can do so by setting P[5] to 7 or P[7] to 5—either one will work; we use the former. At this stage, we have:

P	0	5	0	0	7	0	0	0
	1	2	3	4	5	6	7	8

At the moment, we have the following sets: {1}, {2, 5, 7}, {3}, {4}, {6} and{8}. We introduce the notion of a "set identifier"; this is a chosen member of the set which will be returned in answer to the query "To which set does a given member belong?"

For single-member sets, the set identifier is the member. If a set has more than one member, we follow **P** values from any member until **P[i]** is 0; **i** is the set identifier. For example, to answer "To what set does 2 belong?", we look at **P[2]**, this is 5; we then look at **P[5]**; this is 7; we look at **P[7]**; this is 0 so the set identifier is 7. We get the same answer if we ask to what set does 5 or 7 belong.

Of course, for a single-member set (3, say), we have **P[3]** = 0 so 3 identifies its own set.

In general, if **x** is a member, we can write **getSetID(x)** to return the set identifier of the set to which **x** belongs:

```
public static int getSetID(int[] P, int x) {
  while (P[x] != 0) x = P[x];
  return x;
}
```

How do we join two sets containing members **x** and **y**, respectively? We first find **xi = getSetID(x)** and **yi = getSetID(y)**. We then set **P[xi]** to **yi**. We could also set **P[yi]** to **xi**. Either way will work.

For example, to join {1} and {8}, we set **P[1]** to 8, and we have:

P	8	5	0	0	7	0	0	0
	1	2	3	4	5	6	7	8

We could draw the sets represented as follows:

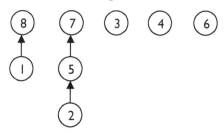

Each set is represented by a tree. We can think of **P[x]** as the "parent" of **x** in the tree representation. From this, we can see that the "set identifier" is simply the root of the tree representing the set. To join two sets, we set the root of one tree to point to the root of the other.

Suppose we want to join the "set containing 1" with the "set containing 5", that is, the sets {1, 8} and {2, 5, 7}. We find **getSetID(1)** (which is 8) and **getSetID(5)** (which is 7). We set **P[8]** to 7 and we have:

P	8	5	0	0	7	0	0	7
	1	2	3	4	5	6	7	8

These values represent the following trees (sets):

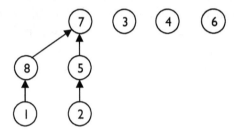

We can "union" the sets containing **x** and **y**, respectively, with:

```
public static void union(int[] P, int x, int y) {
    int xi = getSetID(P, x);
    int yi = getSetID(P, y);
    if (xi != yi) P[xi] = yi; //if x, y are not already in the same set
} //end union
```

To facilitate sorting of the edges, we store them in an array **edgeList**. Each element of **edgeList** is of type **UndirectedEdge**, defined as:

```
class UndirectedEdge {
    int parent, child, weight;
    public UndirectedEdge(int p, int c, int w) {
        parent = p;
        child = c;
        weight = w;
    }
} //end class UndirectedEdge
```

We will implement Kruskal's algorithm as an instance method, **Kruskal**, in the **Graph** class. When **Kruskal** is called, it will be given a value for **MaxEdges**, the maximum number of edges in the graph; the actual number of edges could be less than **MaxEdges**. We declare **edgeList** as:

```
UndirectedEdge[] edgeList = new UndirectedEdge[MaxEdges];
```

and store all the edges of the graph in it. This could be done with code such as:

```
for (int j = 1; j <= numV; j++) {
  GEdge p = vertex[j].firstEdge;
  while (p != null) {
    if (!inEdgeList(j, p.child, list, numEdges)) {
      list[numEdges] = new UndirectedEdge(j, p.child, p.weight);
      numEdges++;
    }
    p = p.nextEdge;
  }
}
```

Keep in mind that, in the representation of an undirected graph, each edge appears twice. For instance, the edge connecting A and H appears as (A, H) and (H, A); H appears on the list of A and A appears on the list of H. Even though the program will work if an edge is processed twice (once as (A, H) and once as (H, A)), we prefer to store and process it once.

So before storing an edge, we check the list to see if it is already there. We use a simple sequential search to check this:

```
private static boolean inEdgeList(int u, int v, UndirectedEdge[] list, int n) {
//search for edge (u, v) in list[0..n-1]
  for (int j = 0; j < n; j++)
    if (u == list[j].child && v == list[j].parent) return true;
  return false;
} //end inEdgeList
```

Note that if the edge (A, H) is already stored, when we meet (H, A), we must check for it by reversing its vertices. If we simply check for (H, A), we will not find it. In **inEdgeList**, **u** is the parent and **v** is the child of the edge we are searching for; we compare **u** with the *child* of a stored edge and **v** with its *parent*.

Once the edges are stored in **edgeList**, we can sort them using any sorting method; our program will use *insertion sort*. For the sample graph, if we print the edges in the format "(parent, child): weight", we will get:

```
(A, B): 2
(B, H): 3
(A, H): 4
(A, N): 5
(H, N): 5
(B, N): 6
(K, N): 6
(B, K): 7
```

The order of edges with the same weight does not matter.

We now write **Kruskal** and all the supporting methods. As each edge in the MST is found (when it is used to join two trees), we store it in the array **MST**. At the end, we print the edges which make up the MST as well as the cost of the tree. For the sample graph, we get the following output:

```
The edges/weights in the MST are
(A, B): 2
(B, H): 3
(A, N): 5
(K, N): 6

Cost of tree: 16
```

Here are the methods which implement Kruskal's algorithm:

```java
public void Kruskal(int MaxEdges) {
   UndirectedEdge[] edgeList = new UndirectedEdge[MaxEdges];
   int[] P = new int[numV+1]; //used to implement disjoint subsets
   for (int j = 1; j <= numV; j++) P[j] = 0;
   int numEdges = getSortedEdges(edgeList, MaxEdges);
   UndirectedEdge[] MST = new UndirectedEdge[numEdges];
   int t = 0; //used to index MST
   for (int j = 0; j < numEdges; j++) {
     int xRoot = getSetID(P, edgeList[j].parent);
     int yRoot = getSetID(P, edgeList[j].child);
     if (xRoot != yRoot) {
       MST[t++] = edgeList[j];
       union(P, xRoot, yRoot);
     } //end if
   } //end for
   printKruskalMST(MST, t);
} //end Kruskal
private void printKruskalMST(UndirectedEdge[] MST, int n) {
//print the n edges in the MST and the total cost
   int cost = 0;
   out.printf("\nThe edges/weights in the MST are\n");
   for (int j = 0; j < n; j++) {
      out.printf("(%s, %s): %d\n", vertex[MST[j].parent].id,
          vertex[MST[j].child].id, MST[j].weight);
     cost += MST[j].weight;
   }
   out.printf("\nCost of tree: %d\n", cost);
} //end printKruskalMST

private static int getSetID(int[] P, int x) {
   while (P[x] != 0) x = P[x];
   return x;
} //end getSetID
```

```
private static void union(int[] P, int x, int y) {
  int xi = getSetID(P, x);
  int yi = getSetID(P, y);
  if (xi != yi) P[xi] = yi;
} //end union
private int getSortedEdges(UndirectedEdge[] list, int max) {
  int numEdges = 0;
  for (int j = 1; j <= numV; j++) {
    GEdge p = vertex[j].firstEdge;
    while (p != null) {
      if (numEdges == max) {
        out.printf("\nToo many edges; exceeds %d\n", max); out.flush();
        System.exit(1);
      }
      if (!inEdgeList(j, p.child, list, numEdges)) {
        list[numEdges] = new UndirectedEdge(j, p.child, p.weight);
        numEdges++;
      }
      p = p.nextEdge;
    } //end while
  } //end for
  sortEdges(list, numEdges);
  return numEdges;
} //end getSortedEdges

private static boolean inEdgeList(int u, int v, UndirectedEdge[] list, int n) {
//search for edge (u, v) in list[0..n-1]
  for (int j = 0; j < n; j++)
    if (u == list[j].child && v == list[j].parent) return true;
  return false;
} //end inEdgeList

private static void sortEdges(UndirectedEdge[] list, int n) {
//sort list[0] to list[n-1] by increasing weight
  int i, j;
  for (i = 1; i < n; i++) {
    UndirectedEdge hold = list[i];
    j = i - 1;
    while (j >= 0 && hold.weight < list[j].weight) {
      list[j+1] = list[j];
      j = j - 1;
    }
    list[j+1] = hold;
  } //end for
} //end sortEdges
```

If graph data has been stored in a file, **graph.in**, and we want to send output to the file, **graph.out**, the statements:

```
Scanner in = new Scanner(new FileReader("graph.in"));
PrintWriter out = new PrintWriter(new FileWriter("graph.out"));
int numVertices = in.nextInt();
Graph G = new Graph(out, numVertices);
G.buildGraph(in);
G.Kruskal(100); //if the maximum number of edges could be 100
```

will read the data, build the graph, construct the minimum-spanning tree using Kruskal's algorithm and send the results to **graph.out**.

Exercises 5

1. Write methods which, given the name of a node, returns the in-degree and out-degree of the node.

2. Given the following graph:

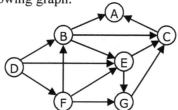

Give the depth-first and breadth-first traversals of the graph starting at D. Edges of a node are processed *in alphabetical order*.

Assume that a depth-first traversal is performed starting at D and that *edges of a node are processed in alphabetical order*. Indicate the discovery and finish times for each node and label each edge with T (tree edge), B (back edge), F (forward edge) or C (cross edge), according to its type.

3. Given the following graph:

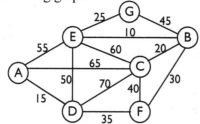

Give the adjacency matrix and list representation of the graph.

Give the depth-first and breadth-first traversals starting at **A**. Edges of a node are processed in alphabetical order.

Starting at **A**, derive and draw the minimum-cost spanning trees obtained using Prim's and Kruskal's algorithms.

Derive the minimal-cost paths from C to every other node using Dijkstra's algorithm. For each node, give the cost and the path to get to the node.

4. Write a non-recursive method for performing depth-first traversal on a graph.

5. The following is the adjacency matrix representation of a directed graph, G, with 5 nodes, assumed numbered 1 to 5 from left to right.

$$
\begin{matrix}
0 & 5 & 8 & -4 & \infty \\
-2 & 0 & \infty & \infty & \infty \\
\infty & -3 & 0 & 9 & \infty \\
\infty & 7 & \infty & 0 & 2 \\
6 & \infty & 7 & \infty & 0
\end{matrix}
$$

The Bellman-Ford algorithm is to be used to find the shortest paths from node 5 to all other nodes. Show the distance and parent values after each of the first 4 passes. (One pass processes *all* the edges of the graph.) The edges are to be processed in the order left to right, top to bottom.

6. A rectangular board is divided into m rows and n columns ($2 <= m, n <= 100$). A robot jumps from one square x to another square y as follows: from x, it moves 2 squares, either horizontally or vertically, and then it moves 1 square in a direction perpendicular to the previous direction to get to y. It can move horizontally either to the left or to the right and vertically either up or down. (A robot move is similar to a knight move in chess.)

Assume that the top-left square is (1, 1) and the bottom-right square is (m, n). The robot is put in the square with coordinates (x, y) ($1 <= x <= m, 1 <= y <= n$) .

The robot wishes to get to a different square (u, v) ($1 <= u <= m, 1 <= v <= n$) using only the jumps described above. Write a program to find the minimal number S of jumps needed to get to (u, v) as well as the sequence of squares visited in reaching (u, v). Data consists of values for m, n, x, y, u and v.

7. On a map there are n cities numbered 1 to n. The map shows the highways leaving each city to neighbouring cities and their respective distances. Highways run in both directions and do not intersect each other.

Write an algorithm to determine the set of highways, with smallest total distance, that connect all cities.

Given the city numbers i and j, write a function to print the shortest travel route from i to j.

8. When a depth-first traversal is performed on an undirected graph, all edges will be classified as either *tree* or *back* only. Verify this. Write a method to perform a depth-first traversal and classify the edges of an undirected graph.

9. A maze has a single entry point and a single exit point. On each corridor there is an item with a known value. If you walk along a corridor, you can pick up the item. However, you cannot retrace your steps and you can walk along a corridor only in the direction of an arrow painted on the floor. Write a program which, given a map of the maze, advises which path to take to collect the most valuable treasure.

10. A telephone network is represented by an undirected graph. Each vertex represents a switching station and each edge represents a communication line with a given bandwidth. The bandwidth on a path between two stations is the lowest bandwidth on the path. Write a method which (a) given a station S, finds the set of stations which can be reached from S using no more than 3 lines and (b) given two stations, finds the maximum bandwidth among all paths between the two stations.

6 Hashing

In this chapter, we will explain:

- the fundamental ideas on which hashing is based
- how to solve the *search and insert* problem using hashing
- how to delete an item from a hash table
- how to resolve collisions using linear probing
- how to resolve collisions using quadratic probing
- how to resolve collisions using chaining
- how to resolve collisions using linear probing with double hashing
- how to link items in order in a hash table

Searching for an item in a table is a common operation in many applications. In this chapter, we discuss a very fast method for performing this search.

6.1 The *search and insert* problem

The classical statement of the 'search and insert' problem is:

> *Given a list of items (the list may be empty initially), search for a given item in the list. If the item is not found, insert it in the list.*

Items can be things such as numbers (student, account, employee, vehicle, etc), names, words or strings in general. For example, suppose we have a set of integers, not necessarily distinct, and we want to find out how many distinct integers there are.

We start with an empty list. For each integer, we look for it in the list. If it is not found, it is added to the list and counted. If it is found, there is nothing to do.

In solving this problem, a major design decision is how to search the list which, in turn, will depend on how the list is stored and how a new integer is added. The following are some possibilities:

1. The list is stored in an array and a new integer is placed in the next available position in the array. This implies that a sequential search must be used to look for an incoming integer. This method has the advantages of simplicity and easy addition, but searching takes longer as more numbers are put in the list.

2. The list is stored in an array and a new integer is added in such a way that the list is always in order. This may entail moving numbers which have already been stored so that the new number may be slotted in the right place. However, since the list is in order, a binary search can be used to search for an incoming integer. For this method, searching is faster but insertion is slower than in

method 1. Since, in general, searching is done more frequently than inserting, this method might be preferable to method 1.

Another advantage here is that, at the end, the integers will be in order, if this is important. If method 1 is used, the numbers will have to be sorted.

3. The list is stored as an unsorted linked list so must be searched sequentially. Since the entire list must be traversed if an incoming number is not present, the new number can be added at the head or tail; both are equally easy.

4. The list is stored as a sorted linked list. A new number must be inserted 'in place' to maintain the order. Once the position is found, insertion is easy. The entire list does not have to be traversed if an incoming number is not present, but we are still restricted to a sequential search.

5. The list is stored in a binary search tree. Searching is reasonably fast provided the tree does not become too unbalanced. Adding a number is easy—only a matter of setting a couple links. An in-order traversal of the tree will give the numbers in sorted order, if this is required.

Yet another possibility is the method called *hashing*. As we will see, this has the advantages of extremely fast search times and easy insertion.

6.2 Hashing fundamentals

We will explain some fundamental ideas in hashing by solving the problem discussed above. The list (of integers) will be stored in an array **num[1]** to **num[n]**. In our example, we will assume **n** is 12.

num

Initially, there are no numbers in the list. Suppose the first incoming number is 52. The idea behind hashing is to convert 52 (usually called the *key*) into a valid table location (**k**, say). Here, the valid table locations are 1 to 12.

If there is no number in **num[k]**, then 52 is stored in that location. If **num[k]** is occupied by another key, we say a *collision* has occurred, and we must find another location in which to try and place 52. This is called *resolving the collision*.

The *method* used to convert a key to a table location is called the *hash function* (**H**, say). *Any* calculation which produces a valid table location (array subscript) can be used, but, as we shall see, some functions give better results than others.

For example, we could use **H1(key) = key % 10 + 1**. In other words, we add 1 to the last digit of the key. Thus, 52 would "hash" to 3. Note that **H1** produces locations between 1 and 10 only. If the table had 100 locations, say, the function would be *valid* but it may not be a good function to use.

Note also that **H(key) = key % 10** would not be a proper hash function here since, for instance, 50 would "hash" to 0 and there is no table location 0. Of course, if locations started from subscript 0, then **key % 10** would be valid, provided there were at least 10 locations.

Another function is **H2(key) = key % 12 + 1**. The expression **key % 12** produces a value between 0 and 11; adding 1 gives values between 1 and 12. In general, **key % n + 1** produces values between 1 and **n**, inclusive. We will use this function in our example.

H2(52) = 52 % 12 + 1 = 5. We say, "52 hashes to location 5". Since **num[5]** is empty, we place 52 in **num[5]**.

Suppose, later on, we are searching for 52. We first apply the hash function and we get 5. We compare **num[5]** with 52; they match so we find 52 with just one comparison.

Now suppose the following keys come in the order given:

> 52 33 84 43 16 59 31 23 61

- 52 is placed in **num[5]**;
- 33 hashes to 10; **num[10]** is empty so 33 is placed in **num[10]**;
- 84 hashes to 1; **num[1]** is empty so 84 is placed in **num[1]**;
- 43 hashes to 8; **num[8]** is empty so 43 is placed in **num[8]**;

At this stage, we have:

num

84				52			43		33		
1	2	3	4	5	6	7	8	9	10	11	12

- 16 hashes to 5; **num[5]** is occupied and not by 16—we have a collision. To resolve the collision, we must find another location in which to put 16. One obvious choice is to try the very next location, 6; **num[6]** is empty so 16 is placed in **num[6]**;
- 59 hashes to 12; **num[12]** is empty so 59 is placed in **num[12]**;
- 31 hashes to 8; **num[8]** is occupied and not by 31—we have a collision. We try the next location, 9; **num[9]** is empty so 31 is placed in **num[9]**;

At this stage, we have:

num

84				52	16		43	31	33		59
1	2	3	4	5	6	7	8	9	10	11	12

- 23 hashes to 12; **num[12]** is occupied and not by 23—we have a collision. We must try the next location, but what is the next location here? We pretend that the table is 'circular' so that location 1 follows location 12. However, **num[1]** is occupied and not by 23. So we try **num[2]**; **num[2]** is empty so 23 is placed in **num[2]**;

- finally, 61 hashes to 2; **num[2]** is occupied and not by 61—we have a collision. We try the next location, 3; **num[3]** is empty so 61 is placed in **num[3]**.

The following shows the array after all the numbers have been inserted:

num

84	23	61		52	16		43	31	33		59
1	2	3	4	5	6	7	8	9	10	11	12

Note that if a number is already in the array, the above method would find it. For example, suppose we are searching for 23.

- 23 hashes to 12;
- **num[12]** is occupied and not by 23;
- we try the next location, 1; **num[1]** is occupied and not by 23;
- we next try **num[2]**; **num[2]** is occupied by 23—we find it.

Suppose we are searching for 33; 33 hashes to 10 and **num[10]** contains 33—we find it immediately.

As an exercise, determine the state of **num** after the above numbers have been added using the hash function **H1(key) = key % 10 + 1**.

We can summarize the process described with the following algorithm:

```
//find or insert 'key' in the hash table, num[1..n]
loc = H(key)
while (num[loc] is not empty && num[loc] != key) loc = loc % n + 1
if (num[loc] is empty) { //key is not in the table
  num[loc] = key
  add 1 to the count of distinct numbers
}
else print key, " found in location ", loc
```

Note the expression **loc % n + 1** for going to the next location. If **loc** is less than **n**, **loc % n** is simply **loc** and the expression is the same as **loc + 1**. If **loc** *is* **n**, **loc % n** is 0 and the expression evaluates to 1. In either case, **loc** takes on the value of the next location.

The alert reader will realize that we exit the **while** loop when either **num[loc]** is empty or it contains the key. What if neither happens so the **while** loop *never* exits? This situation will arise if the table is completely full (no empty locations) and does not contain the key we are searching for.

However, *in practice*, we never allow the hash table to become completely full. We always ensure that there are a few 'extra' locations which are not filled by keys, so that the **while** statement *will* exit at some point. In general, the hash technique works better when there are more free locations in the table.

How does the algorithm tell when a location is "empty"? We will need to initialize the array with some value that indicates "empty". For instance, if the keys are positive integers, we can use 0 or -1 as the "empty" value.

Let us write Program P6.1 which reads integers from a file, **numbers.in**, and uses a hash technique to determine the number of distinct integers in the file.

Program P6.1

```
import java.util.*;
import java.io.*;
public class DistinctNumbers {
   final static int MaxNumbers = 20;
   final static int N = 23;
   final static int Empty = 0;
   public static void main(String[] args) throws IOException {
      Scanner in = new Scanner(new FileReader("numbers.in"));
      int[] num = new int[N + 1];
      for (int j = 1; j <= N; j++) num[j] = Empty;
      int distinct = 0;
      while (in.hasNextInt()) {
         int key = in.nextInt();
         int loc = key % N + 1;
         while (num[loc] != Empty && num[loc] != key) loc = loc % N + 1;
         if (num[loc] == Empty) { //key is not in the table
            if (distinct == MaxNumbers) {
               System.out.printf("\nTable full: %d not added\n", key);
               System.exit(1);
            }
            num[loc] = key;
            distinct++;
         }
      }
      System.out.printf("\nThere are %d distinct numbers\n", distinct);
      in.close();
   } //end main
} //end class DistinctNumbers
```

If **numbers.in** contains

25 28 29 23 26 35 22 31 21 26 25 21 31 32 26 20 36 21 27 24

P6.1 prints

There are 14 distinct numbers

Notes on P6.1

- **MaxNumbers** (20) is the maximum amount of distinct numbers catered for.

- **N** (23) is the hash table size, a little bigger than **MaxNumbers** so that there is always at least 3 free locations in the table.
- The hash table occupies **num[1]** to **num[N]**. If you wish, **num[0]** may be used; in this case, the hash function could simply be **key % N**.
- If **key** is not in the table (an empty location is encountered), we first check if the number of entries has reached **MaxNumbers**. If it has, we declare the table full and do not add **key**. Otherwise, we put **key** in the table and count it.
- If **key** is found, we simply go on to read the next number.

6.2.1 The hash function

In the last section, we saw how an integer key can be "hashed" to a table location. It turns out that the "remainder" operation (%) often gives good results for such keys. But what if the keys were non-numeric, for example, words or names?

The first task is to convert a non-numeric key to a number and then apply "remainder". Suppose the key is a word. Perhaps the simplest thing to do is add up the *numeric value* of each letter in the word. If the word is stored in a string variable, **word**, we can do this as follows:

```
int wordNum = 0;
for (int j = 0; j < word.length(); j++) wordNum += word.charAt(j);
loc = wordNum % n + 1; //loc is assigned a value from 1 to n
```

This method will work but one objection is that words which contain the same letters would hash to the same location. For example, *mate*, *meat* and *team* will all hash to the same location. In hashing, we must try to avoid deliberately hashing keys to the same location. One way around this is to assign a *weight* to each letter depending on its *position* in the word.

We can assign weights arbitrarily—the main goal is to avoid hashing keys with the same letters to the same location. For instance, we can assign 3 to the first position, 5 to the second position, 7 to the third position, and so on. The following shows how:

```
int wordNum = 0;
int w = 3;
for (int j = 0; j < word.length(); j++) {
  wordNum += word.charAt(j) * w;
  w = w + 2;
}
loc = wordNum % n + 1; //loc is assigned a value from 1 to n
```

The same technique will work if a key contains arbitrary characters.

In hashing, we want the keys to be scattered all over the table. If, for instance, keys are hashed to one area of the table, we can end up with an unnecessarily high number of collisions. To this end, we should try to use *all* of the key. For example, if the keys are alphabetic, it would be unwise to map all keys beginning with the same letter to the same location. Put another way, we should avoid systematically hitting the same location.

And since hashing is meant to be fast, the hash function should be relatively easy to calculate. The speed advantage will be diminished if we spend too much time computing the hash location.

6.2.2 Deleting an item from a hash table

Consider, again, the array after all the sample numbers have been inserted:

num

84	23	61		52	16		43	31	33		59
1	2	3	4	5	6	7	8	9	10	11	12

Recall that 43 and 31 both hashed initially to location 8. Suppose we want to delete 43. The first thought might be to set its location to empty. Assume we did this (set **num[8]** to empty) and were now looking for 31. *This* will hash to 8; but since **num[8]** is empty we will conclude, wrongly, that 31 is not in the table. So we cannot delete an item simply by setting its location to empty since other items may become unreachable. .

The easiest solution is to set its location to a *deleted* value—some value which cannot be confused with *empty* or a key. In this example, if the keys are positive integers, we can use 0 for *empty* and -1 for *deleted*.

Now, when searching, we still check for the key or an empty location—deleted locations are ignored. A common error is to stop the search at a deleted location; doing so would lead to incorrect conclusions.

If our search reveals that an incoming key is not in the table, the key can be inserted in an empty location or a deleted one, if one was encountered along the way. For example, suppose we had deleted 43 by setting **num[8]** to -1. If we now search for 55, we will check locations 8, 9, 10 and 11. Since **num[11]** is empty, we conclude that 55 is not in the table.

We can, if we wish, set **num[11]** to 55. But we could write our algorithm to remember the deleted location at 8. If we do, we can then insert 55 in **num[8]**. This is better since we will find 55 faster than if it were in **num[11]**. We would also be making better use of our available locations by reducing the number of deleted locations.

What if there are several deleted locations along the way? It is best to use the first one encountered since this will reduce the search time for the key. With these ideas, we can rewrite our search/insert algorithm as follows:

```
//find or insert 'key' in the hash table, num[1..n]
loc = H(key)
deletedLoc = 0
while (num[loc] != Empty && num[loc] != key) {
    if (deletedLoc == 0 && num[loc] == Deleted) deletedLoc = loc
    loc = loc % n + 1
}
if (num[loc] == Empty) { //key not found
    if (deletedLoc != 0) loc = deletedLoc
    num[loc] = key
}
else print key, " found in location ", loc
```

Note that we still search until we find an empty location or the key. If we meet a deleted location and **deletedLoc** is 0, this means it's the first one. Of course, if we *never* meet a deleted location and the key is not in the table, it will be inserted in an empty location.

6.3 Ways to resolve collisions

In P6.1, we resolve a collision by looking at the next location in the table. This is, perhaps, the simplest way to resolve a collision. We say we resolve the collision using *linear probing*.

6.3.1 Linear probing

This method is characterized by the statement **loc = loc + 1**. Consider, again, the state of **num** after the 9 numbers have been added:

num

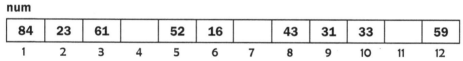

84	23	61		52	16		43	31	33		59
1	2	3	4	5	6	7	8	9	10	11	12

As you can see, the chances of hashing a new key to an empty location decreases as the table fills up. Suppose a key hashes to location 12. It will be placed in **num[4]** after trying locations 12, 1, 2 and 3. In fact, any new key which hashes to 12, 1, 2, 3 or 4 will end up in **num[4]**. When that happens, we will have a long, unbroken chain of keys from location 12 to location 6. Any new key hashing to this chain will end up in **num[7]**, creating an even longer chain.

This phenomenon of "clustering" is one of the main drawbacks of linear probing. Long chains tend to get longer since the probability of hashing to a long chain is usually greater than that of hashing to a short chain. It is also easy for two short chains to be joined, creating a longer chain which, in turn, will tend to get longer. For example, any key which ends up in **num[7]** will create a long chain from locations 5 to 10.

We define two types of clustering:

1. *Primary clustering* occurs when keys which hash to *different* locations trace the *same* sequence in looking for an empty location. Linear probing exhibits primary clustering since a key which hashes to 5, say, will trace 5, 6, 7, 8, 9, etc. and a key which hashes to 6 will trace 6, 7, 8, 9, etc.

2. *Secondary clustering* occurs when keys which hash to *the same* location trace the same sequence in looking for an empty location. Linear probing exhibits secondary clustering since keys which hash to 5, say, will trace the same sequence 5, 6, 7, 8, 9, etc.

Methods of resolving collisions which hope to improve on linear probing will target the elimination of primary and/or secondary clustering.

One may wonder if using **loc = loc + k** where **k** is a constant greater than 1 (e.g. 3) will give any better results than **loc = loc + 1**. As it turns out, this will not alter the clustering phenomenon since groups of **k**-apart keys will still be formed.

In addition, it can even be worse than when **k** is 1 since it is possible that not all locations will be generated. Suppose the table size is 12, **k** is 3 and a key hashes to 5. The sequence of locations traced will be 5, 8, 11, 2 (11 + 3 − 12), 5 and the sequence repeats itself. By comparison, when **k** is 1, all locations are generated.

However, this is not really a problem. If the table size is **m** and **k** is "relatively prime" to **m** (their only common factor is 1), then all locations are generated. Two numbers will be relatively prime if one is a prime and the other is not a multiple of it, e.g. 5 and 12. But being prime is not a necessary condition. The numbers 21 and 50 (neither of which is prime) are relatively prime since they have no common factors other than 1.

If **k** is 5 and **m** is 12, a key hashing to 5 will trace the sequence 5, 10, 3, 8, 1, 6, 11, 4, 9, 2, 7, 12—all locations are generated. A key hashing to any other location will also generate all locations.

In any case, being able to generate all locations is academic since if we had to trace many locations to find an empty one, the search would be too slow and we would probably need to use another method.

Notwithstanding the above, it turns out that **loc = loc + k** where **k** *varies* with the key gives us one of the best ways to implement hashing. We will see how in Section 6.3.4.

So how fast is the linear method? We are interested in the average *search length*, that is, the number of locations that must be examined to find or insert a given key. In the above example, the search length of 33 is 1, the search length of 61 is 2 and the search length of 23 is 3.

The search length is a function of the *load factor*, *f*, of the table, where

$$f = \frac{number\ of\ entries\ in\ table}{number\ of\ table\ locations} = \text{fraction of table filled}$$

For a successful search, the average number of comparisons is $\frac{1}{2}\left(1 + \frac{1}{1-f}\right)$ and for

an unsuccessful search, the average number of comparisons is $\frac{1}{2}\left(1 + \frac{1}{(1-f)^2}\right)$.

Note that the search length depends only on the fraction of the table filled, *not* on the table size.

The following table shows how the search length increases as the table fills up:

f	successful search length	unsuccessful search length
0.25	1.2	1.4
0.50	1.5	2.5
0.75	2.5	8.5
0.90	5.5	50.5

At 90% full, the average successful search length is a reasonable 5.5. However, it can take quite long (50.5 probes) to determine that a new key is not in the table. If linear probe is being used, it would be wise to ensure that the table does not become more than about 75% full. This way, we can guarantee good performance with a simple algorithm.

6.3.2 Quadratic probing

In this method, suppose an incoming key collides with another at location **loc**, we go forward $ai + bi^2$ where a, b are constants and i takes on the value 1 for the first collision, 2 if there is a second collision, 3 if there is a third collision, and so on. For example, if we let $a = 1$ and $b = 1$, we go forward $i + i^2$ from location **loc**. Suppose the initial hash location is 7 and there is a collision.

We calculate $i + i^2$ with $i = 1$; this gives 2 so we go forward by 2 and check location $7 + 2 = 9$.

If there is still a collision, we calculate $i + i^2$ with $i = 2$; this gives 6 so we go forward by 6 and check location $9 + 6 = 15$.

If there is still a collision, we calculate $i + i^2$ with $i = 3$; this gives 12 so we go forward by 12 and check location $15 + 12 = 27$.

And so on. Each time we get a collision, we increase i by 1 and re-calculate how much we must go forward this time. We continue this way until we find the key or an empty location.

If, at any time, "going forward" takes us beyond the end of the table, we wrap around to the beginning. For example, if the table size is 25 and we go forward to location 27, we wrap to location 27 − 25, that is, location 2.

For the next incoming key, if there is a collision at the initial hash location, we set i to 1 and continue as above. It is worth noting that, for each key, the sequence of "increments" will be 2, 6, 12, 20, 30... We can, of course, get a different sequence by choosing different values for a and b.

We can summarize the process described above with the following algorithm:

```
//find or insert 'key' in the hash table, num[1..n]
loc = H(key)
i = 0
while (num[loc] != Empty && num[loc] != key) {
   i = i + 1
   loc = loc + a * i + b * i * i
   while (loc > n) loc = loc – n   //while instead of if; see note below
}
if (num[loc] == Empty) num[loc] = key
else print key, " found in location ", loc
```

Note: we use **while** instead of **if** to perform the 'wrap around' just in case the new location is more than twice the table size. For instance, suppose n is 25, the increment is 42 and we are going forward from location 20. This will take us to location 62. If we had used **if**, the 'wrap around' location would be 62 − 25 = 37 which is still outside the range of the table. With **while**, we will get the valid location 37 − 25 = 12.

Could we have used **loc % n** instead of the **while** loop? In this example, we would get the correct location but if the new location were a multiple of **n**, **loc % n** will give 0. This will be an invalid location if the table starts from 1.

With quadratic probing, keys which hash to different locations trace different sequences hence primary clustering is eliminated. However, keys which hash to the same location will trace the same sequence, so secondary clustering remains.

Other points to note:

- If n is a power of 2, i.e., $n = 2^m$ for some m, this method explores only a small fraction of the locations in the table and is, therefore, not very effective.
- If n is prime, the method can reach half the locations in the table—this is usually sufficient for most practical purposes.

6.3.3 Chaining

In this method, all items which hash to the same location are held on a linked list. One way to implement this is to let the hash table contain "top of list" pointers. For instance, if **hash[1..n]** is the hash table, then **hash[k]** will point to the linked list of all items which hash to location **k**. An item can be added to a linked list at the head, at the tail or in a position such that the list is in order.

To illustrate the method, suppose the items are integers. Each linked list item will consist of an integer value and a pointer to the next item. We use the class:

```
class Node {
  int num;
  Node next;

  Node(int n) {
    num = n;
    next = null;
  }
}
```

to create the nodes in the linked lists. We can now define **hash** as follows:

```
Node[] hash = new Node[n+1]; //assume n has a value
```

and initialize it with:

```
for (int j = 1; j <= n; j++) hash[j] = null;
```

Suppose an incoming key, **inKey**, hashes to location **k**. We must search the linked list pointed to by **hash[k]** for **inKey**. If it is not found, we must add it to the list. In our program, we will add it such that the list is in ascending order.

We write Program P6.2 to count the number of distinct integers in the input file, **numbers.in**. The program uses "hashing with chaining". At the end, we print the list of numbers which hash to each location.

```
                        Program P6.2
import java.util.*;
import java.io.*;
public class HashChain {
  final static int N = 13;
  public static void main(String[] args) throws IOException {
    Scanner in = new Scanner(new FileReader("numbers.in"));

    Node[] hash = new Node[N+1];
    for (int j = 1; j <= N; j++) hash[j] = null;

    int distinct = 0;
    while (in.hasNextInt()) {
      int key = in.nextInt();
      if (!search(key, hash, N)) distinct++;
    }
    System.out.printf("\nThere are %d distinct numbers\n", distinct);
    for (int j = 1; j <= N; j++)
      if (hash[j] != null) {
```

```
                System.out.printf("hash[%d]: ", j);
                printList(hash[j]);
            }
        in.close();
    } //end main

    public static boolean search(int inKey, Node[] hash, int n) {
    //return true if inKey is found; false, otherwise
    //insert a new key in its appropriate list so list is in order
        int k = inKey % n + 1;
        Node curr = hash[k];
        Node prev = null;
        while (curr != null && inKey > curr.num) {
            prev = curr;
            curr = curr.next;
        }
        if (curr != null && inKey == curr.num) return true; //found
        //not found; inKey is a new key; add it so list is in order
        Node np = new Node(inKey);
        np.next = curr;
        if (prev == null) hash[k] = np;
        else prev.next = np;
        return false;
    } //end search

    public static void printList(Node top) {
        while (top != null) {
            System.out.printf("%2d ", top.num);
            top = top.next;
        }
        System.out.printf("\n");
    } //end printList
} //end class HashChain

//class Node goes here
```

If **numbers.in** contains the following numbers:

```
24 57 35 37 31 98 85 47 60 32 48 82 16 96 87 46 53 92 71 56
73 85 47 46 22 40 95 32 54 67 31 44 74 40 58 42 88 29 78 87
45 13 73 29 84 48 85 29 66 73 87 17 10 83 95 25 44 93 32 39
```

P6.2 produces the following output:

```
There are 43 distinct numbers

hash[1]: 13 39 78
hash[2]: 40 53 66 92
hash[3]: 54 67 93
hash[4]: 16 29 42
```

```
hash[5]:  17 56 82 95
hash[6]:  31 44 57 83 96
hash[7]:  32 45 58 71 84
hash[8]:  46 85 98
hash[9]:  47 60 73
hash[10]: 22 35 48 74 87
hash[11]: 10 88
hash[12]: 24 37
hash[13]: 25
```

If **m** keys have been stored in the linked lists and there are **n** hash locations, the average length of a list is $\frac{m}{n}$, and since we must search the lists sequentially, the average successful search length is $\frac{m}{2n}$. The search length can be reduced by increasing the number of hash locations.

Another way to implement "hashing with chaining" is to use a single array and use array subscripts as links. We can use the declarations:

```
class Node {
    int num;    //key
    int next;   //array subscript of the next item in the list
}
Node[] hash = new Node[MaxItems+1];
```

The first part of the table, **hash[1..n]**, say, is designated as the hash table and the remaining locations are used as an *overflow* table, thus:

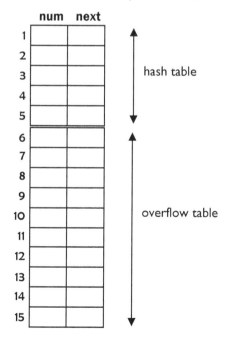

Here, **hash[1..5]** is the hash table and **hash[6..15]** is the overflow table.

Suppose **key** hashes to location **k** in the hash table:

- If **hash[k].num** is empty (0, say), we set it to **key** and set **hash[k].next** to -1, say, to indicate a null pointer.
- If **hash[k].num** is not 0, we must search the list starting at **k** for **key**. If it is not found, we put it in the next free location (**f**, say) in the overflow table and link it to the list starting at **hash[k]**. One way to link it is:

      hash[f].next = hash[k].next;
      hash[k].next = f;

- Another way to link the new key is to add it at the end of the list. If **L** is the location of the last node in the list, this could be done with:

      hash[L].next = f;
      hash[f].next = -1;   //this is now the last node

If deletions are possible, we will have to decide what to do with deleted locations. One possibility is to keep a list of all available locations in the overflow table. When one is needed to store a key, it is retrieved from the list. When an item is deleted, its location is returned to the list.

Initially, we can link all the items in the overflow table as follows:

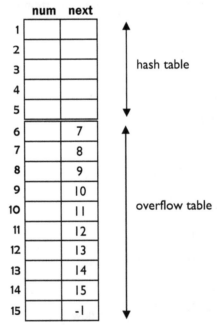

and let the variable **free** point to the first item in the list; here, **free** = 6. Item 6 points to item 7 which points to item 8 and so on with item 15 at the end of the list.

Suppose 37 hashes to location 2. This is empty so 37 is stored in **hash[2].num**. If another number (24, say) hashes to 2, it must be stored in the overflow table. First we must get a location from the "free list". This can be done with:

```
f = free;
free = hash[free].next;
return f;
```

Here, 6 is returned and **free** is set to 7. The number 24 is stored in location 6 and **hash[2].next** is set to 6. At this stage, we have (with **free** = 7):

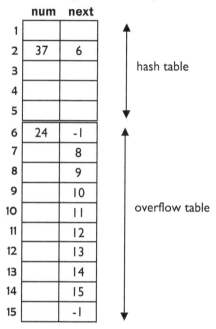

In this scenario, consider how an item may be deleted. There are two cases to consider:

1. If the item to be deleted is in the hash table (at **k**, say) then:
```
if (hash[k].next == -1) set hash[k].num to Empty   //only item in the list
else { //copy an item from the overflow table to the hash table
  j = hash[k].next;
  hash[k] = hash[j];   //copy information at location j to location k
  return j to the free list     //see next
}
```

We can return a location (**j**, say) to the free list with:
```
hash[j].next = free;
free = j;
```

2. If the item to be deleted is in the overflow table (at **curr**, say) and **prev** is the location of the item which points to the one to be deleted, then:
```
hash[prev].next = hash[curr].next;
return curr to the free list
```

Now consider how an incoming key might be processed. Suppose **free** is 9 and the number 52 hashes to location 2. We search the list starting at 2 for 52. It is not found, so 52 is stored in the next free location, 9; **hash[6].next** is set to 9 and **hash[9].next** is set to -1.

In general, we can perform a search for **key** and, if not found, insert it at the end of the list with:

```
k = H(key)     //H is the hash function
if (hash[k].num == Empty) {
  hash[k].num = key
  hash[k].next = -1
}
else {
  curr = k
  prev = -1
  while (curr != -1 && hash[curr].num != key) {
    prev = curr
    curr = hash[curr].next
  }
  if (curr != -1) key is in the list at location curr
  else {  //key is not present
    hash[free].num = key     //assume free list is not empty
    hash[free].next = -1
    hash[prev].next = free
    free = hash[free].next
  }
}
```

6.3.4 Linear probing with double hashing[4]

In Section 6.3.1, we saw that using **loc = loc + k** where **k** is a constant greater than 1 does not give us a better performance than when **k** is 1. However, by letting **k** vary with the key, we can get excellent results.

The most natural way to let **k** vary with the key is to use a second hash function. The first hash function will generate the initial table location. If there is a collision, the second hash function will generate the increment, **k**. If the table locations run from **1** to **n**, we can use the following:

```
convert key to a numeric value, num (if it is not already numeric)
loc = num % n + 1     //this gives the initial hash location
k = num % (n - 2) + 1 //this gives the increment for this key
```

We mentioned before that it is wise to choose **n** (the table size) as a prime number. In this method, we get even better results if **n - 2** is also prime (in this case, **n** and **n - 2** are called *twin primes*, e.g. 103/101, 1021/1019).

---

[4] The technique is sometimes referred to as "open addressing with double hashing".

214

Apart from the fact that **k** is not fixed, the method is the same as *linear probing*. We describe it in terms of two hash functions, **H1** and **H2**. **H1** produces the initial hash location, a value between 1 and **n**, inclusive. **H2** produces the increment, a value between 1 and **n - 1** that is relatively prime to **n**; this is desirable so that, if required, many locations will be probed. As discussed earlier, if **n** is prime, any value between 1 and **n - 1** will be relatively prime to it. In the example above, the second hash function produces a value between 1 and **n - 2**. Here is the algorithm:

```
//find or insert 'key' using "linear probing with double hashing"
loc = H1(key)
k = H2(key)
while (hash[loc] != Empty && hash[loc] != key) {
  loc = loc + k
  if (loc > n) loc = loc - n
}
if (hash[loc] == Empty) hash[loc] = key
else print key, " found in location ", loc
```

As before, to ensure that the while loop exits at some point, we do not allow the table to become completely full. If we wish to cater for **MaxItems**, say, we declare the table size to be bigger than **MaxItems**. In general, the more free locations in the table, the better the hash technique works.

However, with "double hashing", we do not need as many free locations as with normal "linear probe" to guarantee good performance. This is so because "double hashing" eliminates both primary and secondary clustering.

Primary clustering is eliminated since keys which hash to different locations will generate different sequences of locations. Secondary clustering is eliminated since *different* keys which hash to the *same* location will generate *different* sequences. This is so since, in general, different keys will generate different increments (**k**, in the algorithm). It would be a rare coincidence indeed for two keys to be hashed to the same values by both **H1** and **H2**.

In practice, the performance of any hashing application can be improved by keeping information on how often each key is accessed. If we have this information beforehand, we can simply load the hash table with the most popular items first and the least popular last. This will lower the average access time for all keys.

If we do not have this information beforehand, we can keep a counter with each key and increment it each time the key is accessed. After some predefined time (a month, say), we reload the table with the most popular items first and the least popular last. We then reset the counters and garner statistics for the next month. This way we can ensure that the application remains fine-tuned since different items may become popular in the next month.

6.4 Example – word frequency count

Consider, once again, the problem of writing a program to do a frequency count of the words in a passage. Output consists of an alphabetical listing of the words with their frequencies. Now, we will store the words in a hash table using "linear probing with double hashing".

Each element in the table consists of three fields—**word**, **freq** and **next**. We will use the following class to create objects to be stored in the table:

```
class WordInfo {
    String word = "";
    int freq = 0;
    int next = -1;
} //end class WordInfo
```

We declare and initialize the table with:

```
WordInfo[] wordTable = new WordInfo[N+1]; //N - table size
for (int j = 1; j <= N; j++) wordTable[j] = new WordInfo();
```

The table is searched for each incoming word. If the word is not found, it is added to the table and its frequency count is set to 1. If the word is found, then its frequency count is incremented by 1.

In addition, when a word is added to the table, we set links such that we maintain a linked list of the words in alphabetical order. The variable **first** points to the first word in order. For example, suppose five words have been stored in the hash table. We link them, via **next**, as shown below, with **first** = 6:

	word	freq	next
1	for	2	7
2			
3	the	4	-1
4	man	1	3
5			
6	boy	1	1
7	girl	2	4

Thus, the first word is **boy** which points to **for** (1), which points to **girl** (7), which points to **man** (4), which points to **the** (3), which does not point to anything (−1). The words are linked in alphabetical order: **boy for girl man the**. Note that the linking works no matter where the hash algorithm places a word.

The hash algorithm first places the word. Then, regardless of where it is placed, that location is linked to maintain the words in order. For example, suppose, the new word **kid** hashes to location 2. Then the link of **kid** will be set to 4 (to point to **man**) and the link of **girl** will be set to 2 (to point to **kid**).

We print the alphabetical listing by traversing the linked list. Program P6.3 shows all the details.

```
                          Program P6.3
import java.io.*;
import java.util.*;
public class WordFrequencyHash {
  static  Scanner in;
  static  PrintWriter out;
  final static int N = 13; //table size
  final static int MaxWords = 10;
  final static String Empty = "";

  public static void main(String[] args) throws IOException {

    in = new Scanner(new FileReader("wordFreq.in"));
    out = new PrintWriter(new FileWriter("wordFreq.out"));

    WordInfo[] wordTable = new WordInfo[N+1];
    for (int j = 1; j <= N; j++) wordTable[j] = new WordInfo();

    int first = -1; //points to first word in alphabetical order
    int numWords = 0;

    in.useDelimiter("[^a-zA-Z]+");
    while (in.hasNext()) {
      String word = in.next().toLowerCase();
      int loc = search(wordTable, word);
      if (loc > 0) wordTable[loc].freq++;
      else //this is a new word
        if (numWords < MaxWords) { //if table is not full
          first = addToTable(wordTable, word, -loc, first);
          ++numWords;
        }
        else out.printf("'%s' not added to table\n", word);
    }
    printResults(wordTable, first);
    in.close();
    out.close();
  } // end main

  public static int search(WordInfo[] table, String key) {
  //search for key in table; if found, return its location; if not,
  //return -loc if it must be inserted in location loc
    int wordNum = convertToNumber(key);
    int loc = wordNum % N + 1;
    int k = wordNum % (N - 2) + 1;
```

```java
      while (!table[loc].word.equals(Empty) && !table[loc].word.equals(key)) {
        loc = loc + k;
        if (loc > N) loc = loc - N;
      }
      if (table[loc].word.equals(Empty)) return -loc;
      return loc;
  } // end search

  public static int convertToNumber(String key) {
      int wordNum = 0;
      int w = 3;
      for (int j = 0; j < key.length(); j++) {
        wordNum += key.charAt(j) * w;
        w = w + 2;
      }
      return wordNum;
  } //end convertToNumber

  public static int addToTable(WordInfo[] table, String key,
                                     int loc, int head) {
  //stores key in table[loc] and links it in alphabetical order
      table[loc].word = key;
      table[loc].freq = 1;
      int curr = head;
      int prev = -1;
      while (curr != -1 && key.compareTo(table[curr].word) > 0) {
        prev = curr;
        curr = table[curr].next;
      }
      table[loc].next = curr;
      if (prev == -1) return loc; //new first item
      table[prev].next = loc;
      return head; //first item did not change
  } //end addToTable

  public static void printResults(WordInfo[] table, int head) {
      out.printf("\nWords       Frequency\n\n");
      while (head != -1) {
        out.printf("%-15s %2d\n", table[head].word, table[head].freq);
        head = table[head].next;
      }
  } //end printResults

} //end class WordFrequencyHash

//class WordInfo goes here
```

Using a table size of 13 and **MaxWords** set to 10, when P6.3 was run with the following data in **wordFreq.in**:

> The quick brown fox jumps over the lazy dog. Congratulations!
> If the quick brown fox jumped over the lazy dog then
> Why did the quick brown fox jump over the lazy dog?

it produced the following output:

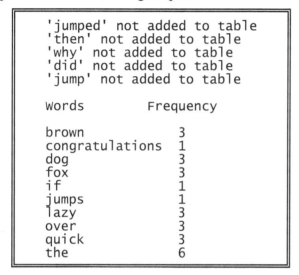

```
'jumped' not added to table
'then' not added to table
'why' not added to table
'did' not added to table
'jump' not added to table

words          Frequency

brown          3
congratulations 1
dog            3
fox            3
if             1
jumps          1
lazy           3
over           3
quick          3
the            6
```

Exercises 6

1. Integers are inserted into a hash table **H[1..11]** using the primary hash function $h_1(k) = 1 + k \bmod 11$. Show the state of the array after inserting the keys 10, 22, 31, 4, 15, 28, 17, 88 and 58 using (a) linear probing (b) quadratic probing with probe function $i + i^2$ and (c) double hashing with $h_2(k) = 1 + k \bmod 9$.

2. Integers are inserted in an integer hash table **list[1]** to **list[n]** using "linear probe with double hashing". Assume that the function **h1** produces the initial hash location and the function **h2** produces the increment. An available location has the value **Empty** and a deleted location has the value **Deleted**.

   Write a function to search for a given value **key**. If found, the function returns the location containing **key**. If not found, the function inserts **key** in the *first* deleted location encountered (if any) in searching for **key**, or an **Empty** location, and returns the location in which **key** was inserted. You may assume that **list** contains room for a new integer.

3. In a hashing application, the key consists of a string of letters. Write a hash function which, given a key and an integer **max**, returns a hash location between 1 and **max**, inclusive. Your function must use *all* of the key and should not deliberately return the same value for keys consisting of the same letters.

4. A hash table of size **n** contains two fields—an integer data field and an integer link field—called *data* and *next*, say. The *next* field is used to link data items in the hash table in ascending order. A value of -1 indicates the end of the list. The variable

top (initially set to -1) indicates the location of the smallest data item. Integers are inserted in the hash table using hash function **h1** and linear probing. The **data** field of an available location has the value **Empty** and no item is ever deleted from the table. Write programming code to search for a given value **key**. If found, do nothing. If not found, insert **key** in the table and *link it in its ordered position.* You may assume that the table contains room for a new integer.

5. In a certain application, keys which hash to the same location are held on a linked list. The hashtable location contains a pointer to the first item on the list and a new key is placed at the end of the list. Each item in the linked list consists of an integer **key**, an integer **count** and a pointer to the next element in the list. Storage for a linked list item is allocated as needed. Assume that the hash table is of size n and the call **H(key)** returns a location from 1 to n, inclusive.

   Write programming code to initialize the hash table.

   Write a function which, given the key **nkey**, searches for it If not found, add **nkey** in its appropriate position and set **count** to 0. If found, add 1 to **count**; if count reaches 10, delete the node from its current postion, place it at the head of its list and set **count** to 0.

6. Write a program to read and store a thesaurus as follows:

   Data for the program consists of lines of input. Each line contains a (variable) number of distinct words, all of which are synonyms. You may assume that words consist of letters only and are separated by one or more blanks. Words may be spelt using any combination of upper and lower case letters. All words are to be stored in a hash table using "open addressing with double hashing". A word can appear on more than one line, but each word must be inserted only once in the table. If a word appears on more than one line then all words on those lines are synonyms. This part of the data is terminated by a line containing the word **EndOfSynonyms**.

   The data structure must be organized such that, given any word, all synonyms for that word can be quickly found.

   The next part of the data consists of several commands, one per line. A valid command is designated by P, A, D or E.

   P *word* prints, in alphabetical order, all synonyms of *word*.

   A *word1 word2* adds *word1* to the list of synonyms for *word2*.

   D *word* deletes *word* from the thesaurus.

   E, on a line by itself, indicates the end of the data.

7. Write a program to compare quadratic probing, linear probing with double hashing and chaining. Data consists of an English passage and you are required to store all the distinct words in the hash tables. For each word and each method, record the number of probes required to insert the word in the hash table.

   Cater for 100 words. For quadratic probing and double hashing, use a table size of 103. For chaining, use two table sizes—23 and 53. For each of the four methods, use the same basic hash function.

   Print an alphabetical listing of the words and the number of probes for each of the four methods. Organize your output so that the performance of the methods can be easily compared.

7 Working with matrices

In this chapter, we will explain:

- how the elements of one- and two-dimensional arrays are stored
- how to conserve storage for matrices with special properties
- how to store triangular matrices to save storage
- how to store symmetric and skew-symmetric matrices to save storage
- how to store band matrices to save storage
- how to store sparse matrices to save storage
- how to store other special types of matrices to save storage

There are many applications in which large matrices are needed. Examples are common in engineering and mathematics. The bigger the matrix, the more storage is required to store it. In some cases, the storage requirement of a program is dominated by that of the matrices it needs to manipulate. In this chapter, we look at ways to take advantage of special properties a matrix may have in order to reduce the amount of memory needed to store it.

7.1 Storing 1-D and 2-D arrays

In previous chapters, we worked with trees and graphs and saw how we could write programs to manipulate these non-linear structures. In all of this, it is useful to remember that the computer's memory (primary storage) has a linear structure. Typically, *memory addresses* range from 0 to some number n where n depends on how much memory our computer has.

When we need to store a graph, say, in memory, we must find a way to translate this non-linear structure into the linear arrangement of a computer's memory. Of course, if our data structure is linear to begin with (like a one-dimensional array), the translation is easier. In this section, we consider how 1-D arrays (linear) and 2-D arrays (non-linear) are stored in memory.

Consider the declaration:

```
int[] A = new int[100];
```

The array **A** contains 100 elements, **A[0]** to **A[99]**, stored somewhere in memory. Each element is an integer which occupies 4 bytes. When we use statements like:

```
A[j] = in.nextInt();
int c = A[j] -3;
```

how does the computer know where to find **A[j]**? When the array is declared, the compiler requests 400 bytes of storage for the array. The address of the first byte of storage is usually called the *base address*, BA. This address is stored as one of the properties of **A**. Other properties would include the size and the type. Thus,

- **A[0]** is stored at memory location BA;
- **A[1]** is stored at memory location BA + 4;
- **A[2]** is stored at memory location BA + 8;
- **A[3]** is stored at memory location BA + 12;

and, in general,

- **A[j]** is stored at memory location BA + 4j;

When your program references **A[j]**, the value of **j** is determined and this value is used to calculate where **A[j]** is stored. Similar remarks apply if the subscript is an expression.

For 1-D arrays of other types, the situation is similar. If each element occupies k bytes, then **A[j]** is stored in location **BA + k * j**.

Consider now the case of a 2-D array:

```
int[][] A = new int[4][5];
```

This array has 4 rows and 5 columns—a total of 20 elements. As before, the compiler requests storage (80 bytes) to store this array and is given the base address where the array can be stored. We can think of the array as:

$$
\begin{array}{ccccc}
A_{0,0} & A_{0,1} & A_{0,2} & A_{0,3} & A_{0,4} \\
A_{1,0} & A_{1,1} & A_{1,2} & A_{1,3} & A_{1,4} \\
A_{2,0} & A_{2,1} & A_{2,2} & A_{2,3} & A_{2,4} \\
A_{3,0} & A_{3,1} & A_{3,2} & A_{3,3} & A_{3,4}
\end{array}
$$

The problem here is how to arrange the elements in a linear order to store them in memory. The two obvious choices are to store them in row order (*row-major* order) or column order (*column-major* order). We will use row order. Thus,

- **A[0][0]** is stored at memory location BA;
- **A[0][1]** is stored at memory location BA + 4;
- **A[0][2]** is stored at memory location BA + 8;
- **A[0][3]** is stored at memory location BA + 12;
- **A[0][4]** is stored at memory location BA + 16;
- **A[1][0]** is stored at memory location BA + 20;

and so on, until

- **A[3][4]** is stored at memory location BA + 76;

Where is **A[i][j]** stored? We can work out the answer as follows:

- each row occupies 20 bytes;
- there are i rows *before* the row in which **A[i][j]** is stored; these rows occupy $20i$ bytes;

- there are j elements *before* **A[i][j]** in its own row; these elements occupy $4j$ bytes;
- hence the total number of bytes before **A[i][j]** is $20i + 4j$;
- hence **A[i][j]** is stored at location BA + $20i + 4j$.

Using this formula, we see that **A[3][4]** is stored at BA + 76.

For the more general declaration:

```
int[][] A = new int[m][n];
```

we can use a similar argument to show that **A[i][j]** is stored at BA + $4(ni + j)$.

And, if each element occupies k bytes, **A[i][j]** is stored at BA + $k(ni + j)$.

7.2 Storing matrices with special properties

There are many applications in mathematics and engineering, among others, which use large two-dimensional matrices. An $m \times n$ matrix (m rows, n columns) consists of mn elements. If each element occupies k bytes, the amount of storage required to store the matrix is kmn bytes.

However, many times, such matrices have special properties which a programmer can exploit to reduce the amount of storage required. In this section, we will discuss triangular, symmetric, skew-symmetric, band and sparse matrices.

7.2.1 Triangular matrices

An $n \times n$ lower-triangular matrix is one in which the non-zero elements are all found on or below the main diagonal, in the "lower triangle"; all elements above the main diagonal are zero. The following shows a 5×5 lower-triangular matrix:

$$
\begin{array}{ccccc}
A_{1,1} & 0 & 0 & 0 & 0 \\
A_{2,1} & A_{2,2} & 0 & 0 & 0 \\
A_{3,1} & A_{3,2} & A_{3,3} & 0 & 0 \\
A_{4,1} & A_{4,2} & A_{4,3} & A_{4,4} & 0 \\
A_{5,1} & A_{5,2} & A_{5,3} & A_{5,4} & A_{5,5}
\end{array}
$$

Note that the matrix must be square—the number of rows is the same as the number of columns. In keeping with the usual mathematical treatment of matrices, we assume that the rows and columns are numbered starting from 1.

An element $A_{i,j}$ above the main diagonal has the property that $i < j$; on the main diagonal, $i = j$; below the main diagonal, $i > j$.

In order to conserve storage, we will store the lower triangle elements in a one-dimensional array, **B[1..m]**, where m is $\frac{1}{2} n(n+1)$, the number of elements in the lower triangle. We will not store the zero elements. We will not use **B[0]**; if you need to use **B[0]**, a minor adjustment to our formula below will be necessary.

The number of elements to store is derived by noting that we store 1 element from the first row, 2 elements from the second row, and so on, until n elements from the nth row. This gives a total of

$$1 + 2 + 3 + ... + n = \tfrac{1}{2} n(n+1)$$

We need to decide the order in which we will store the elements in **B**. We will use row-major order, that is, we store the elements from the first row, followed by the elements from the second row, and so on, until we store the elements from the last row. So, for the sample matrix, we will store the elements in this order:

$A_{1,1}$	$A_{2,1}$	$A_{2,2}$	$A_{3,1}$	$A_{3,2}$	$A_{3,3}$	$A_{4,1}$	$A_{4,2}$	$A_{4,3}$	$A_{4,4}$	$A_{5,1}$	$A_{5,2}$	$A_{5,3}$	$A_{5,4}$	$A_{5,5}$
1	2	3	4	5	6	7	8	9	10	11	12	13	14	15

There are 5*6/2 = 15 elements to store. We store them in **B[1]** to **B[15]**.

Given that the values are stored in **B**, how can we work out the value of $A_{i,j}$? We know that if i is less than j, the value is not stored and hence it is zero. If the value *is* stored, we can work out its position in **B** as follows:

- there are (i-1) rows before the ith row;
- there are $1 + 2 + ...+ (i\text{-}1) = \tfrac{1}{2} i(i - 1)$ elements in these rows;
- there are j elements up to $A_{i,j}$ in the ith row;
- hence, the number of elements up to, and including, $A_{i,j}$ is $\tfrac{1}{2} i(i - 1) + j$.

Thus, $A_{i,j}$ is stored in $B[\tfrac{1}{2} i(i - 1) + j]$. For example, $\mathbf{A_{4,3}}$ is stored in **B[4.3/2 + 3]**, that is, **B[9]**.

We can write a function which, given **i** and **j**, accesses **B** and returns the value of $A_{i,j}$. We assume that the values in the matrix are of type **double**.

```
public static double A(double[] B, int i, int j) {
    if (i < j) return 0.0;
    return B[i * (i – 1) / 2 + j];
}
```

By naming the function **A**, we can work with the matrix in pretty much the same way as if we *had* stored all the elements; instead of the array notation **A[i][j]**, we now use the function call **A(i, j)**.

As an exercise, write the function assuming the elements in the lower triangle are stored in column-major order.

We can treat an *upper-triangular* matrix in a similar manner. A 5 × 5 upper-triangular matrix would look like this:

$$
\begin{array}{ccccc}
A_{1,1} & A_{1,2} & A_{1,3} & A_{1,4} & A_{1,5} \\
0 & A_{2,2} & A_{2,3} & A_{2,4} & A_{2,5} \\
0 & 0 & A_{3,3} & A_{3,4} & A_{3,5} \\
0 & 0 & 0 & A_{4,4} & A_{4,5} \\
0 & 0 & 0 & 0 & A_{5,5}
\end{array}
$$

Here, an element $A_{i,j}$ is zero if $i > j$; it is in the upper triangle if $i \le j$. As an exercise, devise a scheme for storing the upper-triangular elements in a one-dimensional array and write an appropriate access function to return $A_{i,j}$.

7.2.2 Symmetric and skew-symmetric matrices

A *symmetric* matrix, **A**, is one in which $A_{i,j} = A_{j,i}$. If we think of the main diagonal as a mirror, elements which are reflections of each other have the same value. We can take advantage of this property by storing the elements in the lower triangle, say. When we need a value from the upper triangle, we can retrieve its "reflection" from the lower triangle. For instance, if we need $A_{2,4}$ (not stored) we simply retrieve $A_{4,2}$ (stored).

We can write the access function for $A_{i,j}$ based on the following:

- if $A_{i,j}$ is in the lower triangle $(i \ge j)$, retrieve it from $B[\frac{1}{2} i(i - 1) + j]$;
- if it is in the upper triangle, reverse the subscripts and retrieve $B[\frac{1}{2} j(j - 1) + i]$.

Here is the function:

```
public static double A(double[] B, int i, int j) {
    if (i >= j) return B[i * (i – 1) / 2 + j];
    return B[j * (j – 1) / 2 + i];
}
```

A *skew-symmetric* matrix, **A**, is one in which $A_{i,j} = -A_{j,i}$. This impiles that the diagonal elements are zero[5]. We can picture this as:

$$
\begin{array}{ccccc}
0 & A_{1,2} & A_{1,3} & A_{1,4} & A_{1,5} \\
A_{2,1} & 0 & A_{2,3} & A_{2,4} & A_{2,5} \\
A_{3,1} & A_{3,2} & 0 & A_{3,4} & A_{3,5} \\
A_{4,1} & A_{4,2} & A_{4,3} & 0 & A_{4,5} \\
A_{5,1} & A_{5,2} & A_{5,3} & A_{5,4} & 0
\end{array}
$$

Since the diagonal elements are zero, we do not need to store them. And since the elements in the upper triangle can be derived from those in the lower triangle, we do not need to store them.

---

[5] If we want to allow the diagonal elements to be non-zero, we can say $A_{i,j} = -A_{j,i}$, $i \ne j$.

225

We store the elements in the strictly lower triangle in a one-dimensional array, **B**, with $A_{2,1}$ in **B[1]**, $A_{3,1}$ in **B[2]**, $A_{3,2}$ in **B[3]**, and so on, with $A_{5,4}$ in **B[10]**. Based on this, we derive the access formula for $A_{i,j}$ as follows:

- there are $(i\text{-}1)$ rows before the ith row;
- there are $0 + 1 + 2 + ... + (i\text{-}2) = \frac{1}{2}(i-1)(i-2)$ elements in these rows;
- there are j elements up to $A_{i,j}$ in the ith row;
- hence, the number of elements up to, and including, $A_{i,j}$ is $\frac{1}{2}(i-1)(i-2) + j$.

Thus, $A_{i,j}$ is stored in $B[(i-1)(i-2)/2 + j]$. For example, $A_{4,3}$ is stored in **B[3.2/2 + 3]**, that is, **B[6]**.

We can write the access function for $A_{i,j}$ based on the following:

- if $A_{i,j}$ is on the main diagonal, return 0;
- if $A_{i,j}$ is in the lower triangle $(i > j)$, retrieve $B[\frac{1}{2}(i-1)(i-2) + j]$;
- if $A_{i,j}$ is in the upper triangle $(i < j)$, reverse the subscripts and retrieve the negative of $B[\frac{1}{2}(j-1)(j-2) + i]$.

Here is the function:

```
public static double A(double[] B, int i, int j) {
    if (i == j) return 0.0;
    if (i > j) return B[(i - 1) * (i - 2) / 2 + j];
    return -B[(j - 1) * (j - 2) / 2 + i];
}
```

7.2.3 Band matrices

A *band* matrix, **A**, is one in which all the non-zero elements are on a band which includes the main diagonal and subdiagonals on both sides. For example, the following shows a 6×6 *tri-diagonal* matrix (band of width 3):

$A_{1,1}$	$A_{1,2}$	0	0	0	0
$A_{2,1}$	$A_{2,2}$	$A_{2,3}$	0	0	0
0	$A_{3,2}$	$A_{3,3}$	$A_{3,4}$	0	0
0	0	$A_{4,3}$	$A_{4,4}$	$A_{4,5}$	0
0	0	0	$A_{5,4}$	$A_{5,5}$	$A_{5,6}$
0	0	0	0	$A_{6,5}$	$A_{6,6}$

Note that for those elements $A_{i,j}$ *on* the band, we have $|i - j| \leq 1$ and for those elements *off* the band, we have $|i - j| > 1$.

In general, if for some integer m, we have $A_{i,j} = 0$ when $|i - j| > m$, then **A** is a band matrix with a band width of $2m + 1$. When $m = 1$, **A** is tri-diagonal.

Clearly, we can save a lot of storage if we store only the elements on the band.

Consider the case of an $n \times n$ *tri-diagonal* matrix. Except for the first and last rows, each row has 3 elements on the band. The first and last rows have two each. This gives a total of $3n - 2$ elements on the band.

We will store these elements in a one-dimensional array **B[1..3n-2]**. We can choose to store them in row order, column order or even by diagonals. We will use row order.

Thus, we will store $A_{1,1}$ in **B[1]**, $A_{1,2}$ in **B[2]**, $A_{2,1}$ in **B[3]**, and so on, with $A_{n,n}$ in **B[3n-2]**. For the sample 6×6 matrix, we will store the band elements, thus:

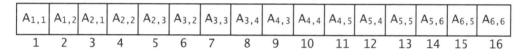

$A_{1,1}$	$A_{1,2}$	$A_{2,1}$	$A_{2,2}$	$A_{2,3}$	$A_{3,2}$	$A_{3,3}$	$A_{3,4}$	$A_{4,3}$	$A_{4,4}$	$A_{4,5}$	$A_{5,4}$	$A_{5,5}$	$A_{5,6}$	$A_{6,5}$	$A_{6,6}$
1	2	3	4	5	6	7	8	9	10	11	12	13	14	15	16

Given this arrangement, we can derive the access formula for $A_{i,j}$ as follows:

- we work out how many elements there are *before* $A_{i,i}$;
- there are $(i\text{-}1)$ rows before the *i*th row, all with 3 elements except the first;
- if we imagine $A_{i,i-1}$ being added to the first row, which has 2 elements, we get $3(i - 1)$ elements *before* $A_{i,i}$; adding 1 takes us to $A_{i,i}$; thus, $A_{i,i}$ is stored in position $3(i - 1) + 1 = 3i - 2$;
- next, consider $j - i$; for elements on the band, this is either -1, 0 or +1; these are exactly the 'offsets' we must add to the position of $A_{i,i}$ to get the positions of $A_{i,i-1}$, $A_{i,i}$ and $A_{i,i+1}$, respectively;
- hence $A_{i,j}$ is stored in position $3i - 2 + j - i = 2(i - 1) + j$.

For example, $A_{4,5}$ is stored in position $2(4 - 1) + 5 = 11$.

We must check whether our formula works for elements in the first row since it was derived based on "rows before the *i*th row" and there are no rows before the first. But when i is 1, the formula reduces to j, which gives the correct position. Hence the formula is valid for all band elements.

We can write the access function for $A_{i,j}$ as follows:

```
public static double A(double[] B, int i, int j) {
  if (Math.abs(i – j) > 1) return 0.0;
  return B[2 * (i – 1) + j];
}
```

As an exercise, work out the access function for a matrix with a band width of 5.

7.2.4 Sparse matrices

While there is no precise definition of a sparse matrix, we think of it as one with many more zeroes that non-zeroes. A useful guide is to think of a matrix as sparse if less than 20% of its elements are non-zero.

The following is an example of a 5 × 6 sparse matrix:

	1	2	3	4	5	6
1	0.0	0.0	2.9	0.0	3.7	0.0
2	5.1	0.0	0.0	0.0	0.0	2.2
3	0.0	0.0	0.0	3.1	0.0	0.0
4	0.0	0.0	0.0	0.0	0.0	0.0
5	0.0	0.0	4.3	0.0	7.6	0.0

Note also that whereas the previous matrices were *required* to be square, that is not the case for a sparse matrix. In general, we will think of it as an $m \times n$ matrix.

There are several ways to store a sparse matrix to minimize storage. Some of these are listed below.

(1) Hash table

We use the (i, j) subscripts of the non-zero elements as the key and store the subscripts and the value in the hash table. We need to store the subscripts since two different pairs of subscripts may hash to the same location.

If each matrix value requires 8 bytes (**double**) and each subscript occupies 2 bytes, this gives a total of 12 bytes for each non-zero value. Storing the matrix normally would take up $8mn$ bytes. If there are k non-zero values, we would save storage if $12k$ is less than $8mn$.

The percentage savings would be $\frac{8mn - 12k}{8mn} \times 100$. For example, if there are 20% non-zeroes, then $\frac{k}{mn} = 0.2$ and the savings is 70%.

(2) Linked lists

In this method, we store the non-zero elements of each row (or column) on a linked list. If there are 5 rows, we use an array (**row**, say) of size 5; **row[i]** points to the first non-zero element in the ith row. If all the elements of the ith row are zero, **row[i]** is set to null.

The following shows how the above matrix can be stored by rows:

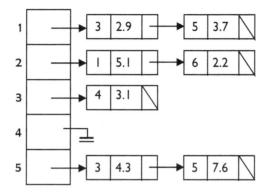

Each item in the list contains the column number and the value. It is natural to store the row elements in increasing order by column number. But this can be changed, if necessary.

The amount of storage required by this method can be easily calculated. Suppose there are m rows and k non-zero elements. Assume that a pointer value occupies 4 bytes, a column number occupies 2 bytes and a matrix value occupies 8 bytes. The array takes up $4m$ bytes and the list elements take up $14k$ bytes for a total of $4m + 14k$ bytes.

Retrieving element $A_{i,j}$ requires you to search the list starting at **row[i]** for a column value of **j**. If found, the value is returned; if not found, the value is 0.

Suppose a linked list element is a **Node** object, where **Node** is defined as:

```
class Node {
    int column;
    double value;
    Node next;
}
```

We can write the access function as follows:

```
public static double A(Node[] row, int i, int j) {
    Node curr = row[i];
    while (curr != null && j > curr.column) curr = curr.next;
    if (curr == null || j < curr.column) return 0.0;
    return curr.value;
}
```

This method is efficient if **A** will be accessed primarily by rows; for example, if we need to calculate the matrix product $A \times B$. It is also easy to accommodate changes to matrix values. A value which goes from non-zero to 0 just has to be deleted from the appropriate list and one which goes from 0 to non-zero just has to be added. Both these operations are simple and efficient.

Some matrix operations require that rows be interchanged. This is almost trivial to do here; to interchange rows i and j, all we need to do is swap **row[i]** and **row[j]**.

But suppose we need the matrix product **B** × **A**? Now we will need to access **A** by columns. In this case, it is better to store **A** by columns, rather than rows. If there are n columns, we can use an array (**col**, say) of size n such that **col[j]** points to the list of non-zero elements in the jth column.

What if we need A by both rows and columns? We can combine the two representations using **row** and **col** pointers; **row[i]** points to elements in the ith row and **col[j]** points to elements in the jth column. Now, however, each list element will contain a row number, a column number, a pointer to the next non-zero element in the same row and a pointer to the next non-zero element in the same column.

Other variations are possible. Depending on how the matrix is to be processed, we can, for instance, have pointers to *previous* elements in the same row or column.

(3) Arrays

Instead of linked lists, we can use arrays to store the matrix by rows or columns. Suppose we want to store the non-zero values in the sample matrix by columns. We first store the values in column-major order; with each value, we store the row in which it appears (we will explain item 1 shortly):

value	0.0	5.1	2.9	4.3	3.1	3.7	7.6	2.2
row	1	2	1	5	3	1	5	2
	1	2	3	4	5	6	7	8

Thus, **5.1** is in row **2**, **2.9** is in row **1**, **4.3** is in row **5**, and so on. We assume this array is called **B**; **B[i].value** and **B[i].row** refer to the value and row at position i.

Next, we must fill in "access arrays" which tell us *where* in **B** the elements of each column are located. Since there are 6 columns, we will need an array (**col**, say) of size 6. Each element will have two fields—**start** and **end**; **col[j]start** is the location of the first element of column **j** in **B** and **col[j].end** is the location of the last element of column **j** in **B**. Here are the values for the sample matrix:

start	2	1	3	5	6	8
end	2	1	4	5	7	8
	1	2	3	4	5	6

For example, there are 2 non-zero elements in column 5; they are stored in **B[6]** and **B[7]**. Hence, **col[5].start** is set to 6 and **col[5].end** is set to 7.

Of particular interest is column 2; this is a column of all zeroes. Instead of having to do something special for zero columns, we choose to store a single zero in **B[1]** and set **start** and **end** to 1 for any column that contains all zeroes. Doing so will enable zero columns to be processed in the same way as non-zero columns.

In effect, we are saying that a zero column contains one "non-zero" element, stored in **B[1]**; its value is 0. This is a small penalty to pay for simpler processing.

This method is very efficient if we need to process the matrix by columns or if we need to interchange two columns. To interchange columns **j** and **k**, we just swap the values in **col[j]** and **col[k]**.

If there are k non-zero values and n columns, the amount of storage required by this method is $10(k + 1) + 4n$ bytes.

If we need the matrix by rows, a similar scheme can be employed.

One of the big advantages of storing a sparse matrix this way is that some kinds of processing are speeded up greatly. Consider the matrix product **C** × **A** where **C** is $m \times p$ and **A** is $p \times n$. Conventionally, we multiply, pairwise, each row of **C** by each column of **A**. The product (**T**, say) is an $m \times n$ matrix. The following pseudocode shows how:

```
for i = 1 to m
  for j = 1 to n
    //multiply row i of C by column j of A; this give T[i, j]
    T[i, j] = 0
    for k = 1 to p
      T[i, j] += C[i, k] * A[k, j]
```

This gives a total of mpn multiplications. (There are also mpn additions.)

But suppose a column of **A** has only one non-zero element. Since we *know* that, except for this one element, all the other multiplications will give 0, we need perform only one multiplication when multiplying by this column. Hence, the number of multiplications involving this column is reduced from mp to m. The following shows how to do the multiplication assuming **A** is stored as above:

```
for i = 1 to m
  for j = 1 to n
    //multiply row i of C by column j of A; this give T[i, j]
    T[i, j] = 0
    for u = col[j].start to col[j].end
      T[i, j] += C[i, B[u].row] * B[u].value
```

Here, we ensure that only the non-zero elements of **A** are multiplied by the corresponding elements in **C**.

In general, if there are k non-zero elements in **A**, the number of multiplications is reduced from mpn to mk. For example, if $m = p = n = 1000$ and k is 100000 (10% non-zeroes), the number of multiplications is reduced from one billion (10^9) to 100 million (10^8), a savings of 900 million. Put another way, storing **A** as sparse will perform the matrix multiplication in about one-tenth of the time that it would take if **A** were stored normally.

7.2.5 Other special types of matrices

Sometimes a matrix is defined by some special relation among its elements. For example,

$$\mathbf{A}_{i,j} = \mathbf{A}_{u,v} \text{ if } i+j = u+v$$

As the following shows, elements on the diagonals going from south-west to north-east are equal since their subscripts add up to the same value:

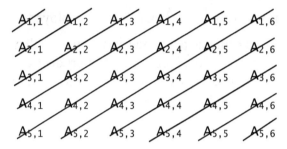

There are at most 10 distinct values in the matrix. Another way to look at it is that the sum of subscripts ranges from 2 to 11, a range of 10 values. In general, for an $m \times n$ matrix, there will be at most $m+n-1$ distinct values.

For such a matrix, all we need is an array **B[1..m+n-1]**. We store values starting from $\mathbf{A}_{1,1}$, going across the first row then down the last column:

$A_{1,1}$	$A_{1,2}$	$A_{1,3}$	$A_{1,4}$	$A_{1,5}$	$A_{1,6}$	$A_{2,6}$	$A_{3,6}$	$A_{4,6}$	$A_{5,6}$
1	2	3	4	5	6	7	8	9	10

The access function is almost trivial:

```
public static double A(double[] B, int i, int j) {
    return B[i + j - 1];
}
```

As an exercise, write the access function for a matrix **A** where

(a) $\mathbf{A}_{i,j} = \mathbf{A}_{u,v}$ if $i-j = u-v$

(b) $\mathbf{A}_{i,j} = \mathbf{A}_{u,v}$ if $|i-j| = |u-v|$

Exercises 7

1. The elements in the lower triangle of a lower-triangular matrix, **A**, are stored in column-major order in a one-dimensional array, **B**. Write a function which, given **i** and **j**, accesses **B** and returns the value of $\mathbf{A}_{i,j}$.

2. The elements in the upper triangle of an upper-triangular matrix, **A**, are stored in column-major order in a one-dimensional array, **B**. Write a function which, given **i** and **j**, accesses **B** and returns the value of $\mathbf{A}_{i,j}$.

   Write the function if the elements are stored in row-major order.

3. The elements on the band of a tri-diagonal matrix are stored as follows: the upper diagonal, followed by the main diagonal, followed by the lower diagonal. Write the access function for $A_{i,j}$.

4. Show how to store a sparse matrix by columns using linked lists.

5. A sparse matrix is stored by rows using linked lists. Write code to print the matrix in its normal form.

6. Write code to read the non-zero values of a sparse matrix (each element is supplied as *row, column, value*) and create the linked list representation (i) by rows (ii) by columns (iii) by rows and columns.

7. Write code to read the non-zero values of a sparse matrix (each element is supplied as *row, column, value*) and create the array representation (i) by rows (ii) by columns.

8. An $n \times n$ matrix **A** is used to store the rate per minute for telephone calls between any two of n towns. **A[i, j]** is the rate per minute for calling from town i to town j and vice versa. Within a town, calls are free. Devise a scheme to store the information in **A** in a one-dimensional array **B**, conserving storage as much as possible. Write a function which, given **i** and **j**, accesses **B** and returns the value of **A[i, j]**.

   Using the function, write another function which, given j, returns the town with the highest rate of calling from town j. Assume there is only one such town.

9. For any pair (i, j, i ≠ j) taken from n persons, it is known whether person i is younger than, older than or the same age as person j. Explain how this information can be represented using an $n \times n$ matrix, **A**. State any special properties of the matrix.

   Explain how the information in **A** can be stored in a one-dimensional array **B**, conserving storage as much as possible.

   Write a function which, given i and j, accesses **B** and returns -1, 0 or 1 depending on whether person i is younger, same age as, or older than person j, respectively.

10. An $n \times n$ matrix **A** is used to store the points obtained in football matches among n teams. A team gets 3 points for a win, 1 point for a draw and 0 points for a loss. **A[i, j]** is set to 3 if team i beats team j, to 1 if the match is drawn and to 0 if team i loses to team j. In order to conserve storage, the values in the (strictly) lower triangle of **A** are stored in an array **B[1..m]** in row order. What is the value of **m**?

    Write a function which, given **i** and **j**, accesses **B** and returns the value of **A[i, j]**. If **i** or **j** is invalid, the function returns -1.

11. A matrix **A** has the property that $A_{i,j} = A_{u,v}$ if $i - j = u - v$. How many distinct elements are there in **A**? Store the distinct elements in a one-dimensional array **B** and write the access function for **A[i, j]**.

    Repeat the above when $A_{i,j} = A_{u,v}$ if $|i - j| = |u - v|$.

12. **A** is an $m \times n$ sparse matrix. **B** is an $n \times n$ tri-diagonal matrix. It is required to find the product ABA^T. Devise schemes for storing **A** and **B**, conserving storage as much as possible. Using your schemes, write code to find ABA^T.

Index

www.ingramcontent.com/pod-product-compliance
Lightning Source LLC
Chambersburg PA
CBHW080403060326
40689CB00019B/4113

* 9 7 8 1 4 3 8 2 7 5 1 7 8 *